DEVELOPING COMMUNITY-LED PUBLIC LIBRARIES

Developing Community-Led Public Libraries
Evidence from the UK and Canada

JOHN PATEMAN
Thunder Bay Public Library, Canada

KEN WILLIMENT
Halifax Public Libraries, Canada

ASHGATE

Published by
Ashgate Publishing Limited
Wey Court East
Union Road
Farnham
Surrey, GU9 7PT
England

Ashgate Publishing Company
110 Cherry Street
Suite 3-1
Burlington, VT 05401-3818
USA

www.ashgate.com

British Library Cataloguing in Publication Data
Pateman, John, 1956-
Developing community-led public libraries : evidence from
the UK and Canada.
1. Public libraries--Aims and objectives--Great Britain.
2. Public libraries--Aims and objectives--Canada.
3. Libraries and people with social disabilities--Great
Britain. 4. Libraries and people with social disabilities--
Canada. 5. Library outreach programs--Great Britain.
6. Library outreach programs--Canada. 7. Public
libraries--Great Britain--Administration--Citizen
participation. 8. Public libraries--Canada--
Administration--Citizen participation.
I. Title II. Williment, Ken.
027.4'41-dc23

Library of Congress Cataloging-in-Publication Data
Pateman, John, 1956-
Developing community-led public libraries : evidence from the UK and Canada / by John Pateman and Ken Williment.
    pages cm
Includes bibliographical references and index.
ISBN 978-1-4094-4206-6 (hardback) -- ISBN 978-1-4094-4207-3 (ebook)
1. Libraries and community--Great Britain. 2. Libraries and community--Canada. 3. Libraries and society--Great Britain. 4. Libraries and society--Canada. 5. Public libraries--Great Britain--Administration. 6. Public libraries--Canada--Administration. 7. Public services (Libraries)--Great Britain. 8. Public services (Libraries)--Canada. I. Williment, Ken. II. Title.
Z716.4.P375 2013
021.20941--dc23

2012034187

ISBN 9781409442066 (hbk)
ISBN 9781409442073 (ebk – PDF)
ISBN 9781472402745 (ebk – ePUB)

Printed and bound in Great Britain by the
MPG Books Group, UK.

Contents

List of Figures

Acknowledgements

John Pateman: Looking back on my long career in public libraries I have no doubt that my greatest achievement was helping to produce *Open to All?* because this has shaped public library policy and practice in the UK in terms of tackling social exclusion and creating needs-based library services. I would like to thank all those library services which have been brave enough to implement *Open to All?* ideas and recommendations. I would particularly like to pay tribute to John Vincent who set up and sustained The Network to keep *Open to All?* ideas alive within the library profession. John has also provided invaluable and challenging advice and comments on the contents of this book and has been our unofficial proofreader and reference checker! Finally, I would like to thank my comrades in Canada – particularly Brian Campbell, Annette DeFaveri and my fellow author Ken Williment – who have put *Open to All?* ideas into action via the Working Together Project.

Ken Williment: I was fortunate to be one of the Community Development Librarians working at one of the four Working Together project sites. Over the last six years I have been able to learn about the context of the work completed with Working Together prior to my arrival. I sincerely hope my colleagues from this project feel that the book accurately reflects the major findings and learnings, and provides a superficial summary of the extensive work completed from each of the four sites from 2004 to 2008. It is important to acknowledge that, while a majority of the content I provided for this book was based on the Working Together Project, additional content was also provided based upon my personal experiences using the community-led approach. Undoubtedly, some of the content will reflect my personal perspectives – after working with this approach over the past six years.

Clearly, community-led work has had a major impact on library systems across Canada and will continue to expand in its importance and influence. It is my deepest wish that this book will help to contribute to libraries working closely with communities to collaboratively determine and develop relevant services for underserved communities.

This book would not have been possible without the amazing work completed by all the Working Together staff acknowledged at the end of the *Toolkit*. The amazingly comprehensive and precise national evaluation conducted by Jill Atkey at the Social Planning and Research Council of British Columbia (SPARC BC) was heavily referenced in this book. I must personally acknowledge the strong support I received from Tracey Jones-Grant, Susan McLean, Annette DeFaveri, Sandra Singh, Halifax Public Libraries, Toronto Public Library, Regina Public

Library, Vancouver Public Library and Edmonton Public Library. Special thanks to Melissa and my children for supporting me through this lengthy process. To my co-author John Pateman – although we have never personally met – I feel honoured to have been given this opportunity to learn from such an inspirational leader in the library profession.

The Working Together Project was funded as a demonstration project by Human Resources and Social Development Canada (HRSDC). This funding allowed participating library systems with the opportunity to both understand and begin developing library specific community development techniques and approaches. HRSDC's funding has proven to be invaluable in the development and progression of this work.

Finally, to my dear friend Mike Robinson, I wish you were still with us. I know you would have read this book from cover to cover, calling me with many questions and great observations – you are deeply missed and I dedicate the content I have contributed to you.

List of Abbreviations

ALP	Annual Library Plan
AV	audio and visual
BME	black and minority ethnic
BPK	body of professional knowledge (as defined by CILIP)
CDL	community development librarian
CILIP	Chartered Institute of Library and Information Professionals
CIPFA	Chartered Institute of Public Finance and Accountancy
CPLIS	Centre for the Public Library and Information in Society
EPL	Edmonton Public Library
F4F	*Framework for the Future: Libraries, Learning and Information in the Next Decade* (DCMS 2003)
ICT	information and communication technology
IT	information technology
LAA	Local Area Agreement
LGA	Local Government Association
LGBT	lesbian, gay, bisexual and transexual
LIS	library and information services
LNA	Library Needs Assessment
LSP	Local Strategic Partnership
MLA	Museums, Libraries and Archives Council
MLIS	Master of Library Information Studies
NIS	National Indicators Set
PC	personal computer
PLA	public library authority
PLSS	Public Library Service Standards
PLUS	Public Library Users Survey
PN	People's Network
RFID	Radio Frequency Identification
VPL	Vancouver Public Library
WTP	Working Together Project

Chapter 1

Introduction

This book came about as the result of a dialogue between its authors. John Pateman was part of the research team who produced *Open to All? The Public Library and Social Exclusion* and he went on to develop needs-based library services in two UK public library services, Merton and Lincolnshire. Ken Williment was a member of the Working Together Project which developed community-led approaches to public library services in Halifax, Toronto, Regina and Vancouver. What started as an email exchange about needs-based libraries in the UK and community-led libraries in Canada developed into an idea for this book. Each chapter reflects this dialogue, with John talking about *Open to All?* ideas and best practice in the UK and Ken responding with Working Together application, findings and learnings in Canada. The outcome is a synthesis of different experiences but basically the same approach.

While this book provides an overview of *Open to All? The Public Library and Social Exclusion* and Working Together, the intent is to provide a practical road map for library staff to begin integrating and sustaining community-led approaches in libraries.

A needs-based library service is predicated on the assumption that all people have needs and everyone has different needs. A needs-based library service has the strategy, staffing and service structures, systems and organizational culture which enable it to identify, prioritize and meet community needs. These needs cannot be second-guessed via professional intuition. These needs must be comprehensively and holistically assessed using a systematic Library Needs Assessment process. This will determine who has the greatest needs (often those who use the library least) and who has the least need (often those who use the library most). The service can then focus on those with the greatest needs.

While we advocate for the identification and targeting of services to those with the greatest need, it is important to focus on increasing the total number of users by retaining existing users, attracting back lapsed users and engaging new users. A needs-based approach does not mean that we abandon our 'core' users, some of whom may have extensive or complex needs. In fact, in each community there is often a big overlap between poverty and exclusion but there are also people who are not poor and excluded (for example, because of discrimination) and others who are poor and not excluded (for example, because they have good social networks). All of these nuances have to be built into a needs-based approach to prevent stereotyping and the pursuit of 'quick wins'.

When developing a community-led approach, it is important to identify target groups, or specific communities within which the approach will be used to initially develop services. Since a community-led approach is based upon the development of relationships with individuals from various communities, by initially focusing on a geographical community or specific community of interest (for example, seniors, people with disabilities, etc.), it provides a library system with a viable and practical introduction to using community-led services. In addition, this highly adaptable and non-prescriptive approach lends itself well to the numerous and varied social contexts of each library system and the communities they serve.

Once needs have been identified and prioritized they can be met by using a community development approach. This is very different from an outreach approach which simply takes library services (which have been designed, planned, delivered and evaluated by library staff) out of the library and into community settings. A community development approach is based on creating meaningful and sustained relationships with local communities, while acknowledging that the community is the expert on its members' own needs. Library staff become listeners rather than tellers, and staff and community co-produce library services. Community-led work is not prescriptive, which is a major strength, as it is highly adaptable and applicable to all contexts and communities which librarians are working in, or could be working in.

A needs-based and community-led approach enables library services to be targeted at the underserved and the library becomes an agent of social change and social justice.

Open to All?

Public libraries are, at present, only superficially open to all. They provide mainly passive 'access' to materials and resources and they have service priorities and resourcing strategies which work in favour of existing library users rather than excluded or disadvantaged communities or groups. An Information Communication Technology (ICT)-led 'modernisation' of the library service is doing little to change this pattern: our research concludes that this will simply replicate existing inequities of use in an 'information age'.

The core conclusion of the study is therefore that public libraries have the potential to play a key role in tackling social exclusion, but in order to make a real difference they will need to undergo rapid transformation and change. (Muddiman et al. 2000a)

The Working Together Project had two main objectives. The first objective was to use a community development approach to build connections and relationships in the community. These connections facilitated a better understanding of what socially excluded communities want and need from public libraries. They also ensured that socially excluded people defined and articulated their own wants and needs. Understanding what the community wants and needs from the library is a significant step toward building relevant and inclusive libraries that respond to the needs of all community members.

> The second objective was to identify and investigate systemic barriers to library use. Many socially excluded people see and feel barriers that may not be evident to librarians and library staff. The Working Together Project wanted to identify those barriers and then, rather than try and convince socially excluded people that these barriers either do not exist or are being perceived incorrectly, attempt to remove the barriers by influencing internal policy and procedural changes. In other words, the Project attempted to change the library's understanding and awareness of socially excluded people. (Working Together 2008a)

The theoretical approaches to working with socially excluded community members developed by *Open to All? The Public Library and Social Exclusion* (Muddiman et al. 2000a) and the direct application and approaches developed through the Working Together Project (2004–08) provide the international library community with a powerful and persuasive case for adopting this approach in library systems.

Since the completion of the Working Together Project in 2008, there have been ongoing discussions about the potential impact that the newly developed community-led service model will have on public libraries across Canada and internationally. At the same time, the future direction of public libraries in the UK has been debated within the context of a rapidly shrinking public sector. The time is now right to combine *Open to All?* recommendations and Working Together Project learnings to showcase good practice and challenges to community development work in public library services in Canada and the UK. In doing so, our aim is to provide:

- a comparative analysis between the approaches of Canada and the UK to developing community-led library services
- an overview of public library policy and practice from 2000 to 2012 with a focus on what has changed and what still needs to be changed
- a thorough analysis of each of the main recommendations put forward by *Open to All?* and the learnings of the Working Together Project
- a call for action on nine key public library policy areas (from community engagement to service standards and evaluation) in the light of public sector cuts and the threat of wide-scale public library closures.

Overview of Open to All?

Open to All? was a study of the public library and its role in and capacity to tackle social exclusion. It assessed the ways in which public libraries addressed exclusion, and it explored how public libraries might focus their services more effectively in the future on excluded social groups and communities. It aimed to suggest how public libraries might contribute towards developing a more inclusive society in the UK.

The study was the product of an 18-month research project based at Leeds Metropolitan University and conducted in partnership with the London Borough of Merton (Libraries), Sheffield Libraries and Information Services and John Vincent, an independent consultant. The research was conducted between October 1998 and April 2000, with financial support from, successively, the British Library Research and Innovation Centre, the Library and Information Commission, and Resource. It formed part of the 'Value and Impact of Libraries' Research Programme developed by these organizations.

The research was organized to include the following elements:

- working papers which explored the issues around social exclusion itself, and public library responses to it
- a survey of all UK public library authorities, which assessed the nature and extent of current UK public library activity and initiatives relevant to social exclusion
- detailed case studies of eight UK public library authorities and their social exclusion strategies and initiatives
- the development of a Social Exclusion Action Planning Network which has organized workshops, conferences and other events facilitating dissemination and feedback
- conclusions and recommendations which suggest how public library exclusion strategies might be strengthened both through practical innovations at local level and new policy developments.

Open to All? reviewed the context of social exclusion and the scale of the problems which the public library, and other public services, faced. It pointed to:

- the importance of *exclusion* as a concept because of its focus on the excluded and their needs
- the very varied nature of exclusion and its roots in the material inequalities of capitalist society, as well as discrimination linked to race, gender and disability
- the global dimensions of exclusion, and its manifestations in the global 'information society'
- the accelerating problems of exclusion in the UK, and the widening gap between rich and poor
- the contrast between weak, voluntary approaches to exclusion by public services, and stronger, more interventionist approaches

Open to All? also reviewed the record of public library provision for 'disadvantaged' or 'excluded' individuals, social groups and social classes. The 150-year history of the public library revealed that UK libraries have adopted only weak, voluntary and 'take it or leave it' approaches to social inclusion. The core rationale of the public library movement continued to be based on the idea of developing universal access to a service which essentially reflected mainstream middle-class, white and British values. Attempts to break out of this mould, such as the 'community librarianship' of the 1970s and 1980s, had been incorporated back into this mainstream. Attempts to target services towards excluded people remained patchy, uneven and were often time-limited. Some key consequences of this approach to service provision were:

- a continuing under-utilization of public libraries by working-class people and other excluded social groups
- a lack of knowledge in the public library world about the needs and views of excluded 'non-users'
- the development in many public libraries of organizational, cultural and environmental barriers which effectively excluded many disadvantaged people.

A small minority of authorities and librarians had in the past adopted strategies and initiatives which had taken the needs of excluded people as their starting point. These were exceptions, however, and public libraries could claim to have been inclusive institutions in a limited sense only.

Survey

There was a clear imperative for the public library, like other public services, to seriously address social exclusion. The project survey examined the extent to which this policy impetus was being reflected in activity in public library authorities (PLAs). Overall, the survey findings suggested that there were wide differentials between UK public library authorities in terms of activity relevant to social inclusion:

- The survey estimated that only one sixth of PLAs approximated to a comprehensive model of good practice for social inclusion. Most PLAs (60 per cent), although having developed some initiatives, had no comprehensive strategy, with uneven and intermittent activity. A final group of one quarter of PLAs were those with little apparent strategy and service development.
- Targeting of disadvantaged neighbourhoods and social groups was used comprehensively by only approximately one third of PLAs. Recent service developments in libraries, such as the development of ICT networks and literacy initiatives, tended to be targeted at socially excluded people in only a small minority of cases.
- Most PLAs reported fairly high levels of community involvement by their staff but this tended to be at a general level, rather than focused on disadvantage or exclusion.
- Most PLAs had no consistent resource focus on exclusion, and this was sometimes very marginal indeed. A minority of PLAs were very active in

developing partnership projects but this was not a dominant factor in most PLA social exclusion strategies.
- Many of the UK's most marginal and excluded people were not considered to be a priority in PLA strategy, service delivery and staffing. This applied especially to a number of social groups who commonly faced stigma and discrimination, such as refugees, homeless people and travellers.

Case Studies

The project case studies illustrated some innovative initiatives and service developments, but overall they suggested that such activity was patchy and uneven. The case studies also highlighted barriers and problems which hindered PLA attempts to tackle exclusion. Some of these were a result of external factors, like lack of money and equipment, but others were linked to the internal procedures, cultures and traditions of library services themselves. The case studies highlighted:

- some successes in addressing social exclusion, most frequently linked to targeted initiatives employing community development, partnerships and other proactive ways of working
- problems in developing an overall, PLA-wide policy framework with exclusion issues 'mainstreamed' only exceptionally
- a reluctance to adopt resourcing models that consistently prioritized excluded communities or social groups
- limits on the ability of library staff to work with excluded people because of lack of skills and training and sometimes negative attitudes
- a tendency to suggest that any 'community' activity automatically addressed exclusion and a tendency to consult with communities and excluded groups only sporadically
- a preoccupation with libraries as a 'passive' service which prioritized 'access' rather than with proactive and interventionist ways of working
- an ongoing concern with the ICT-led 'modernization' of the library service which was only exceptionally linked to exclusion issues.

Transformation

Open to All? suggested that much more than modernization was needed. If public libraries were to seriously address social exclusion, they needed to become much more proactive, interventionist and educative institutions, with a concern for social justice at their core. The following strategies were needed for such a transformation:

- the mainstreaming of provision for socially excluded groups and communities and the establishment of standards of service and their monitoring

- the adoption of resourcing strategies which prioritize the needs of excluded people and communities
- a recasting of the role of library staff to encompass a more socially responsive and educative approach
- staffing policies and practices which address exclusion, discrimination and prejudice
- targeting of excluded social groups and communities
- the development of community-based approaches to library provision, which incorporate consultation with and partnership with local communities
- ICT and networking developments which actively focus on the needs of excluded people
- a recasting of the image and identity of the public library to link it more closely with the cultures of excluded communities and social groups.

Recommendations of *Open to All?*

Open to All? concluded with a series of general recommendations and suggestions designed to initiate and support change. These recommendations had implications for a wide range of stakeholders in the public library community:

- *Public library authorities* (PLAs) were urged to adopt long-term strategies for tackling social exclusion involving reviews of resourcing, staffing, community development, ICT, materials provision, partnership and joint provision and monitoring. PLAs were urged to mainstream social exclusion throughout all their activities.
- Those parts of *central government* concerned with the public library and social exclusion (such as the Department for Culture, Media and Sport) were urged to assist PLAs by developing a coordinated policy framework. This would include national service standards for public library activities relevant to social exclusion, and arrangements for monitoring library authority performance.
- *Professional organizations*, particularly the Library Association (later renamed the Chartered Institute of Library and Information Professionals, or CILIP), were urged to improve access to the profession for socially excluded people and to establish mechanisms which represented the interests of disadvantaged groups.
- *Research institutions and research funding bodies* were urged to fund detailed research into library-related needs of excluded groups and to undertake detailed statistical monitoring of the use of libraries by categories of excluded people.
- *Training organizations*, especially schools of information and library studies, were urged to ensure that their courses and programmes were relevant to public library work for social inclusion.

There is significant evidence to indicate that all of these stakeholders were influenced by the ideas and recommendations of *Open to All?*

Professional Organizations

The first stakeholder group to respond to *Open to All?* was CILIP, who commissioned a Social Inclusion Executive Advisory Group (SIEAG) to produce *Making a Difference: Innovation and Diversity* (SIEAG 2002). This report used *Open to All?* as its starting point and recommended that CILIP should:

- Lead the mobilization of the Library and Information Services (LIS) sector's response to social exclusion and diversity through a reassertion of the LIS social justice value base.
- Encourage LIS organizations to mainstream services to socially excluded people and promote diversity, recognizing that for most this will mean organizational transformation.
- Encourage and help facilitate LIS organizations to engage effectively in partnerships and community activities to ensure that the voice of the excluded is centre stage in the planning and delivery of services. (SIEAG 2002: 32)

Research Institutions and Research Funding Bodies

Open to All? also had an impact on the research programmes of funding bodies such as the Local Government Association and the Laser Foundation. Consultation with hard-to-reach communities was one of the dominant themes of the public library research commissioned by the Laser Foundation and published in *Public Libraries: What Next?* (2007):

> To have a sustainable future, public library services must be relevant to the communities they serve and consultation is an essential element in the planning of future services or new libraries. It can be very difficult to consult effectively with groups in the community that are hard to reach, or that may think library services are not for them, in order to find out how we can meet their needs and expectations. (Laser Foundation 2007: 14)

Therefore the Laser Foundation funded three consultation projects that showed particular imagination and innovation in overcoming such barriers. Two projects related specifically to the planning process for new libraries in socially deprived areas, whilst the third was an important national survey into the attitudes and expectations of young people in relation to public libraries:

- Bolton Libraries collaborated with Planning for Real to engage hard-to-reach communities in a bold and imaginative way in the planning of the new High Street library for one of Bolton's most deprived areas.

- Birmingham Libraries consulted with young people to plan for a new library in Birchfield, a diverse inner-city community in one of Birmingham's most economically and socially disadvantaged areas.
- *Destination Unknown: A Research Study of 14–35-Year-Olds for the Future Development of Public Libraries* (Laser Foundation 2006) defined a baseline which libraries need to achieve if they are to attract young users.

The Local Government Association (LGA) commissioned *Extending the Role of Libraries* (2004) as part of its educational research programme: 'The challenge for libraries in the future appears to be to draw in those harder-to-reach groups. These groups, which may include travellers, refugees and asylum seekers, and migrant workers, may only be reached by more radical provision.' The LGA placed a strong emphasis on the need for workforce development:

- The changing role of staff in libraries is taking them out from behind desks and away from books to deal directly with a wide variety of user groups. This has considerable implications, not just for the training and development of existing staff but for the recruitment of future staff and the structuring and deployment of the workforce:
- Sufficient funding and appropriate training need to be put in place to ensure that staff are fully supported and equipped to deal with groups that can be challenging in their attitudes and behaviour.
- Staffing structures need to reflect the changing roles of library staff and efforts must be made to match staff skills to appropriate types and levels of work.
- Policy makers and library service senior managers need to address the issue of what kind of people, with what kind of skills, the librarians of the future should be? (LGA 2004: 44)

Training Organizations

The need to reform the public library workforce had been a key recommendation of *Open to All?* and this challenge was also taken up by the Centre for the Public Library and Information in Society (CPLIS) who recognized that schools of information and library studies needed to provide courses and programmes which were relevant to public library work for social inclusion. *The Right 'Man' for the Job?* (Wilson and Birdi 2008) considered the role of empathy in community librarianship and suggested that the following skills were required to work in socially inclusive services:

- communication, listening and negotiating skills
- influencing relationships and reflective practice
- improved confidence and assertiveness and dealing with conflict.

CPLIS concluded that 'The future recruitment of the right "man" for the job will be intrinsic to the effectiveness of public libraries' contribution to the social inclusion agenda, and should be an absolute priority for the future of community librarianship' (ibid.: 111).

Central Government

Open to All? had a significant impact on national public library policy and strategy. The 1964 Public Libraries and Museums Act made the provision of a 'comprehensive and efficient' library service the statutory responsibility of every local authority. But, apart from some specifics such as the free provision of books and information, the 1964 Act did not define the role and purpose of a library service, so each local authority was left to determine this in the light of local requirements. This created a postcode lottery whereby the quality and range of library services could vary widely across the country.

The first serious attempt to provide a common modern mission for all library services was *Framework for the Future: Libraries, Learning and Information in the Next Decade* (DCMS 2003). This was a long-term strategic vision for the public library service based on three key areas of activity:

- the promotion of reading and informal learning
- access to digital skills and services including e-government
- measures to tackle social exclusion, build community identity and develop citizenship.

Open to All? had a direct influence on this strategic agenda, particularly the emphasis on tackling social exclusion and identifying community needs. *Framework* recognized that for libraries to be open to all they had to:

- Engage groups and individuals that are hard to reach by identifying them and establishing what are their particular needs and then by redesigning services when necessary so that there are no barriers to inclusion.
- Remain relevant to the needs of all within the community. Those needs cannot be assumed or taken for granted. Libraries must be adept at seeking, understanding and serving the needs of non-users, some of whom may be ill-at-ease in a library setting.
- Survey and review the needs of the communities they serve, focusing particularly on the needs of the people who do not currently use libraries. (DCMS 2003: 41–2)

This focus on identifying community needs and reaching out to non-users was a direct legacy of the *Open to All?* project.

The next major attempt to define the strategic direction of public libraries was *The Modernisation Review of Public Libraries: A Policy Statement* (DCMS 2010a), which built on *Framework for the Future* and made 54 recommendations across 19 policy areas, including:

- guidance on processes of engagement and consultation
- attracting new members, engaging effectively with the community and community outreach
- providing an accessible library service.

This review emphasized that effective engagement was key to understanding community needs and local authorities had a duty to involve local people:

> We recognize that there is no single way of making an appropriate assessment of the general needs of a community and the specific needs of adults, children, families and young people. However, we would expect a library authority to devise a comprehensive vision and development plan for their service based on some common types of information and data. When reviewing their service, library authorities should consider the following questions:
>
> - What resources are available and how does this match the needs of the community? Have you analysed and considered need and demand? What are the specific needs of adults, families and young people of all ages? Would members of the community be able and willing to contribute to the delivery of library services as volunteers or joint managers? What are the needs of those living, working and studying in the area?
> - How accessible is the service? Is public transport appropriate? Are there barriers to physical access of library buildings that should be removed? Have local people been consulted? How? What are the views of users and what are the views of non-users?
> - Have you done an Equality Impact Assessment? What implications are there for other strategies e.g. educational attainment, support for those seeking work, digital inclusion, adult social care? Are there other partnerships that can be explored – e.g. with the third sector, community and development trusts or town and parish councils? (DCMS 2010a: 15–16)

This emphasis on community needs assessment was another direct legacy of the *Open to All?* project.

Public Libraries

In addition to having an impact on national public library policy and strategy, *Open to All?* also influenced library practice across the UK. One of the most important legacies of the *Open to All?* project was the Social Exclusion Action Planning Network. The aim of this network was to keep the ideas of *Open to All?* alive and current within the library profession. There had been too many research projects which produced reports, organized launch events and then sank into obscurity. The research team who produced *Open to All?* were determined that their work would have a lasting impact on public libraries in the UK and beyond.

The mission statement of The Network, as it became known, is to assist the cultural sector, including libraries, museums, archives and galleries, heritage and other organizations, to work towards social justice. We do this by providing:

- information on initiatives that tackle social exclusion, contribute to community engagement and social/community cohesion, including publishing a monthly newsletter
- training and other opportunities for the cultural sector and related local services to explore, develop and promote their role in this field
- a forum to advocate for partnership approaches to tackling social exclusion and contributing to the wider social agenda. (www.seapn.org. uk)

The majority of PLAs in the UK belong to The Network, as do many regional and national libraries, museums and galleries. The monthly *Network Newsletter* and regular e-bulletins are a unique source of information about social exclusion issues and initiatives. The Network also disseminates good practice and facilitates partnership working.

Open to All? has also had an impact on public libraries in other countries, most notably in Canada where it provided the inspiration for the Working Together Project.

The Working Together Project

During times of economic turmoil and downturn, those with the least are impacted the most. The conclusion of the Working Together Project in 2008 coincided with the worldwide economic crisis of the same year. The timing for *Open to All?* and the Working Together Project (WTP), and the subsequent development of this book could not be better.

When Brian Campbell, from Vancouver Public Library (VPL), initiated the *Libraries in Marginal Communities: A Demonstration Project Proposal*, he had the foresight to both acknowledge and approach existing progressive library branches across Canada, located in Toronto, Vancouver, Regina and Halifax, that had already worked extensively with socially excluded community members. By bringing together library staff working within their respective library systems to collaboratively discuss and continue to develop emerging models of innovative work, specifically targeting disadvantaged communities, the intent was to provide a context in which project learnings could be documented and distributed to libraries across Canada. There was recognition that 'Working with marginal communities is different from providing library service to middle-class communities. The costs are much higher, the standard measurement of service of service delivery, such as circulation, do not apply and personal relations developed over time are much more important' (Campbell 2003).

Funding for the Working Together Project (2004) was initially approved by the Office of Learning Technologies and later transferred to Human Resources and Social Development Canada (HRSDC). Vancouver Public Libraries initiated the project and was responsible for the administration, coordination and evaluation of the project. A call was put out to potential participating library systems, with four large urban library systems from across Canada taking part in the project. Each of the four participating library systems – Toronto, Vancouver, Regina and Halifax – chose one library branch as a pilot site. These branches were physically located in or next to socially excluded and underserved community members.

There were two phases to the Working Together Project, Phase I (2004 to November 2005) and Phase II (November 2005 to April 2008). Along with specific goals and objectives that were negotiated with the federal funder (discussed below), each of the four project sites worked closely with the national administrators of the project in Vancouver to ensure that adequate support was in place to ensure the deliverables were met.

Each participating library system provided substantial in-kind contributions for a number of items including, but not limited to, office space, administrative staffing activities etc. In addition, each of the participating library systems had a site supervisor, hired community development librarians (CDLs) and hired additional support staff.

The project 'Working Together: Library-Community Connections' was undertaken to develop better ways of serving socially excluded individuals who do not traditionally use library services. As identified by Singh et al. (2008), the project had two main objectives:

- Use a community development approach to build connections and relationships with socially excluded communities and individuals. These connections facilitate a better understanding of what socially excluded communities want and need from public libraries. These connections also ensure that socially excluded people define and articulate their own wants and needs.
- Identify and investigate systemic barriers to library use. Many socially excluded people see and feel barriers that may not be evident to librarians and library staff. We want first to identify those barriers, and then, rather than trying to convince socially excluded people that these barriers are either non-existent or perceived incorrectly, we want to break the barriers by influencing internal policy and procedural changes. In short, we are attempting to change the library's understanding and awareness of socially excluded people. (Singh et al. 2008: 52)

Phase I

At the onset of the project, during Phase I which ran from 2004 until November 2005, a number of deliverables were negotiated with the funder. The activities of the project were measured against two goals and five objectives, consisting of:

- *Goal 1* – VPL and its partners seek to develop and test alternative community development models to connect libraries with marginalized communities in order to identify what these communities expect from libraries and to work together in determining various approaches on what and how services may best be delivered.
- *Goal 2* – To transform the way libraries work with marginal communities by providing experience models, tools and a philosophy which encourages working with these communities as an important part of library services.
- *Objective 1* – Each library will select a specific marginal community within which the community development model will be developed (based on community consultations).
- *Objective 2* – Each library will complete and document an inventory of Community Learning Assets to establish the assets and gaps within each community.
- *Objective 3* – Establish a seven-member Community Advisory Committee consisting of representatives from both the library and the target community within each area.
- *Objective 4* – Each library will deliver and test its models of service within its respective targeted community.
- *Objective 5* – Develop and implement a toolkit to transfer service models and skills to all Canadian libraries. (Atkey 2008: 237–8)

Major Outcomes from Phase I

Some of the learnings from this period have been publicly documented (DeFaveri 2005a, DeFaveri 2005b, Campbell 2005, Muzzerall et al. 2005). A number of community development librarians (CDLs) discussed the experiences of working outside the branch and the process taken to begin developing relationships and addressing some of the many identified barriers the socially excluded experience when trying to access library services (Muzzerall et al. 2005). Additionally, there were a number of learnings over this same period regarding the role which outreach plays in comparison to community-led work in communities. Campbell (2005) described these as being mutually exclusive processes, which can be thought of as:

- *either* outreach – where library staff take existing library created services into the community and deliver them,
- *or* community development approaches – where relationship-building plays a central role in beginning to work with the community to determine need and developing services to meet community-identified needs.

Two of the most important learnings from this phase were:

- differentiation of community development approaches to working with communities from traditional outreach approaches (discussed in Chapter 5), and

- starting a process whereby community development concepts were being adapted for work in a library context.

It was important (for project staff, participating branch staff and each of the four respective library systems) to develop a working definition of community development in a library context. This definition provided project staff with key wording to describe the approaches they were undertaking and how they differentiated from current library practices:

> Community development in a library context means connecting, consulting and working collaboratively with community members to understand the needs of the community and to inform the direction of library work and policies.
>
> Community development in libraries focuses on building relationships with community members as a first step toward understanding the needs of the community. The second step is discussing those needs with the community in order to define the library's role in the community. An ongoing and continuous dialogue between the library and the community is necessary to evolve and evaluate the library's participation and contribution to the relationships and partnerships that have been established.
>
> Community development in a library setting also means using the information and stories that community members provide to better understand how to build a more inclusive and accessible library for those who find the library unwelcoming and do not use library services.
>
> A community development approach encourages and promotes philosophies, strategies and empathies that reduce the rigidity of the relationships between socially excluded community members and the library. At the same time a community development approach contributes to the growth of responsive and relevant library services and models that focus on library-community connections. (Singh and DeFaveri 2005)

Phase II

Phase II of the WTP took place between November 2005 and April 2008

Goals

The primary project goal for this second phase was to:

Develop and assess new alternative service models for libraries to work with socially excluded communities and individuals using community development techniques and community-based learning initiatives.[1] These models provide the targeted participants with:

- access to the resources of the library
- an increase in their sense of self-confidence
- new skills oriented to greater community participation
- employment opportunities.

Objectives

Ten objectives and a broad range of activities and deliverables to meet the objectives are outlined in the funding agreement (Schedule A). The funding agreement provided the basis for the evaluation framework, which outlines objectives, the expected results, the activities and the methods by which they will be evaluated.

Several key contractual activities [included] program and service development, toolkit development, partnerships and relationships, community entry, advisory committee, model branch development, [develop a course for university instruction, government web-based pathfinders], and initiatives to ensure project sustainability, and institutional change. (Atkey 2008: 23)

Major Outcomes from Phase II

By far the most significant outcome from this phase of the project, and of the whole WTP, was the development of a universal service planning model, which can and has been adapted to fit within local community and library contexts (Working Together 2008a). While preliminary discussions were focused on the development of different service models being created for different communities and contexts, the development of a universal service model which can be adapted to different contexts was a major breakthrough for both the project and the library profession.

For the first time, the service planning process traditionally undertaken by library staff was formally conceptualized and documented. Referred to as 'Traditional library service planning' (see Figure 1.1), this approach is primarily an insular process where library staff are central in assessing the community, identifying needs, planning and delivering services, and creating instruments or techniques for evaluation at the end of the planning process.

After a baseline understanding of 'traditional' library service planning was created, the approaches and learnings from CDLs was fed into the development of what has become known as the 'Community-led library service planning model' (see Figure 1.2). This model builds upon the traditional service planning model, providing

---

1   'Working Together ultimately developed a universal service model that can be adapted to various local contexts' (Atkey 2008: 3).

	Community Assessment & Needs Identification		Service Planning and Delivery		Evaluation
	Community Assessment	Needs identification	Service Planning	Delivery	
Traditional Planning	Staff reviews Demographic data Library use statistics Comment cards Community survey results	Staff identify service gaps or under-served communities	Staff review literature Staff consult with other staff and service providers Staff develop service response	Staff deliver service; develop the collection, hold the program, design facilities	Staff review various inputs Feedback forms Program attendance Collection use Library card enrolment [And] other statistics

Figure 1.1   Traditional planning

Source: Working Together 2008a.

	Community Assessment & Needs Identification		Service Planning and Delivery		Evaluation
	Community Assessment	Needs identification	Service Planning	Delivery	
Community-Led Planning	Staff review all of the traditional measures and Staff spend time in community developing relationships with community members. Staff hear from community about what is important to them.	Staff discuss with community members and hear from the community what their priorities are.	Service ideas are the community's ideas. Community is engaged in the planning of the service. Staff act as partners and facilitators rather than as creators and teachers.	Community members and staff work together to deliver the service. Community partners involved in selecting collection materials. Community partners active in hosting the program. Community partners working collaboratively with the library to develop policy recommendations.	Staff review various inputs. All of the traditional measures and Community and staff discuss: How did the process work? Did the service/ policy etc. actually address the need? What could have been done differently?

Figure 1.2   Community-led planning

Source: Working Together 2008a

library staff with additional skills and techniques to work collaboratively with the community to develop relationships, identify community needs, plan and deliver services together, and evaluate services with both staff and community input.

A very thorough overview of this service planning model can be found in an equally important deliverable developed at the conclusion of the WTP. The project coordinator, Annette DeFaveri, worked tirelessly to coordinate information from the four-year project from each of the four sites into the *Community-Led Libraries Toolkit* (Working Together 2008a). This toolkit now serves as a starting point for other library systems to both learn and build upon the community-led approach. The toolkit also provides an overview of tools which can be adapted and refined for each specific local context for working with socially excluded community members. The toolkit includes chapters on community entry, community mapping, relationship-building, partnerships, programme planning, computer training, collection development and customer service.

Singh and DeFaveri (2007) also discuss some additional key components which must be in place if library staff are to connect and develop relationships with socially excluded individuals. These include:

- Library staff must enter the community space and be open to learning from them.
- Library staff must be able to build trusting and respectful relationships as equals.
- Library staff must be able to work with individuals directly, and library staff should not confuse or substitute service provider relationships with individual community members.
- Library staff need to begin viewing communities as the experts on their own needs and library staff as facilitators. (Ibid.: 52–4)

Key Messages

A number of key messages were also developed during this second phase. These messages provide a range of important lessons learned from the four years of in-depth community-based work with socially excluded community members. Any library system considering developing programmes and services from a community-led approach should consider the implications of these key messages:

- As librarians we learn from, adapt and evolve techniques used in the community development field. We do this in order to better work with socially excluded communities.
- Librarians are not the experts on what our communities need or want in terms of library services – the community is the expert. It is our job to ensure that we develop a library service that reflects the community's needs and vision. We do this *with* them, not *for* them.
- The type of relationships we're building and the framework for how we are working with socially excluded community members can also be applied to socially included community members.

- Community Development in a library context represents a different approach to working with our communities: it represents a philosophical and practical shift from being a service provider for our communities to being a partner with our communities in service development and provision. This approach shifts the emphasis from our staff to our communities as the key initiators and/or drivers of service innovation and enhancement.
- Consultation is the necessary first step toward community development-based librarianship. Consultation must evolve into collaborative service prioritization, development, planning and evaluation.
- Reaching socially excluded community members and learning from them means meeting them in the places they are most comfortable and being open to learning from them. This means leaving the library and building trusting, respectful and equitable relationships. Only then, will we be able to learn what social excluded people need and want from their communities and library.
- A community development approach necessities working directly with, and building relationships with, socially excluded individuals in the community. Libraries often have relationships with service providers but service provider goals and objectives should not be confused with direct consultation and collaboration with community members themselves. Nor should service provider priorities be substituted for priorities defined by community members. The priorities and needs expressed by our community members must drive our library services.
- Public libraries need to change how they interact with socially excluded people. It is not the role of public libraries to teach people to be 'responsible' or 'good citizens'. Rather their role is to make services more welcoming, supportive and responsive to the needs of socially excluded people. Public libraries need to change for communities. Communities should not be expected to change for public libraries. (Singh and DeFaveri 2007)

Impacts after the Working Together Project

As with any 'project', some people may view the WTP as having finite beginning and end dates. Although the various library systems involved in the WTP were not obligated to incorporate and integrate the community-led approach into the way in which they worked, many of them began and continue to develop programmes, services and policies while taking this approach into account. There have been a number of major impacts which have arisen from the WTP. These include, but are not limited to:

- Raising the awareness of libraries that traditional service planning approaches did not take into account the perceived needs of a large portion of their communities, specifically members of socially excluded communities. This raised consciousness has expanded beyond those participating in the project, to other library systems throughout Canada and internationally.

- Some library systems have begun to adopt and integrate community-led principles, practices and language into their operations. (Canadian Library Association 2012, Williment et al. 2011b, Edmonton Public Library 2012)

Community-Led Libraries

We believe that failure to implement the recommendations of *Open to All?* and the learnings of the Working Together Project may have dire consequences for libraries in North America and Europe. With tightening budgets, there is a real danger that library management and decision-makers will react by entrenching themselves in traditional service approaches. We offer an alternative way forward based on a community-led approach to developing needs-based library services:

- consultation – the different approaches used to consult and engage with local communities to ensure that they are fully involved in the design, planning, delivery and evaluation of library services
- needs assessment and research – the methods by which community needs can be identified, prioritized and met
- library image and identity – how public libraries are perceived as a reflection of their buildings, staff and services
- outreach, community development and partnerships – the differences between outreach and community development in the context of traditional and community-led service planning
- ICT and social exclusion – the role of new technology in tackling social exclusion
- materials provision – the development of holistic collections policies to ensure that library stock reflects the needs of local communities
- staffing, recruitment, training and education – the skills and competencies that library workers must have to build relationships with excluded communities
- mainstreaming and resourcing for social exclusion – how to place community needs at the heart of public library strategy, structures, systems and organizational culture
- standards and monitoring of services – how to work with local people to create meaningful performance indicators and evaluation systems.

Each of the remaining chapters follows the same format:

- *Open to All?* recommendations
- an overview of UK public library policy and practice in relation to social exclusion, 2000 to 2012
- WTP findings

- the development of a community-led service philosophy in public libraries in Vancouver, Regina, Halifax and Toronto, 2004 to 2008.

The final two chapters are a synthesis of *Open to All?* recommendations and WTP learnings which provide a blueprint and road map for developing needs-based and community-led public library services.

Chapter 2
Consultation

In this chapter we examine the approaches which needs-based and community-led library services can use to consult and engage with local communities to ensure that they are fully involved in the design, planning, delivery and evaluation of library services. Consultation has become a very important issue for public library services in the UK and Canada. The drivers for this are partly statutory (for example, the Local Government and Public Involvement in Health Act 2007) and partly professional, but the overriding imperative is to give people what they want so that usage levels are maintained or increased to ensure future funding and sustainability.

Of course, there are many different types of consultation, from the very passive ('here is the information, what are your views?') to the very active ('how do you think library services should be delivered?'), and we are passionate advocates of the more dynamic approach. It is clear that coming up with a decision and asking the community to just 'rubber-stamp' it is not the basis of needs-based and community-led services. *Open to All?* (Muddiman et al. 2000b) made it clear that consultation must be both real and continuing and that social exclusion strategies and services should be developed with the active engagement of socially excluded people who should be involved in the planning, implementation and monitoring of services.

These ideas have been put into action in Canada through the Working Together Project, which has encouraged library staff to shift from just giving information to partnering and collaborating with the community. A number of key questions were asked to determine how well library staff were engaging with the community; for example, 'how is the community involved in identifying needs and then developing a service response?' Relationships were developed with community members and staff became aware of how uncomfortable the library environment could be for some socially excluded people.

The Consultation Spectrum

When *Open to All?* was published in 2000, community consultation was still in its infancy in the UK. There was no requirement to consult local communities about public services and, when consultation did occur, it was very often at the passive/reactive end of the engagement spectrum described in Figure 2.1:

PASSIVE	REACTIVE	PARTICIPATIVE	EMPOWERMENT	LEADERSHIP
Local residents and organizations are informed of issues by library service	Local residents and organizations provide input into the priorities and resource use of library service	Local residents and organizations influence the priorities and resources of library service	Local residents and organizations work in shared planning and action with library service	Local residents and organizations initiate and lead on issues with support from library service

Figure 2.1   Community engagement

The UK government's White Paper *Strong and Prosperous Communities* (DCLG 2006) set out wide-ranging proposals for supporting the improvement of local services. This included giving people who use local services opportunities to influence the way these are run, strengthening the way councils provide leadership and encouraging all those involved in delivering local services to work together more effectively. This has been enshrined in law through the Local Government and Public Involvement in Health Act 2007.

Councils, as part of their community leadership role, are required to undertake high-quality engagement with all local communities. They have an obligation to understand and act on the needs of the communities they serve and to promote equality and tackle inequalities. Public library services needed to review their approach to community engagement to ensure it was helping to deliver improved outcomes for local communities. This required public consultation which was towards the empowerment/leadership end of the engagement continuum.

Community Engagement

Community engagement is about the way in which the library service and its partners engage with their communities, and it focuses on the needs of local people. It requires good awareness of the range of different communities within an area. Systems and processes are in place to monitor and ensure a full understanding of the different needs and aspirations of these communities. This is reflected in strategy, policy and service delivery. Genuine community engagement ensures that everyone in the local area is given an opportunity to participate and be involved in setting local priorities and shaping the delivery of local library services. It helps to:

- challenge the types of library services and the way they are provided
- identify root causes of any community tensions and contribute to better community cohesion: this term refers to the aspect of togetherness and bonding exhibited by members of a community, the 'glue' that holds a community together, and it might include features such as a sense of common belonging or cultural similarity

- improve local knowledge and develop local capacity, confidence and ownership
- build communities that are strong and empowered.

It includes a wide range of methods for engaging local people and ensures there is regular dialogue with local communities.

A library service which effectively and meaningfully consults and engages with its local community should see these outcomes:

- Increased levels of involvement across all community groups with increasing levels of pride in the local area and communities contributing effectively to the library service.
- Local people influence the setting of library priorities and participate in decision-making. They have a clear understanding of the library service ambitions and priorities and actively support these.
- A wide and diverse range of engagement methods, that cater for the needs of local people. The needs and aspirations of different communities are successfully balanced.
- A track record of change and improvement following community engagement.
- Good relations between people from different communities as a result of effective community engagement.
- People from diverse groups feel they can participate in decision-making and do not feel excluded.
- Local people report being satisfied with their level of involvement in the development of library services.
- Library services that meet the diverse needs of its users. Services users can identify where services have improved.
- High levels of access to, and satisfaction with, library services amongst all sections of the community, including those that are vulnerable or 'hard to reach'.
- Targeted community development work to protect the most vulnerable and reach those at highest risk.
- Local people report that they play a significant role in shaping the development of new and changing library services.
- Effective targeting of resources and providing services that meet the needs and wishes of local communities.

A Community-Led Approach

A community-led library service requires mutually supportive strategies, structures, systems and cultures which can identify, prioritize and meet community needs. This section, based on the Audit Commission's *Knowing Your Communities*

Toolkit, outlines the issues which should be considered when a community-led approach to community engagement is being developed.

Has the library service and its partners developed a clear vision?

The vision sets out long-term outcomes for the library service which fully takes into account the needs and aspirations of diverse citizens and communities. Ambitions build on developing integrated and cohesive communities and on improving outcomes. There is clear evidence of achievement in improved access to, and satisfaction with, library services. Inequalities in outcomes are being addressed by targeted actions specified in partnership agreements. The library service and its partners can demonstrate increased community engagement and the integration of communities through their actions.

What use is made of demographic data?

The library service and its partners have a strong knowledge base of the diverse communities they serve. Using shared intelligence processes, they regularly monitor the changing profile of the local community and assess its impact on community cohesion. This information is also used to set priorities and measure improvements for local people. Data analysis is used to map inequalities, identifying current and future needs, and tailor library services accordingly. The library service and its partners can demonstrate that they have successfully adapted community engagement processes to engage the different communities being served, including those from vulnerable groups. There are effective information-sharing arrangements to ensure seamless and integrated service provision to local people.

Is information gathered through consultation?

The library service and its partners employ a comprehensive and creative range of methods and mechanisms to engage and involve all citizens and local communities. This includes current and potential users. They go beyond the usual consultation mechanisms to include targeted community development with disadvantaged, vulnerable or marginalized groups. The information gathered is converted into good intelligence used in decision-making. Outcomes are always fed back to those who have been consulted.

To what extent are local people involved?

Clear strategies have been developed to increase levels of participation from under-represented and vulnerable groups. Local people have actively influenced policy and decision-making and there has been demonstrable improvement in library services as a result of public involvement. There is increased representation of diverse communities involved in local libraries. This has contributed to good community cohesion. Information from engagement activities is shared regularly between partners and this has reduced the likelihood of consultation fatigue.

Are decision-making processes inclusive?

There is a well-established culture of public participation across all library and partner services. Support is available to enable local people, including those from vulnerable groups and communities, to regularly contribute to decision-making processes. There is widespread awareness amongst local people of their contribution to service design and delivery and how they have influenced changes.

Are there shared library, partner and community priorities?

Library priorities have been drawn up and widely consulted upon using extensive consultation, engagement and involvement with all sections of the community. All partners have been involved in priority-setting and this has resulted in clear alignment with partners' priorities. They include robust strategies for promoting community empowerment and community cohesion. The library service has successfully combined library and community priorities with the result that outcomes for local people are being achieved.

Are staff supported to deliver the priorities?

Library service and partner staffing strategies have resulted in a workforce that is broadly representative of the communities served. Diverse staff groups and local communities recognize that staffing policies are providing opportunities for recruitment, retention and progression. There is equality of access to training and employment which has led to a demonstrable improvement in the retention of staff from local communities. Investment in staff training has resulted in high satisfaction levels. Surveys clearly demonstrate frontline staff are responding flexibly to meet the needs of all service users. There is excellent working across library service and partner boundaries resulting in improved access to services and equality of access for diverse community groups. ICT has been used to increase access for all communities to library and partner services.

Are partners able to support these priorities?

Partners both deliver high-quality services for local people from diverse communities and provide community benefits. They are sufficiently flexible to respond to the changing needs of the community being served. Users are regularly consulted about service provision and satisfaction with these partner services is high. Partners provide local employment opportunities and their staff are broadly representative of the local communities.

Is information useful to local people and service users?

Satisfaction levels from a range of community and user groups regarding the quality and type of information produced is high. Service users, including those from diverse and vulnerable groups, report that the information produced is clear, easy to understand and meets their information needs. Performance information is reported in a clear and transparent way. A wide range of formats ensures that information is accessible to all diverse groups within the community.

Are the library service and its partners communicating well with local people?

Regular two-way dialogue with all communities enables the library service and its partners to fully understand the wishes and needs of local people. All stakeholders feel fully informed about changes to library services and priorities as a result of regular communication.

Are community impact assessments in place?

Community impact assessments identify the costs and benefits of a policy proposal and the risks of not acting. They are intended to inform the policy decision-making process and communicate clearly the objectives, options, costs, benefits and risks of proposals to the public to increase the transparency of the process.

Information is drawn from a range of sources to support community impact assessments including engagement and consultation with a wide range of community groups. Action plans resulting from community impact assessments are fully implemented. The library service and its partners can demonstrate that community impact assessments have led to improved outcomes and equality of access for diverse groups. Community impact assessments are used at service level to inform library service provision.

Is there a system in place to measure the impact of these priorities?

The library service and its partners can demonstrate a strong track record of using evaluation and assessment to measure quality of life and understand levels of satisfaction of local people. They have improved and adapted service delivery to reduce inequalities. The library service and its partners are using impact and outcome measures to assess progress against community engagement priorities and have incorporated the findings from surveys to improve performance.

Have library service users been able to influence how impacts and outcomes are measured?

A diverse range of local people report that they have been fully involved in service evaluation and assessment in areas they have identified as priorities. This process has increased confidence in the library service and its partners and their efforts to improve services and reduce inequalities.

Do the library service and its partners use their own information about use of library services?

The library service and its partners routinely collect information about use of, and satisfaction with, their services, and have a strong knowledge base developed over time about service usage. This includes clear analysis across diverse user groups and localities, which is used to address inequalities in provision and to understand where contact with local communities needs to be improved.

Are complaints and feedback used to drive improvement?

The library service and its partners have a strong learning and improvement culture, which is open and supportive. They positively encourage local people and staff to tell them where they need to improve. Staff and local people feel that their views are valued and this is evidenced through assessments which demonstrate consistent improvement in satisfaction levels across all groups. Monitoring information and complaints knowledge is being consistently used by the library service and its partners to improve outcomes for all local people, including those from vulnerable groups, and to reduce inequalities.

Are the library service and its partners open to community scrutiny and review?

The library service and its partners view community scrutiny as a key driver to improvements in the quality of life for local people. They welcome community review and can show how it has been used to hold the library service to account. There is regular scrutiny of library services which engages users, non-users, staff, partners and other stakeholders. The library service and its partners ensure there is the information and capacity necessary to hold them to account.

Community Cohesion

UK government policies for community engagement have been high profile, as have community cohesion agendas – but these have been developed in parallel. *Community Engagement and Community Cohesion* (Mayo et al. 2008) explored the challenges of bringing them together.

The UK government is committed to promoting community engagement. But services are being delivered by an increasingly diverse range of providers, with correspondingly diverse opportunities for user and community involvement. There is growing concern about how to join up these different service providers to provide integrated services which meet community needs.

There has been less focus upon the implications of engaging service users and communities effectively when communities are themselves diverse, with differing needs and priorities. Globalization has been associated with increasing migration, although these changes are difficult to measure. This poses major challenges for the community engagement and community cohesion agendas.

Local communities want their views to be heard, and they want to participate. For many local people 'being heard' means being recognized, having a safe space to meet, providing mutual support and gaining the knowledge, confidence and skills to engage more widely. 'Being heard' also means being listened to with respect, knowing that resources are being allocated with visible fairness. Established communities typically share this view of community engagement, and they also face problems in getting their views heard, but newer communities find it even harder.

New communities face practical barriers, such as lack of information (exacerbated by the fluidity and fragmentation of governance structures), personal barriers such as difficulties in the use of English or a lack of time to participate due to working long/unsociable hours, and barriers to recognition (for example, newer communities often do not have formally constituted community organizations so are not being consulted and are not eligible to receive public funds).

Groups particularly at risk of not having their views heard effectively are asylum seekers and refugees, undocumented migrants and new migrant workers from the European Union. Amongst these groups, women and younger people were identified as having even less chance of being listened to than older men. Meanwhile, some established minority communities and some established white working-class communities had been less successful than others in making their views heard.

These findings highlight the importance of linking strategies that promote community engagement with strategies that promote community cohesion. Otherwise, the result could be increased competition for scarce resources between established communities and newer arrivals.

The research also highlighted the importance of continuity and sustainability in governance structures. It is difficult enough for local communities to get their views heard and this fluidity in structures exacerbates these difficulties.

Much of the emphasis on community engagement has been directed at the neighbourhood. But the research found that neighbourhood forums are not necessarily the most appropriate levels for some issues, such as the transport infrastructure. The neighbourhood level is particularly problematic for communities that are geographically dispersed across towns and cities, as many new arrivals are, and given that many of their concerns – such as jobs, refugee/ asylum status and language skills – are managed outside the neighbourhood.

A range of good practices addressing these challenges were identified, involving local communities as part of wider strategies to promote cohesion. Community development work emerged as a critical factor. These 'promising practices' can be used to inform the development of community-led library services:

- Ensure that community and citizen engagement strategies take account of diversity and the dynamics of population change and turnover.
- Provide clear and comprehensive guides to services and the criteria for allocating resources fairly and transparently, with welcome packs for new service users, explaining where and how their concerns can be addressed, and including information about how to get involved.
- Develop proactive communication strategies, including challenging negative stereotyping within and between communities.
- Provide support to community organizations, groups and informal networks, both directly through library workers and indirectly through resourcing partner organizations, ensuring that equalities issues are prioritized.
- Support the organization of shared events, including community festivals, sports events, outings and welcome events, as part of wider strategies to promote community cohesion and community engagement.
- Recognize the limitations of neighbourhood participation structures and support the complementary development of effective city/borough-wide structures.

Attracting New Members and Engaging Effectively with the Community

Attracting new members, engaging effectively with the community and community outreach were also key recommendations in *The Modernisation Review of Public Libraries* (2010) which identified the importance of engaging in outreach activities in order to attract new, often hard-to-reach, library users: 'All library authorities should consider how they can shape services to respond to the locally identified needs of their community – including families. This, in turn, helps develop services which appeal to new users and which might be cost effective in a constrained financial environment' (DCMS 2010a: 24).

There are a number of schemes operating at national and local level which were successful in attracting new library members and promoting reading. Led by the National Literacy Trust and the Reading Agency, the National Year of Reading in 2008 encouraged 2.3 million people to join the library, and Bookstart baby packs successfully encouraged parents to enrol their children as library members. In 2009 the Summer Reading Challenge, involving 95 per cent of libraries and spearheaded by the Reading Agency during the long school holiday, saw 725,000 children participating, with 47,000 becoming new library members.

In Manchester, when funding from existing budgets was identified to create a temporary outreach and promotions assistant, a new approach was taken to targeting the 72 per cent of residents who did not already have a library ticket. A portable mini-library with wheeled shelf units and bearing a selection of seasonal stock was taken round to potentially fruitful recruiting grounds including the town hall, large private companies and higher education institutions. By summer 2009 the library service had held 45 'Meet the Neighbours' sessions and recruited 3,750 new members.

When Leeds Library and Information Service was awarded £1.4 million from the Big Lottery Fund Communities Libraries Programme to extend and refurbish a dull 1960s library in Garforth into a new vibrant creative space and one-stop centre, a comprehensive community engagement plan was adopted to ensure that communities could influence the service the new building would provide. Parents, business representatives, children of primary school age, older people and representatives from the voluntary sector were consulted and focus groups were held. A community Steering Group selected a large proportion of the book stock for the new library. The success of the project is illustrated by visitor statistics – 1,600 people attended the first family day at the library.

Working Together: Moving from Informing to Public Involvement

From the onset of the Working Together Project (WTP) there was recognition that a new set of tools needed to be developed in order to actively include socially excluded community members in service development. It was quickly confirmed that barriers to accessing library services existed and it was essential for consultation activities to occur in community spaces, outside of library branches, where socially excluded people felt comfortable gathering. Community development librarians (CDLs) were tasked in each of the four different sites to develop, implement and test different consultation approaches, in order to determine how to begin working with community members who have historically been excluded from library provision development.

Experimentation was essential, and learning occurred through trying, succeeding and at times failing while attempting to implement these new consultation techniques. It is essential to note that while community engagement usually began within the scope of consultation, many of the relationships which were developed allowed the interaction between library staff and the community to become sustained and led to collaborative service planning, development, implementation and evaluation.

Much like the passive/reactive engagement spectrum (as discussed in the table earlier) similar conceptual work was also developed through the Working Together Project (WTP) on how best to involve members of the public in the information exchange process (see Figure 2.2). As library staff move from the left side of the public involvement continuum to the right, members of the public are more involved in the information exchange – thus changing information flows from being primarily information-giving processes to collaborative two-way conversations (Working Together 2008a).

The most common approach used in library systems to interacting with the community is to *give information out* to the community about services which have been created by library staff. By initiating conversations with socially

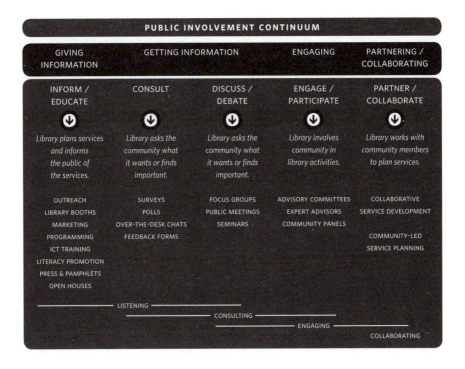

Figure 2.2   Public involvement continuum

Source: Working Together 2008a, p. 16.

excluded community members, it became apparent to CDLs that marketing existing programmes and services were ineffective in making library services relevant to them, since the development of these existing services did not take their needs into account (Williment 2009). Giving information inherently led to a one-way flow of information that did not provide mechanisms for the community to contribute to the interaction. As a result, library staff were not taking advantage of opportunities to learn about and begin responding to the needs of socially excluded communities.

Prior to WTP, discussions and consultation were also well-tested techniques for involving the community. In each of these processes, library staff were *getting information* from the community about what it wants or finds important. Most times this information is collected by library staff who have pre-developed and determined questions to ask the community, based on library staff perceptions of community need. Library staff are asking questions because they have something they want to 'find out' from the community. This begs the question: are library staff asking the right questions in order to 'find out' the right information? Additionally, the validity and reliability of passive techniques, such as feedback forms, or other written responses should be questioned. Many of these information-gathering techniques are biased towards those who have the confidence to fill them out, to those who raise their voices (primarily existing library users), and limited to those who have the literacy skills to fill them out. Each of these techniques may work well for existing library users who feel they have a voice in library service development, but do not work well for the socially excluded.

Consultation techniques, found on the right side of the community involvement continuum, which actively involve community members, are discussed in more length below.

Consultation – Collaborative Techniques: Working Together

The consultation techniques developed when using a community-led approach necessitate the development and maintenance of relationships. *Relationships are the basis of community-led services – if relationships with individuals are not built and maintained, community-led service planning cannot occur*. These should not be considered one-off interactions with community members, but ongoing and sustained interactions. The engagement techniques also need to be active, not passive. It is important to actively speak, listen, verify and learn from people. One of the major advantages of using community-led engagement techniques is that they are not prescriptive. When each engagement approach is applied it has be adapted to work within the different social contexts.

When consulting it is important for library staff to resist the temptation to immediately develop a service response or 'solution' for the community. Traditionally, librarians initially respond to interactions with community members by trying to formulate programmes and services to meet library staff members' perceptions of community need. By focusing on the end point, instead of how librarians can interact with the community to discover needs, they are doing a disservice to both the community and the library. By using a community-led approach for engagement, the techniques provide a means to understand and differentiate between an individual request and a community need.

Initially, there was a great deal of hesitation on the part of CDLs to 'go out into the community without anything to offer' (Atkey 2008: 114). It was a very humbling experience to consult with community members, while resisting the allure of offering what the library had already created for the community.

> We as library staff are not the experts on what our communities want or need in terms of library services – the community is the expert. It is our job to ensure that we develop a library service that reflects the community's needs and vision. We do this with them, not for them. (Working Together 2008a: 28)

Ultimately, when developing services library staff need to ask themselves 'who came up with the idea and who was involved in the putting together' (DeFaveri, personal correspondence 2007). If 'library staff' is the response, this should give library staff pause to reconsider how they are engaging with the community.

Initial Assessment of Community – Entering the Community

An initial activity which was taken by most CDLs was to walk and move about the community. One of the first tasks many of the CDLs undertook when starting out in each community was to walk the targeted community and take public transport around it. While this activity did not provide an opportunity to establish ongoing and sustained relationships, it provided librarians with an overall feel of the community, while also providing the community with the opportunity to see a new, soon-to-be familiar face. In an urban environment it was important to take the role and to explore the community from the perspective of community members. Social exclusion impacts mobility, and by moving about the community in the same mode as socially excluded community members, librarians began to understand the distances between services, such as where they picked up their groceries, took their children to daycare, accessed local municipal services, and of course the distance to the local library.

Door-to-Door Knocking

Where communities are densely populated, one way to begin building relationships with socially excluded community members is to go directly to where they live. CDLs in multiple locations went door-to-door in communities. The purpose of doing this was not to market library services, but instead to provide a brief introduction and develop a sense of community use and perceptions of library services. Thus it was important to develop a script with a set of questions or speaking points. For example, in one targeted community consisting of 255 city housing townhouses, the CDL developed a set of speaking points in order to explore barriers to library services. By going directly into the community and having these discussions, the library quickly learned about the impact of library fines and fees, transportation and opening hours. This provided the library with a solid grounding for beginning to work with the community to develop service responses to address these and other identified barriers.

Access to Community Members through Service Providers

While community-led service planning focuses on developing relationships with individual community members, the rationale for working with community service providers (also commonly referred to as community agencies) is that many of them are providing spaces where socially excluded community members frequently gather. It was very important to clarify that the rationale for developing relationships with service providers was to gain access to individual community members. CDLs in each of the four sites undertook a community asset-mapping project, which focused on identifying service providers who provided space for community members to gather and meet (McLeod 2006). In addition, this process allowed for the identification of existing skills, abilities, talents and strengths in each community (Working Together 2008a).

At times the initial reaction from staff at these organizations was that the library could potentially play a role in filling a programme or service requirement for the organization. However, after establishing relationships with them it provided an opportunity to engage with service providers and share community-led techniques and approaches to working with the community. A surprising consequence was that other non-library service providers also started to develop programmes and services using community-led approaches.

Hanging Out

Conceptually, 'hanging out' was possibly one of the most difficult community engagement techniques to envision implementing, but also one of the most effective approaches to consulting with the community. Librarians, individual community members and service providers are used to engaging with the community on the left side of the public involvement continuum (Figure 2.2) – information is provided to the community. There can be a sense of disbelief that 'hanging out' can be permitted as part of our library work. However, as illustrated by the example below, hanging out in community spaces where socially excluded community members are comfortable gathering provides a unique opportunity to learn about community needs – from the community members themselves.

> In one community agency there was discomfort with the CDL 'just hanging out' in the lobby. However, the librarian had recognized there was a common seating area and decided to bring a tactile activity in where the librarian could participate as an equal with community members. Some of these 'activities' included bringing in clay for making handmade pottery and origami paper and books. When people are busy doing something, conversations begin and people start talking about their lives. These discussions and the underlying stories were the basis for discovering community needs. According to participants who worked with the clay, conversations went from 'it feels empowering to do something creative' to 'what other creative things can we do?'. What started out as an outreach strategy turned into collaborative service planning, and developed into a not-for-profit arts society. (Atkey 2008: 25)

This hanging-out activity became known as the '100 pounds of clay', and since making pottery required follow-up, these follow-ups led to ongoing conversations, the development of relationships, and was the beginning of the librarian learning about community interests and existing capacities.

Another example from a CDL illustrates the power of hanging out.

> At one site, I entered a location where youth were gathered. As the youth were living on the street, I felt a little uncomfortable, and once I introduced myself as a

librarian one of the youth said to me 'you here to educate me?' In the meantime, the other librarian I was with had brought some astrology and origami books and paper with him (he had heard them discussing these topics as being interesting). The next thing I know, the one youth who thought I was there to educate him, was teaching me how to make origami. The next thing you know, we were busy talking about his life, what it was like living on the street, etc. (Author's personal notes, unpublished)

Informal and Formal Group Discussions

Focus groups are traditionally structured and are quite formal. Informal small group discussions involve going into groups where informal discussions are already happening. This approach was used by the Vancouver CDL to consult with a teen group.

Community roundtables are also an important consultation mechanism for service providers to talk to other service providers and form alliances. They tend to provide perceptions of community needs and are an outreach-based means of sharing existing programmes.

Advisory Committees

Throughout the four-year project each of the four sites tried to establish advisory committees, with varying success. While advisory committees were successfully implemented in two locations, the community capacity to participate through formalized advisory committees was abandoned. As identified by Atkey (2008):

> The advisory committees in two cities had successes hosting community events and the committee structure was effective in informing Working Together and branch staff about the experiences of people living in their communities. The particular difficulties in establishing the committee in two cities ... are largely the result of the community's capacity for participating through formalized structures. While both sites continued to get community feedback about community needs and interests, the pursuit of establishing formal committees was largely abandoned. It is unclear, however, how the needs identification through these alternate processes differed from other needs identification processes carried out through Working Together.

> The lack of clarity highlights the importance of making a clear distinction between an advisory body's advisory function and their role in identifying access barriers. It does not appear as though this distinction existed within the project, which may have hampered the efforts to establish functional committees at two sites. It is equally possible that advisory committees are the wrong model for community-led service planning, a viewpoint that was generally supported by interviewees. (Atkey 2008: 32)

As discussed in the evaluation above, one of the major limitations to consulting with community members is that capacity to participate in a formalized structure such as an advisory committee may be limited by the very same factors that make someone socially excluded. Most advisory committees require people to attend a scheduled meeting, in a specific location, and to participate in meetings, which may not feel natural.

Additionally, advisory groups also run the risk of attracting spokespersons for the community. One way to mitigate this is by having term-based participants on advisory committees, thus continually changing members of the committee to ensure numerous, diverse voices are heard.

Attending Regular Meetings and Events

When attending events it is important to engage with the community. Standing behind booths with information waiting for communities to approach you does not work. You need to be proactive by walking amongst the people participating and having discussions with them.

Taking Existing Services into the Community

Chapter 5, focusing on outreach versus community development, provides a more extensive overview of this approach. Since CDLs were not taking out existing programmes and services, one difficulty that every librarian experienced when first going out into a community was 'what could be used to initially engage with the community?' In response a number of different approaches were taken. For example, in one community the CDL took laptops into a community agency where people gathered. While community agency staff initially took a lot of interest in the technology, individual community members were hesitant to interact with the technology (Atkey 2008: 81). However, within a few weeks community members expressed interest in learning more about computers. While laptops provided a focal point for conversations, it also restricted conversations to technology and limited discussions about other potential needs.

Final Thoughts

The consultation techniques discussed above are just the tip of the iceberg. There are numerous community-based engagement techniques which were piloted through the Working Together Project. Most of these techniques expanded beyond simplistic one-time consultations, instead focusing on creating sustained and ongoing relationships, which served as the basis for community-led service planning.

There is no one right engagement technique and the technique used needs to be tailored to the specific group being targeted. The Working Together

Toolkit provides a much more in-depth analysis and should be referred to when contemplating the use of consultation techniques in a library context.

Helpful Hints[1]

#1: When working with library staff, introduce them to the first two rows of Figure 2.2. Place these two rows on a large flipchart and ask library staff individually to write down at least two different things they are currently doing which involve the community. Have them place their answers below the relevant section in the involvement continuum. Most responses will probably fall on the left side of the involvement continuum. Ask staff how the activities could be changed so they can be moved to the right.

#2: A number of key questions can be used to determine how well library staff are engaging with community. It is important to identify where ideas are initiated. When working with a targeted community ask:

- How were they engaged?
- Who identified the community need?
- Who placed the identified need in a library context? If it was library staff, did they re-engage the community to verify if they were interpreting the library-based need correctly?
- How was the community involved in the identification and then developing the service response?

#3: After relationships are established with individual community members, ask them if they would be willing to walk through the community with you, and introduce you to other community members.

#4: The discomfort that librarians may initially experience being in an unfamiliar place where socially excluded community members gather should be viewed as having only one tenth of the discomfort that socially excluded members face when entering libraries.

#5: Public libraries need to develop methods for real and continuing consultation with socially excluded communities, groups and individuals.

---

1 The intent of helpful hints, which will be found in each chapter, is to provide the reader and their respective library systems with a number of exercises or additional items to think about when considering the application of community-led work within their specific organization and community contexts.

#6: Social exclusion strategies and services should be developed with the active engagement of socially excluded people, who should be involved in the planning, implementation and monitoring of services.

#7: Public libraries should ask socially excluded people when they would like libraries to be open and offer imaginative and creative opening hour patterns which meet these needs.

Chapter 3
Needs Assessment and Research

In this chapter we consider the methods by which community needs can be identified, prioritized and met. This is probably the most critical chapter in our book, because needs assessment and research is at the very heart of a community-led library service. If we do not know what the community's needs are, then how can we meet those needs? We take a critical view of library services in the UK and Canada who assume that they know what the community wants and needs, based on their professional knowledge and/or official statistics. We argue that professional knowledge is premised on a narrow set of values which cannot understand or comprehend community needs. We also argue that official statistics are, at best, inaccurate and incomplete and, at worst, misleading.

Open to All? (Muddiman et al. 2000a) recommended for the first time that public libraries should go beyond passive community profiles (compiled exclusively by staff using statistical data) and work in partnership with the community to develop holistic methodologies for identifying needs. Critically, it was suggested that libraries need to stop talking only to library members and open up a dialogue with non-users as well. There was an urgent need to understand community perceptions of libraries (many of which were negative) and reduce barriers to use.

There is evidence that some UK library authorities (such as Lincolnshire and Southend) have adopted a more needs-based approach to service delivery. In Canada this approach has been piloted in four authorities (Halifax, Vancouver, Regina and Toronto) where staff have been trained to recognize that different communities have different needs and that a 'one size fits all' approach is not appropriate. Use of library jargon, for example, can be a major barrier which can disrupt the relationship-building process. This is a very sensitive area and Working Together put great time and effort into ensuring that staff had the right mix of skills and sufficient structural support to enable them to engage with the community and identify needs.

Community Profiles

Community profiles had been a feature of the more progressive UK public library authorities since the 1970s. The wave of community librarianship which swept across London and other metropolitan areas was informed by an attempt to understand the needs of local communities. The major flaw in this early approach to needs assessment was that the information about local communities was taken by many library services from official sources such as the ten-yearly national census. The census did not fully reflect local needs because some people – particularly the marginalized and disadvantaged – were either not recorded on the census or gave false information because they mistrusted (with good reason) the purposes for which this information was being gathered and how it could be used by those in positions of power. Immigrants and people who were on state benefits, for example, wanted to keep a low profile and not offer up too much personal information to the state. These fears were fully realized when Margaret Thatcher introduced the much-hated Poll Tax which charged everyone – regardless of their income – the same amount of money to pay for local council services. Many people tried to avoid paying this regressive tax, which hit working-class communities very hard, and the government implemented a raft of measures to ensure that the Poll Tax was collected. One of these powers included the ability to sequester public library membership records to check who was living at a particular address. The effect on working-class people was to make them more reluctant to give their personal details to the authorities, including library membership information. The other major flaw with relying on census data was that it quickly went out of date and it was not supplemented by information and intelligence garnered from staff, other service providers or the local community themselves. So these early community profiles were a very statistics-based and one-dimensional view of the world which sometimes bore little resemblance to the real situation on the ground. This was particularly so in local communities which were dynamic and fast-moving, with people flowing into and out of the area on a constant basis, such as refugees, migrant workers and asylum seekers. The needs of these communities were not fully understood or met by public libraries before the Welcome to Your Libraries Project.

With a few notable exceptions (in particular the pioneering work carried out by Lambeth Libraries in the 1970s and 1980s, where there was huge community involvement and input), this flawed data was used, at best, to inform outreach activities which were planned, designed, delivered and assessed by professional librarians without any community involvement or input. As we point out in our chapter on community development, this passive approach to delivering services outside of the library is unlikely to meet community needs.

These early attempts at community profiling and needs assessment were voluntary and carried out by a handful of authorities who saw the value in community engagement and involvement. The great majority of library services did not profile their local communities or carry out any needs assessment – they relied, instead, on 'professional judgement' which was based on the individual (often white middle-class) values of qualified staff. This led to stereotyping, assumptions and second-guessing of local needs, and the professionals often got it very wrong. It was assumed, for example, that migrant communities wanted books in their own languages, when in fact they were desperate for books in English so that they could assimilate and get jobs.

The Needs-Based Library Service

Developing a Needs-Based Library Service (Pateman 2003) took as its starting point Maslow's hierarchy of needs, proposed by Abraham Maslow in *A Theory of Human Motivation* (1943). This theory suggests that the most basic levels of needs must be met before the individual will strongly desire (or focus motivation upon) the secondary or higher level needs. The table here suggests how this theory can be applied to the public library context.

Maslow's hierarchy of needs	Needs-based library services
Self actualization – realizing a person's full potential	Co-producing library services by combining the skills, knowledge and experience of local communities and library staff
Esteem – recognition, acceptance, self-respect	Sharing power and resources with local communities to give them a genuine stake in library service planning, design, delivery and evaluation
Love/belonging – friendship, intimacy, family	Building relationships with local communities; creating an inclusive public library environment where people feel welcome and there is a sense of belonging
Safety – personal and financial security, health and well-being	Working with partners and/or signposting to agencies which can provide financial advice and assistance and meet health and education needs
Physiological – food, clothing, shelter	Working with partners and/or signposting to agencies which can meet food, clothing and housing needs

Figure 3.1   Hierarchy of needs

A needs-based library service will seek to identify, prioritize and meet community needs, with a focus on those who have the greatest needs. These needs will include library and information needs but will also include those more basic needs in the lower levels of Maslow's hierarchy. People who do not have enough food to eat or nowhere to live are not going to have high library and information needs. But, if the library service can help people to meet their basic needs (through partnership working and signposting to agencies who can meet those needs), then a relationship is developed between the library service and local communities. Over time, as lower-level needs are met and trust and respect is developed through relationship-building, the library service can work with local communities to meet their higher-level needs, including their library and information needs.

Library Needs Assessments

In 2009 Wirral Council threatened to close 11 of its libraries. There was a vociferous local campaign to keep these libraries open, which became a national cause célèbre. The challenge was not that Wirral Council could not make changes to its library service, but that local communities should be consulted before these changes were made. The New Labour government was not sure how to respond and did not want to invoke the limited powers of the 1964 Public Libraries Act. New Labour had come into office on the promise to give greater freedom to local councils and local people to determine which services would best meet local needs. Some of these initiatives are covered in our chapter on community engagement. So, rather than intervene, New Labour decided to commission an enquiry into the Wirral Library Service.

The UK government has only conducted a formal public inquiry into a local council's plans for library closures twice – once in Derbyshire in 1991, and in the Wirral in 2009. The role of the inquiry was to:

> Gather information and provide advice in order for the Secretary of State to assess whether, in taking the decision to implement the proposed changes to their library service, The Wirral was in default of their statutory duties under the Public Libraries and Museums Act 1964, including the provision of a comprehensive and efficient library service. (Charteris 2009)

In formulating this advice and recommendations the inquiry considered the following questions:

- Did Wirral make a reasonable assessment of local needs in respect of library services and, in any event, what are those needs?
- On assessment of local needs, did Wirral act reasonably in meeting such needs through their proposals in the context of available resources and their statutory obligations?
- In considering the question of local needs, the inquiry considered what assessment was made by Wirral (through the process of consultation) of local needs, and commented independently upon the following local factors:
  - local authority context: equalities and population (including deprivation, geography, demography), budget, local priorities and sustainability
  - service operation: infrastructure (including buildings, mobiles, digital and outreach services), resources, staffing, opening hours, service budget
  - service delivery: value for money, performance data (including visits, book issues, user satisfaction), library leadership/management capacity, local partnerships and cross-authority working
  - strategic vision: links between library service and key local strategies, current and future vision for the service.

In considering statutory obligations, the inquiry considered and made an assessment, with reference to best practice where appropriate, on how effectively

Wirral's library service addressed and met the 'guidance factors' contained in the 1964 Act relating to the desirable elements of all library services, which can be summarized as follows:

- securing and keeping a wide range of free resources (including books and other printed matter, pictures, sound recordings, films and other materials), to browse and borrow in sufficient number, range and quality to meet the general requirements (and any special requirements) of both adults and children (living, working or studying in the local area)
- free independent information and advice from staff
- encouragement for use and participation of the service; for example, through clear and easy ways to join, access, shape and influence the service.

The Wirral Inquiry gave interested parties the opportunity to comment, and took their views into consideration. Particular emphasis was placed on securing the contribution of the following groups:

- local communities – those resident, working or studying in the area – including representative organizations
- community leaders including local members of Parliament and councillors
- key partner organizations
- council officers – leadership, library managers, library staff and their unions.

The Wirral Inquiry found that if Wirral Metropolitan Borough Council went ahead with its proposals to close 11 of its libraries, it would be in breach of the Public Libraries and Museums Act and the council withdrew its proposals. The inquiry's conclusions included:

- The Council's decision to reform its library service in the manner proposed placed it in breach of its statutory duties.
- The Council failed to make an assessment of local needs in respect of its library services.
- The Council was not able to demonstrate that it had had due regard to the general requirements of children.
- Because the Council did not demonstrate that it had made an adequate assessment of local needs, the Council did not act reasonably in meeting such needs through their proposals.
- There was an absence of a strategic plan or a development plan for the service.
- Without adequate plans for outreach services, the library service as a whole would not be compliant.

The evidence submitted to the inquiry indicated a demonstrable need for a physical presence of a service in some areas for the following reasons:

- where libraries were located in an area of significant deprivation
- where the Council's decision on which libraries to close changed
- where the Council identified an area of need but subsequently chose to ignore this information
- where the Council had failed to meet its own standards in terms of a reasonable distance to travel
- where libraries had interdependent links with schools and/or children's centres.

Guidance on Processes of Engagement and Consultation

This Wirral Inquiry represented a quantum leap forward for UK public libraries, many of whom had paid lip service to the issue of assessing community needs. Better still, the findings of the Wirral Inquiry were incorporated into *The Modernisation Review of Public Libraries* (DCMS 2010a) which included guidance on processes of engagement and consultation. There was a general consensus that decisions about services, opening hours and locations must be based on consultation and research in the community. The decision to close a library should always be part of an agreed strategy which ensures there is a clear plan for the development of the library service as a whole and that arrangements to cater for the local community through alternative provisions (especially the vulnerable or disadvantaged) should be agreed and be in place before the closure:

> Sue Charteris's inquiry into library service provision in the Wirral made a number of recommendations about a local authority's duties as set out in the 1964 Act. The Government recommends that all library authorities familiarize themselves with their statutory duties. Library authorities may also wish to consider the findings of the Charteris Report on the Wirral Library Service when developing their library policy and particularly when considering significant changes to library provision. Government recognizes that library closures may sometimes be necessary, but closures must form part of a strategic approach to service provision and decisions must only be taken after consultation with the community. (DCMS 2010a: 15)

Effective engagement is key to understanding community needs and, under the Local Government and Public Involvement in Health Act 2007, local authorities have a statutory duty to involve local people. There is no single way of making an appropriate assessment of the general needs of a community and the specific needs of adults, children, families and young people. However, library authorities were expected to devise a comprehensive vision and development plan for their services based on some common types of information and data. When reviewing their service, library authorities should consider the following questions:

What resources are available and how does this match the needs of the community?

- Have you analysed and considered need and demand? What are the specific needs of adults, families and young people of all ages? Would members of the community be able and willing to contribute to the delivery of library services as volunteers or joint managers?
- What are the needs of those living, working and studying in the area?
- How accessible is the service? Is public transport appropriate? Are there barriers to physical access of library buildings that should be removed?
- Have local people been consulted? How?
- What are the views of users and what are the views of non-users?
- Have you done an Equality Impact Assessment?
- What implications are there for other strategies, such as educational attainment, support for those seeking work, digital inclusion, adult social care?
- Are there other partnerships that can be explored – for example, with the third sector, community and development trusts or town and parish councils?

How efficient is the current service?

- Are the arrangements for the delivery of the library service (such as buildings, staff, service provision, facilities, online presence. etc.) meeting the demand of the community and are they cost-efficient?
- What other delivery partnerships could be formed inside and outside the library authority or region to make the library service more efficient and effective?
- Can the facilities be used more flexibly?
- What are you doing to encourage use and maximize income?
- What scope is there for integrating or co-locating the library service with other services in the public or private sector (for example, council services, post offices, schools, children's centres, etc.).

This was another major step forward. For the first time since 1964 the government was actively trying to define a 'comprehensive and efficient' public library service. More importantly, it was saying that this should not be defined by the local council alone, but in consultation with the local community.

It was hoped that the Wirral Inquiry would lead to greater community engagement and rigorous needs assessments. When a new Conservative/Liberal Democrat coalition government came into power in May 2010 it was feared that the Wirral Inquiry would be kicked into the long grass and its recommendations quietly dropped. But the Wirral Inquiry still has some currency and is being invoked by local campaign groups who are trying to prevent wholesale library closures which have been triggered by swingeing and unprecedented public service spending cuts.

Working Together

> Instead of suggesting, ask. You think you know what they want but you don't. It seems to work a lot better when you know what they really want (Williment et al. 2011b).

The Community-Led Service Model can be thought of as a circular path which both library staff and community can travel together, with the ultimate goal of developing relevant programmes and services for the community. The first stage of this process is the identification of a specific community where relationships are developed and sustained. As discussed in Chapter 2 on consultation, relationships are premised on library staff interacting with a targeted community on an ongoing and regular basis. This is key to the next phase of community-led service planning – library staff conducting effective individual and community-based needs assessments.

As the second phase of community-led service planning, it was important at the beginning of the Working Together Project for librarians to conceptualize how library systems were identifying and conducting need assessments. It was soon discovered that library staff's perception of community needs was narrowly focused on one section of the community – existing users. Since most programmes and services are primarily delivered to a small segment of community members, comprising existing library users, needs identification had become so specialized that active and participatory engagement rarely if ever occurred. Since library staff reflected many of the same social, racial and economic characteristics as existing library users, needs assessment was primarily occurring through internal library-based processes (DeFaveri 2005a, Williment 2009). Programmes and services were being developed for a small proportion of community members by librarians who closely resembled those members – in terms of predominantly middle-class values. Community needs were assessed purely on the basis of library staff perceptions of those needs.

Assessments were primarily conducted using quantitative data collection techniques. These techniques focused on capturing and analysing information collected from existing library users, such as circulation statistics, gate counts, demographic profile, etc. (see Figure 3.2) Additionally, any data collection techniques which tried to capture information about non-users were exclusionary in nature since, for instance, telephone surveys could only be completed by people who had phones and handwritten surveys could only be completed by people with adequate literacy levels. Since librarians and socially excluded community members tend to live drastically different lives, internally based processes were inevitably exclusionary.

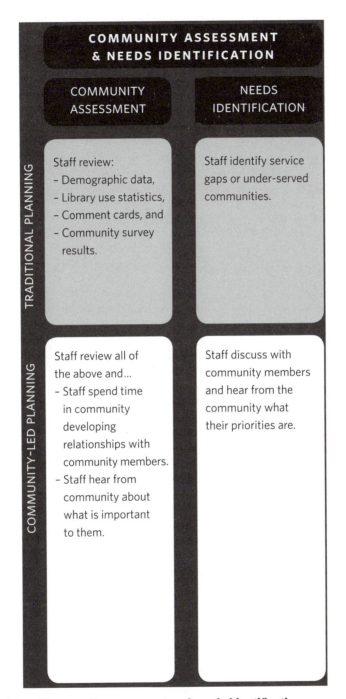

Figure 3.2   Community assessment and needs identification

Source: Working Together 2008a, p. 30.

A significant amount of library staff energy is spent working with other library staff developing and delivering a service to community members, with minimal external community contact or collaboration. This becomes a major issue when working with community members whose life circumstances do not reflect the same lived realities as middle-class librarians. Thus, when a service is being designed, developed and delivered, library staff hope that community members will attend, without actually knowing if the service is actually meeting the specific needs of that community. The *major flaw* in this approach is that library staff will rarely, if ever, be able to predict what others' needs are without actually – at a minimum – consulting or collaborating with the community. By quickly jumping to the development of programmes and services, without doing a comprehensive needs assessment, there is an increased likelihood that whatever is developed will not be relevant to the targeted group, will not have the intended impact, and will not be sustainable.

Community-led needs assessment should be viewed as an approach which does not replace traditional assessments, but as an approach which builds on traditional assessment techniques. By conducting a traditional assessment, while also completing a community-led assessment, it provides library decision-makers with additional information from local communities and provides library systems with a greater understanding of the needs gap that is identified by community-based assessments.

A Need or an Asset?

Over the past thirty years community development workers have shifted their approach to working with the community, from primarily focusing on the discovery of needs to identifying strengths. This occurred because when entering communities and asking people what they 'needed', it was easy to come up with long and ever-increasing lists of problems or needs that should be addressed. This approach lends itself to the false premise that service providers go into communities to discover community needs, and then go back into their organizations and magically create 'solutions' to community issues, problems and needs.

By shifting the process, so the identification of existing community assets and strengths are identified and acknowledged, libraries as local community information centres are strategically positioned to work collaboratively with community members and organizations to identify the new roles libraries can play in building upon these strengths.

While this sounds good in theory, application is quite different. When community development librarians (CDLs) entered socially excluded communities and began interacting with people on a one-on-one basis, individuals' day-to-day focus is not on assets but on needs. This is because individual life circumstances, social factors and the multi-dimensional causes of

	Socially included		Socially excluded	
Services	You phone or visit any office that you need to do business with, and you expect good service	You have good working relationships with some service providers such as your doctor, staff at your bank, or your children's teachers	You feel anxious about making appointments or visiting government offices or service providers, but you have worked out a system for dealing with it, such as having a friend come with you to speak for you	You miss out on services you are entitled to (such as the heating fuel rebate) because staff might question you or you might have to fill out a form
Information for decision-making	You get information you need by using the Internet, the library, or contacting organizations	You get information from TV and radio, from books and magazines that you have on hand, and by phoning 'experts' that you know	You base your decisions on what you already know, and what you expect will happen	You ask for and follow a friend or relative's advice, regardless of their experience *or* you avoid making decisions because you do not know enough, and hope the situation will work out

Figure 3.3   Inclusion/exclusion continuum

Source: An internal piece of work created by Ken Williment in 2009.

exclusion compound the difficulties that people experience daily. For much of the time, meeting survival-based needs is the central focus of individuals, who are trying to live life from day to day.

Listening to and Communicating Need with Community

The first key step, which is imperative to implement when conducting a needs assessment, is the development of sustained relationships. Sustained relationships, built upon trust, are central to community-led needs identification. By engaging people where they feel comfortable, many times outside the four walls of library branches, library staff ensured they were meeting people where they felt comfortable. In this context, library staff were placed in locations where they could begin to hear what people were saying, and begin to learn.

Since one of the key information skills that library professionals in the North American context traditionally rely on is continuously marketing and communicating information about library services out to the community, active listening can be a difficult concept to put into action. Being inquisitive and acting on curiosity about the unknown outside of library branches was a new skill developed through the Working Together Project. In order to create the environment for relationships to develop, the role of library staff shifted from library staff being *identifiers* of need and services to address community need, to being *facilitators* of a process which assisted community members in identifying and articulating their needs (Working Together 2008a: 29). Using this approach, library staff learnt how to actively listen when in communities. Active listening is a process whereby library staff:

- receive information and begin to conceptualize an understanding of community need
- repeat and rephrase what they have heard in order to clarify and shed assumptions
- actively probe, and
- allow others to lead the conversation and finish their thoughts. (Working Together 2008a: 119)

Through informal, non-leading conversations library staff began to hear about peoples' lives. By actively listening to what people were talking about, and 'without articulating people needs for them', library staff began to find new roles which the library can play in collaboratively assisting people to meet their information and other needs. This is a humbling experience, to step back and listen to important issues being discussed within a community, and at times discovering just how disconnected library staff perceptions of need are from socially excluded community members' needs. One of the most important benefits of using a community-led approach is that the power of listening, exploring the unknown, and documenting need, leads to library staff becoming connected to the needs of local people.

At times these conversations can lead to library staff helping to develop a service which is not traditionally thought of as a library service. For instance, as told by one CDL:

> We continuously heard from the community that daily needs were hard to meet. We heard about the high cost of food and clothing. While the library was not a place where clothes could be sold or purchased, we soon discovered through the community that a large number of sewing patterns were located in a not very visible location in the library. Word quickly spread amongst other community members and they were very excited to find out they could get patterns at the library. They were un-catalogued, so they could freely take them out and bring them back at their own leisure. Library staff helped to locate a sewing machine and worked with a community partner to have the machine placed in the community, so people could have access to it at different times of the day.

In the above example, it would have been easy either to dismiss the need because it did not fall within a library systems mandate, or point the community to items which library staff felt would address the needs – such as books. Actively listening to the community is an ongoing process, *not* a onetime event. In fact, 'It is understandable that Working Together staff desire[d] ongoing feedback from participants rather than determining at the end of a programme that it was not meeting client needs' (Atkey 2008: 179).

Through active listening library staff may see changes to community needs becoming more refined, complex, or even dissipate over time. As pointed out in the national evaluation: 'The needs of any given community evolve over time … [making it essential to develop] a framework for working with the community to identify needs in an ongoing way and collaborating with the community to develop services' (Atkey 2008: 73).

Systemic Implications of Need Identification

While it is important to be keenly aware of the impact of existing internal barriers to change, it is also important to move beyond initially responding with a 'no' to a need which does not initially seem to fit within the library mandate or role. A willingness to shift library-based responses, from 'no' to 'how can we work with the community to fit their needs within the libraries mandate', creates opportunities for libraries. If community members are expressing that they see a link between the library and their needs, staff should be encouraged to find the linkage – otherwise it is another lost opportunity for library service development. As observed by the national evaluator of the Working Together Project:

Community development by its very nature is uncertain because it does not necessarily follow typical patterns. Being responsive to community-identified needs requires both flexibility and the ability to adapt to what takes shape in the community (both on the part of the librarian and the library system). It also requires letting go of tight control of the process. One of the most profound learnings for most CDLs was the ability to *respond to community needs with fluidity*, rather than control, and taking risks not typically associated with library work.

The community *can teach the library about itself, its assets, its challenges and its needs* and library staff can educate the community about library systems and where change can most readily happen. It is not that librarians are without expertise, it is that they must also recognize that the community has its own particular expertise. (Atkey 2008: 8)

If an information need clearly does not fit within the libraries' mandate, if they have worked closely within the community, the information that the library has learned about the community will allow them to link the need to other community members or organizations whose role it *is*.

As a result of conducting a successful needs assessment, when a specific need arises and is collaboratively identified, it is very tempting for library staff to try to create a solution for the community. It is important not to jump the gun, and to view community-led service planning as incorporating collaboration through each stage of the service planning process.

A Brief Overview of Approaches used for Community-Led Needs Assessment

Throughout the time period of Working Together a number of different approaches to entering local communities and relationship-building were developed, which led to the assessment and identification of community needs. These approaches are thoroughly spelled out and reviewed in the Working Together *Toolkit*. As discussed in the national evaluation: 'Interests and needs continued to be identified through informal focus groups, drop-in or open-house sessions and attendance at community meetings in addition to the needs identified through the community entry strategies' (Atkey 2008: 26).

An entire chapter in the *Toolkit* is dedicated to asset mapping, which is a process that allows for community-based needs to be identified by service providers. However, the main purpose of conducting a needs assessment using this approach should be from the perspective that 'While service providers can provide insight into the *perceived* needs of individuals, only the individuals themselves can discuss their *actual* needs' (Atkey 2008: 120). Building relationships with service providers may potentially allow library staff to have direct access to individual community members.

Another avenue used was to try to discover needs through an existing programme developed through Working Together. The digital divide and use of technology was a major focus of the project, but a major challenge was to identify needs that went beyond the topic of IT:

> Although the intake procedure tries to elicit information about other interests or needs, 'people tend to brush those things off'. As one interviewee noted, 'we had to lay off talking about library services during the intake process because people thought we were trying to sell them on it'. Once the relationship and a sense of rapport has been built between the instructor and participant, this information emerges more organically and the instructor documents what other types of services could be offered. (Atkey 2008: 47)

This reinforces the central and essential place that trust and relationships play in the implementation of community-led needs assessment.

Final Thoughts

In order to implement a community-led needs assessment, library staff need to be confident, because it takes time, patience, and new skill sets to explore, document and contextualize need; and it also takes trial and error when trying new and different approaches when implementing a service or programme response *with* the community. Library staff also need to be confident that they can learn as much from failure as from success. Learning to listen does not dismantle librarians' professional identity nor the legitimacy of libraries, but can build upon them.

Helpful Hints

#1: When developing a programme or service, ask yourself where the evidence has come from for the activity you are proposing in your library system. If you cannot provide evidence from direct consultation or collaboration with the community, ask yourself: How was the programme or service identified? Where did the need come from? Was the need identified by library staff or the community?

#2: Broad generalizations about how socially excluded people access services and information can be presented to library staff, so they can start to contextualize the differing approaches people take to address their needs,

#3: There are a number of issues which library staff should be aware of when engaging and listening to conversations. These include:

- Being sensitive to the context in which the conversation is occurring. The same person in a different location or in a different role (a person can simultaneously have multiple roles such as a parent, a student and a homeless person) can identify different needs, based on the context of the conversation.
  - In [one library system] CDLs heard different needs from the same people when they talked with them at a college and at a community centre.
  - It was also learned that participants may express their needs and interests in the context of the service they are accessing from a partner agency when the CDL is talking to them (for example, they might express needs related to food security when accessing a food bank). It then becomes important to ask probing questions of participants in any context to ensure that they are being challenged to identify a range of needs and interests. It also illustrates the need to access a broad range of service providers and community groups when identifying community needs (Atkey 2008: 29).
- Using plain language. Library jargon is a major barrier which can disrupt the relationship-building process.

Being wary of the Hawthorne Effect, which is a common concern in research, because people react to the researcher based on what they believe the researcher is looking for. Until relationships and trust are deeply developed, people will likely tell you a need based upon what they think it is that the library is seeking from them. If it is your first time out in the community, think about what you have heard during these initial conversations and give the relationship time to develop. What you will hear from the same people will probably change as the initial interaction develops into strong and sustained relationships.

#4: If the community or target group does not continue to work with library staff beyond the needs assessment, and you find just yourself or other library staff developing and implementing the programme/service, alarm bells should be sounding that something may have gone amiss.

#5: When working with library staff there are a number of different issues which should be addressed when starting and going through a needs identification process:

- define who the target is
- determine the skills which staff need to develop
  - This can be trial and error – best to try it in the community (for example, shifting from information out to information in).

- – Understanding and taking the perspective of others (for example, how is information usually shared in the community? If it is primarily through talking, this may be the best method to approach a needs assessment. When engaging with community members, library staff may not want to use written surveys or written materials where there are low literacy levels, or where English is not the first language).
- Structural support: develop policies or procedures which support 'non-traditional' needs assessments.

#6: At local level all groups and individuals that are socially excluded or at risk of exclusion should be identified through community profiles and other methodologies such as needs analysis.

#7: More research is needed into the perceptions of libraries by non-users and how barriers to access can be removed.

#8: Detailed statistical monitoring of levels of library use by disadvantaged and working-class users needs to be undertaken.

Chapter 4
Library Image and Identity

In this chapter we consider how public libraries are perceived as a reflection of their buildings, staff and services. The saying 'perception is reality' is very true when it is applied to public library services, which have a strong brand and image. This can be a double-edged sword – everyone knows what a library is (so no need to spend vast amounts on expensive marketing campaigns) but many people also have an outdated and sometimes negative image of a boring institution filled with dusty books and even dustier staff! While this image may sometimes be unfair or plain wrong, unfortunately there are still many libraries which conform to the stereotype. We argue that the modern public library needs a new image and identity if it is to appear relevant to socially excluded communities.

Open to All? (Muddiman et al. 2000b) recognized that public libraries were often viewed as municipal, bureaucratic, unwelcoming and passive state institutions. This image could sometimes be changed simply through a renaming or rebranding exercise to give them a more modern look and feel. But renaming and rebranding was often not enough and library processes and practices also needed to be changed to remove or reduce barriers to use. Better signing and guiding was also needed and libraries should be located or, better still, co-located in community settings. There have been some interesting examples of public library makeovers in the UK from the Idea Stores in Tower Hamlets to the Discovery Centres in Hampshire.

In Canada the Working Together Project focused on creating a new image and identity for libraries by changing the language which staff use to develop relationships with local communities. For example, staff were asked to identify library jargon which community members might not understand. Staff were also asked to review specific policies and procedures which might create confusion, misunderstanding or even conflict with library users. One powerful technique used by Working Together was to have non-library users take staff on a 'silent tour' (the staff stayed silent) of the library. This enabled staff to understand how some members of the community (particularly non-users and irregular users) perceived the library and pointed out issues which staff and regular users did not see, as they used the library every day.

Barriers to Library Use

Public libraries are often described as welcoming, neutral spaces which are open to all who chose to walk through their doors. For people who regularly use public libraries they are safe havens of free information staffed by friendly and familiar faces. Regular users know their way around the library, understand the library systems and feel confident in their use of the library. Their views are listened to by the staff and they feel that they have a stake in the library service. They are very much a part of the status quo and organizational culture – 'the way that we do things around here'. They do not want things to change, even if those things are barriers to other people who want to use the library.

There are many different types of barriers to library use. These may be:

- institutional
- personal and social
- environmental
- related to perceptions and awareness.

Institutional Barriers

Institutional barriers are those that authorities, libraries and library staff themselves may create and which may discourage or restrict usage by certain people or sections of the community. They include:

- unsuitable or unduly restrictive opening hours or restrictions upon the availability of library services
- inappropriate staff attitudes and behaviour
- inappropriate rules and regulations
- charging policies which disadvantage those on low incomes
- book stock policies which do not reflect the needs of the community or are not in suitable formats
- lack of signage in buildings so that people cannot easily find their way around
- lack of a sense of ownership and involvement by the community.

Personal and Social Barriers

Social barriers exist either in personal terms or because of cultural or community circumstances. They include:

- lack of basic skills in reading, writing and communication
- low income and poverty
- direct and indirect discrimination
- lack of social contact
- low self-esteem
- lack of permanent fixed address.

Environmental Barriers

Environmental barriers include:

- difficult physical access into and within buildings
- problem estates and urban decay
- the isolation problems experienced by rural communities
- poor transport links.

Perceptional Barriers and Lack of Awareness

Perceptions that 'libraries are not for us' exist both in individual and community terms. This perception causes difficulties for:

- people who are educationally disadvantaged
- people who live in isolation from wider society
- people who do not think libraries are relevant to their lives or needs
- people with a lack of knowledge of facilities and services, and how to use them.

This is a daunting list but the issue which is of most interest to our work is the barrier created for those who do not see how the library can reflect their lives or needs. This is a tough challenge because in the main public libraries reflect mainstream society which is white, middle-class and middle-aged. Libraries offer services and stock which match the tastes, values and attitudes of this 'dominant reader' and create an exclusive paradigm for those who do not fit the majority stereotype. So, in order to change the library image and identity there have to be some fundamental changes which are likely to upset the regular users.

The word 'library' is an incredibly strong brand because the word immediately conjures up an image of what a traditional library is and does – shelves, books and prim-looking staff. Whether libraries actually reflect this image – and unfortunately many still do – this is how libraries are often represented in the popular media. A well-known UK situation comedy was centred around a character called Timothy who wore thick glasses and worked at the public library. He lived at home with his mother and a cat and he was shy and retiring and unable to get a girl friend. Very funny, perhaps, but not so good for the public image of libraries.

Idea Stores

Some libraries have tried ditching the 'L' word to attract a wider user base. Tower Hamlets, a highly diverse and poor inner London borough, was driven to rebrand its libraries when usage fell to very low levels. Tower Hamlets faced a series of significant social problems. Of its residents, 30 per cent needed help with basic skills, while at the same time over 80 per cent of the population never used the library services on offer. Tower Hamlets used a radical new design for their libraries as a means of bridging this gap and to:

- make libraries more attractive to those people who did not normally go there
- provide the facilities for life-long learning.

The new Idea Stores mirror the retail approach, both in their location on the high street and also in their open building style. They are open 7 days a week for 71 hours. The concept was imaginative and the buildings are certainly visually stunning, but did this experiment work? On a purely statistical level they have been a success. Visitor figures have quadrupled and issues are up by 40 per cent and rising. But on another level, as agents of social cohesion, they have failed, as witnessed by my visit to the Bow Idea Store.

On entering the building there is a large vestibule with chairs where people can just sit and talk. It is a pleasant, well-lit space which encourages rest and conversation. On the day of my visit this area was full of what I would call local white, elderly working-class people. These are the original East Enders who lived in crowded tenements long before the arrival of newer communities from Pakistan and Bangladesh. As I eavesdropped on their conversations it was mostly about the 'good old days' before the advent of multiculturalism. These communities were studied in some groundbreaking community research by Michael Young and Peter Willmott in *Family and Kinship in East London* (1957). Public libraries are not mentioned in the index and did not seem to have much relevance to working-class lives even in the late 1950s.

On the ground floor of the Idea Store there is a Learning Centre, full of the latest computer technology. This area was the domain of predominantly young black men, mostly of African descent, studying accountancy, management and business studies. Upstairs there is the public library with traditional adult lending collections, reference and children's sections. This vibrant area was full of young Asian men and women making full use of the wide range of services on offer. The Idea Store was clearly very busy and it was obviously meeting the needs of a wide range of local communities, but it had not succeeded in bringing these communities together to achieve greater understanding and mutual support. At the end of the day Idea Stores are conventional (but very modern) public libraries combined with traditional (but very ICT-focused) learning centres. And local people still refer to them as 'the Library'.

Discovery Centres

Another attempt at changing the image and perception of libraries is taking place in Hampshire, a large, affluent, English rural county. Here the challenge is not falling levels of use but the need to make best use of limited resources. The solution is to house a range of cultural facilities – public library, museum, heritage centre, art gallery, performance space, community café – under one roof and call it a Discovery Centre. According to the Hampshire County Council website:

> They are modern, welcoming and friendly with a modern library service at the heart of each Discovery Centre with books, information, music, DVDs and talking books for all ages and tastes. There are rooms for community groups and well equipped learning suites. Free internet allows access to the most up to date information. There are areas for children and young people to read, study or just browse and a coffee bar with comfortable seats is a good place to relax or meet friends. Discovery Centres are an exciting new development providing an opportunity for more people to use a wide range of services.

While the intention is that people will use more than one service within the Discovery Centre – a type of 'one-stop shop' for cultural services – during my visit to Winchester Discovery Centre I observed that most people only used one of the services on offer. For example, the library users did not visit the heritage centre or art gallery, and vice versa. The only facility which seemed to be used in common by all users was the café, which served delicious cakes and coffee!

Idea Stores and Discovery Centres are two brave attempts to break the mould of UK public libraries, reduce barriers and attract a wider range of users. But we need to go further and completely break down the walls of the library into open flexible spaces. If library services are going to enable community cohesion then they will need to engage local communities to determine how library spaces (both physical and interactive) can be created to facilitate exchanges between communities. For this to work it is important to involve rather than impose on the community. Many people already feel that these spaces can be used by individuals and groups other than those designated by staff. It is often the library staff who set the conditions for differentiation. In addition:

- Each library will develop its own bespoke programme and service priorities.
- Future libraries will be developed in partnership with other services.
- Adaptability of internal design, circulation, access and hours of services will be a key factor in building layout and design.
- Reading development and literacy are likely to become even more central to what libraries offer communities.
- Libraries will become key communications centres for mobile populations by providing access to emails and the Internet.
- Long-stay use of libraries for study purposes requires friendly and efficient support services such as toilets, catering and recreational quiet zones.
- Electronic links between homes and libraries will increase.
- Children's services will grow in importance as the library becomes a secure, electronic safe haven in the city.

- Virtual library services will be provided 24 hours a day.
- Librarians will change their roles from custodians of culture to knowledge navigators and community developers.

Modern Library Architecture

The need for *Better Public Libraries* (2003) was recognized by Resource (the Council for Museums, Archives and Libraries) and the Commission for Architecture and the Built Environment:

> The location, design and services offered by public libraries are changing in unprecedented ways, and will continue to do so in the future. After decades of gradualism and small-scale adaptation, the UK is now witnessing a radical step-change in thinking about public libraries, and how they are re-positioning themselves in the expanding educational and cultural networks of villages, towns and cities throughout the UK. (CABE 2003: 4)

The implications for the design of libraries are thus even more significant and can be represented schematically as follows:

Traditional library architecture	Modern library architecture
Neoclassical pattern	Modern free style
Imposing steps and entrance halls	Street level, retail entrances
Needs of disabled people unmet	Good disability access
Domes and rotunda	Atriums and top-floor cafés
Galleries and mezzanines	Escalators and lifts
Clerestory light	Atrium light
Restricted access to books	Open access to books and other materials
Bookshelves requiring ladders	Bookshelves at human scale
'Temple of knowledge'	'The living room in the city'
Institutional furniture	Domestic or club furniture
Stand-alone building	Shared space with other services
Hierarchical design and circulation	Open-plan design and circulation
Canonical stock holding	Contemporary cultural marketplace
Individual study carrels	Seminar rooms and computer suites
Defensive space	Networked space
Librarians as knowledge custodians	Librarians as knowledge navigators
The rule of silence	The culture of mutual respect
Child-free	Child-friendly

Figure 4.1   Modern library design

Communities should have access to welcoming, high-quality library buildings in the right place and open at the right times for their users. There are some fantastic new libraries with iconic designs, innovative services and inventive links to local people. The popularity of new builds confirms the 'pulling power' of the buildings' infrastructure. For instance, the new library in Bournemouth town centre is 3.5 times larger than the library it replaced and includes retail units. In its first year alone visits increased by 120 per cent and stock issues increased by 50 per cent. Almost 5,000 new borrowers registered in the first week. In 2007 the Big Lottery Fund awarded £80 million investment to build and refurbish libraries across 58 authorities with a key requirement to engage communities in planning.

Two major public refurbishments are showing how library location and design can deliver increased usage. Mansfield and Dorking Libraries have both recently reopened following extensive re-fits. Both libraries have now released figures showing dramatic increases in the numbers of people using them. Figures from Nottinghamshire's Mansfield Library show that visitor numbers more than doubled after a major refurbishment and the number of loans increased from 31,688 to 52,598. In Surrey, the figures are equally encouraging, with a 168 per cent increase in visitors when Dorking Library was re-located in the heart of the town's shopping area. Dorking also saw an extra 250 people join the library. Surrey County Council said: 'The way people use libraries is changing so it's vital we evolve and adapt to meet the needs of the twenty-first-century visitor. We've invested in providing a bigger, brighter and better library for Dorking to encourage more people to use it' (*CILIP Update* 2012b: 11).

While it is always encouraging to see old libraries being refurbished and new libraries being built, it is important to sound a warning note about the fixation with erecting super-buildings. These are often monuments to a particular councillor's vanity, and, in themselves, may become just as daunting as Carnegie buildings. We have heard much about the new public central library in Newcastle, for example, but my experience of visiting it (and Norwich) shows significant activity in the 'entrance' areas (especially the cafés) which diminishes as you get into the building. It is quite possible that scarce resources are being ploughed into future white elephants. A case in point was the new Hertfordshire Library built in Welwyn Garden City. It was huge, a real monument, but now 40 years later it is barely used because people do not need such a vast facility.

Fit-for-Purpose Libraries

21st Century Libraries: Changing Forms, Changing Futures (2004) also looked at the changing role of library buildings:

> In order to design libraries for the needs of future users, we need to examine the varied elements involved in the complex range of libraries we have today. If libraries that are on the drawing board now can integrate the needs of the future

into those of the present they will be fit for purpose up to and beyond 2024. (CABE 2004: 4)

There are four crucial elements to today's public library: the people for whom the library service is intended (along with the staff providing the service); the programme of services, events and activities required to fulfil that obligation; the partners with whom the library authority might wish to undertake a joint development or venture; and the place of the library itself (along with the spaces it offers to meet its designated programme most efficiently and effectively). This interconnected set of strategic themes creates a virtuous circle:

People	Programmes
• Socio-demographic profile of catchment area • Profile of existing users • Profile of new target users • Weighting given to children's services • Skills of the library staff • Administration and management of premises	• Core library stockholding • ICT services and training • Public information services • Basic literacy and numeracy provision • Children's events and activities • Writers' groups/cultural events • E-government facilities • Time-management and opening hours
Places	**Partners**
• A town centre location? • A civic landmark? • A neighbourhood facility? • A safe and secure sanctuary in the city? • The living room in the city? • Imbued with life-long learning ethos?	• Town planners • Major retailer wishing to share premises • Local education services • Museums and art galleries • Local radio station • Tourist information providers

Figure 4.2   People, programmes, places and partners

Imaginatively designed and responsive public library services can play a pivotal role in promoting greater social cohesion and a stronger sense of civic pride and local identity. For this to happen the local community must be actively involved in the planning and design of new libraries.

A case in point is the new Boultham Library in Lincolnshire, which replaced an older building which was literally falling to pieces. The location was ideal, at the heart of the community and next to a health centre, but the key to success was engaging young people in the design of the library building and the services which it provides. Working in partnership with the Youth Service, library workers sought to engage young people who lived in the local area. Their target was not the 'usual suspects' – well-educated and well-behaved children and young people;

instead they wanted to reach out to disaffected youth and street kids who needed the library the most but used it the least. Boultham is an urban area, with few facilities for young people, on the outskirts of the city of Lincoln. Engaging this group was not easy because they did not see the library as being a cool place to go. Continuity was also a problem – the group which was initially engaged changed over time and young people dropped in and out of the project, but the outcome was successful. The initial brief was to design a library which could meet the needs of young people and this remained the core of the project. Young people wanted their own space in the library but they also wanted access to all other areas of the building. This led to an open-plan design with no ghettoes or no-go areas. What came as a real revelation was the concern of the young people for other service users. Contrary to the media myth that all young people are inherently selfish, the contact group also wanted good services for children and older people. As one young person put it, 'The library is not just for me but for my little sister, my mum and my grandfather.' The resulting design was truly open to all and usage levels went through the roof. The library became a source of civic pride and a natural hub for community events.

Public Libraries – What Next?

The key role of young people in planning library services was also identified by the Laser Foundation who funded three consultation projects that showed particular imagination and innovation in overcoming barriers to library use. Two projects related specifically to the planning process for new libraries in socially deprived areas (Bolton and Birmingham), whilst the third was an important national survey into the attitudes and expectations of young people in relation to public libraries.

Destination Unknown (Laser Foundation 2006) reported a 'deeply entrenched negative perception' of libraries by young people aged 14–35. The majority of existing and un-modernized libraries were seen as dirty, uncared for, with old and poor stocks and an oppressive atmosphere. The researchers found that there is a baseline which libraries need to achieve if they are to attract younger users:

- Improve stock to place a greater focus on contemporary material.
- Refreshed library interiors (décor and furnishing) to be welcoming, comfortable and up to date
- Roll out or extend – and raise awareness of – up-to-date borrowing processes (email reservation, loan extensions, 'drop boxes', IT services, etc.).
- Improve the destination value of the library by attaching or combining additional services.
- Allow for some variety and separation within the library (in terms of more or less noisy areas) to accommodate the range of users but also to reduce inhibitions of those with more barriers.

Bolton Libraries collaborated with Planning for Real to engage hard-to-reach communities in a bold and imaginative way in the planning of the new High Street library for one of Bolton's most deprived areas. Bolton Libraries used innovative consultation methods to find out what the community would like to see in the High Street of the future. Five local artists used a range of different art forms and techniques to work with the local community to explore what they wanted from a modern library service. Both the process and the outcomes of this work were fascinating and helped the staff significantly in planning a library that will have a vital role in the local community. The outcomes of this project included a Good Practice Guide and DVD.

Birmingham City Council used community engagement to plan for an innovative signature building to replace the recently demolished Birchfield Library. Birchfield is a diverse inner-city community in one of Birmingham's most economically and socially deprived areas. Birmingham Libraries undertook a community consultation project – with a particular focus on young people who were actively involved as project researchers. The initial consultations and research drove forward a networking and outreach programme to access diverse and often difficult-to-reach community groups to collect their views and ideas to inform the design of the new library. These in their turn drove forward three further consultative activities: more consultation with young people; a heritage and archives project; and community consultations with architects. The project successfully addressed the complexity of engaging a diverse community and gathering the views of people of many different ages, backgrounds and skills. In doing so it tested a variety of methods for raising the profiles and plans for the new library and its services. A major outcome of the project has been the lessons which have been learned about the choice of approaches appropriate to different circumstances. The Laser Foundation concluded that:

> It can be very difficult to consult effectively with groups in the community that are hard to reach, or that may think library services are not for them, in order to find out how we can meet their needs and expectations. To have a sustainable future, public library services must be relevant to the communities they serve and thus consultation is an essential element in the planning of future services or new libraries. (Laser Foundation 2007: 14)

Communicating the Library Offer

The importance of communicating the Library Offer (see Chapter 7, Materials Provision) to the community effectively was emphasized by *The Modernisation Review of Public Libraries* (DCMS 2010a). More needs to be done to promote the benefits of libraries to those who do not currently use them. Communities need to know what they can expect from their local library service, yet many public libraries are not publicizing their offer in terms that the public can understand,

and there are too many perceived barriers to use. The Library Offer to the public represents a commitment to the community and can help communicate library services to users and non-users alike. It also reflects the importance of giving people guarantees of high-quality public services, as set out in the *Smarter Government* White Paper (HM Government 2009). The modernization review recommended that all library authorities make their Library Offer to the public clear and visible to all the citizens in the area – on their websites, in library buildings and through any other local marketing opportunities. The modernization review also made a number of proposals to provide an accessible library service in terms of opening hours, buildings infrastructure and co-location.

Small libraries can make an important contribution to local communities and mobile libraries, and 'library access points' in community spaces can be an attractive alternative in some communities to dedicated library buildings. This approach has been successful in the East Riding of Yorkshire where, until a fundamental review of the mobile library service was carried out in 2000–01, communities were missing out on a modern library service due to the predominantly rural nature of the area and lack of dedicated library buildings. The new mobile vehicle provides a broad range of services and now many somewhat isolated rural communities have the equivalent of a one-stop shop on their doorstep. The modernization review recommended that local authorities should regularly review the footprint of the library service to determine whether they have the right buildings in the right place.

Co-Location

Co-location of services can help to widen usage and make valuable links for the user. Co-location works particularly well when it brings together complementary services on an equal footing. Effective co-location of libraries with other services – such as health or employment services, post offices, leisure services, schools, early years settings and children's centres, universities or other educational institutions – enables innovation, offers value for money and delivers a coherent, joined-up approach to the community. Co-located libraries can be used as community hubs. Libraries are viable and valued partners for co-location because:

- Libraries are a universal service.
- Libraries are free, community spaces.
- They are widely used by the individuals and community groups other partners want to reach.
- They provide free access to quality information, reading and information and communication technology (ICT) resources which support and complement the work of many partners, particularly in health, education and learning.
- Library spaces are relatively inexpensive to fit out in a shared building.

Co-location can completely change the image and identity of a public library. Co-location was a key recommendation of *Open to All?* which has been widely adopted by many UK library authorities. The age of the stand-alone library building is quickly passing and the age of the flexible, open space multi-purpose library has started to arrive.

Working Together

As discussed in the first section of this chapter, library staff are well aware of the perceptions that existing library users have regarding library services. On an ongoing basis within library branches, library staff and regular library patrons are constantly interacting and library staff are continually reminded about the needs of existing library users. There are a number of attributes which existing library users possess which position them as strong advocates for their personal and community interests. These include: having the confidence to approach staff and voice their opinions; high literacy levels; and previous interactions and existing relationships with library staff (DeFaveri 2005b).

Working Together sought to explore the unknown: the impact that the existing public library image has on socially excluded members' use of libraries. Library staff held basic conceptions or preconceived notions of the 'image' of library services as seen by non-library users and socially excluded community members. At the onset of the Working Together Project community development librarians (CDLs) began to ask library staff about their perceptions of why socially excluded community members do not use public library services. There were two regular responses which librarians provided. They believed that socially excluded community members choose not to use library services primarily because:

- they do not know what the library has to offer – so libraries need to market existing services better to the community, or
- socially excluded community members actively choose not to use library services (Williment 2009).

However, when CDLs began to directly develop sustainable trusting relationships with individuals in the community it became possible for Working Together staff to begin to truly understand both the perceptional and experiential barriers that impeded socially excluded community members' access to public library services.

Throughout the Working Together Project a number of barriers were identified that impeded library access for socially excluded communities. These barriers can be broadly categorized into a number of different areas, including:

- library-created and -sustained barriers to access
- perceptional barriers
- negative staff attitudes

- non-representation (DeFaveri 2005a).

Each of these barriers creates and perpetuates negative views and sustains non-use of library services by socially excluded communities.

Library-Created and -Sustained Barriers

There are a number of barriers that are intentionally or unintentionally created by library services which significantly impact on socially excluded community members' abilities to access and navigate public libraries. These barriers impede access to the libraries' physical spaces and collections. For instance, as identified by one CDL who developed relationships with socially excluded community members, 'the barriers identified through these contacts were: poor signage in the library, lack of specific interest materials at local branches, and library fines' (Atkey 2008: 215).

Many socially excluded individuals accrue fines and fees for late or lost library materials for a number of reasons, often outside the person's control. For instance, many socially excluded people are living in precarious and at times transient living conditions, and so they are much more likely to have experiences where materials are not returned on time. 'Fines were particularly significant barriers for people living in poverty and emerged most strongly for members of [a service agency] because borrowed books are often stolen or thrown out by landlords trying to control bedbug outbreaks' (ibid.: 215).

The impact of library fines should not be understated or underestimated. As discovered during a focus group with low-income individuals, even the basic perception that a person had a minimal fine was enough to keep the person from entering a library branch for over five years, only to discover after coming to the library that no fine had actually existed (Williment 2009).

DeFaveri (2005a) explains that the long-term impacts and consequences of fines being imposed on socially excluded people hurts not only individuals trying to access library services, but also libraries as public institutions:

> Fines, replacement costs and processing fees are affordable for the middle classes, but represent significant and often overwhelming costs for poor people. As a result, poor patrons with fines over $10.00 who cannot pay the fines are excluded from accessing library resources ... When the library fails to recognize situations where charging replacement costs means losing library patrons, it loses the opportunity to participate in the life of the patron and the patron's family ... It will cost the library more than [$10.00] to convince this mother:
>
> - to return to the library,
> - to persuade this mother that the library is a welcoming community place willing to meet her needs and support her family,
> - to mount literacy programs aimed at her children, who will not benefit from

regular library visits and programs, and
- that the library is a welcoming and supportive place for their children.

Many of the features which are intended to provide better functionality and accessibility to library collections for existing library users and library staff, are also imposing and excluding individuals from using library services. These factors include:

- the design of the library (physical structure), such as the imposing nature of the electronic sensors near the door (ibid.: 213)
- the nature of library-related technology (for example, electronic catalogues)
- library language (such as 'getting a card').

As identified by DeFaveri (2005a) the reasons people have for not using the library are extensive, including:

- Reading is hard. 'You have to be a good reader to use the library.'
- Feeling as if the library is a club and 'I'm not a member of the club'.
- Feeling as if the library is like school and school is hard and not much fun.
- Believing that the library has good things, but feeling too stupid to find them or ask for help.
- Fear of asking the wrong question, or asking the wrong person the wrong question.
- Believing that the library is only for smart people.
- Feeling stupid at the library.
- Not understanding how the library works.
- Being afraid to go in and ask for something in case it is something that everyone else knows how to find.
- Believing that the library is about books and 'I do not read too many books'.

Working Together staff also found that some of these systemic and organizationally created barriers are maintained because of the perceived need to treat everyone equally. Unfortunately, equality does not take into account the differing life circumstances and socioeconomic conditions which people experience, such as unequal resource distribution and restricted access to income, education and transportation. Library services need to focus on equitable access to ensure that barriers stemming from policies and procedures based on false notions of equality are addressed.

In response to this, management at Vancouver Public Library (VPL) decided to focus its efforts on increasing the understanding and implementation of values-based service so that patrons were treated equitably rather than exactly the same (Atkey 2008: 105). Another significant activity was undertaken to address systemic barriers when Working Together staff and public library managers reviewed the customer service training curriculum in order to 'infuse the courses with sensitivity and awareness of the impacts of rigid policy and procedure on socially-excluded individuals' (Atkey 2008: 105).

Perceptions of Libraries

Socially excluded individuals have a broad range of perceptions about the inclusivity or non-inclusivity of public library services. Most community members, both socially excluded and included, have come to view libraries as being synonymous with books, reading and literacy. These perceptions assist in contributing to an imposing view that many people have of public libraries, which seem to be almost exclusively focused on middle-class service development and implementation (Atkey 2008: 239). Additionally, public libraries are viewed as another government-based institution, much like other institutions where socially excluded people have not had positive interactions – such as schools, policing or social services.

DeFaveri (2005a) began to hear people 'reveal that they associated the library with school, which was often hostile and isolating. They felt that, like their schools, the library was an authoritarian institution imposing its values and behavioural norms on them.' This was also reflected in the national evaluation:

> A number of respondents emphasized that the library is often seen as a 'government building,' or a 'white-bread, middle class institution.' One interviewee suggested that there is a perception that 'libraries are full of well-read, well-educated people who might look down on people who aren't well read and well-educated.' The same respondent also noted that library employees are well-paid, and this might be an inhibiting factor for members of the North Central community who are not well-off financially. (Atkey 2008: 307)

In addition to viewing public libraries as inflexible government institutions, which favour the well-read, socially excluded community members discussed alternative community-based agencies which were serving the same purpose for them that a library could serve. These locations clearly provided community members with alternative settings where they did not have to worry about library late fines and 'appropriate' use of library materials.

> The youth that access the agency[1] are intimidated by the library because of its institutional nature, whereas at the agency 'kids will lie there and read the books and nobody walks through that area so they can get some quiet time.' The agency does not concern itself with whether or not the books are returned because if 'there are returned books laying around the house, then people will read them but they have to be there because people won't go looking for them.'

---

1   In this case an 'agency' refers to an organization which provides services to people.

> Interestingly, the youth at the agency have started to show ownership of the collection by organizing and maintaining the bookshelves themselves. (Atkey 2008: 84)

While there was some acknowledgement that there was a lack of understanding of existing library services or what libraries are about, the more important point was the relevance of existing library services to their lives. Interestingly, the negative previous experiences that many socially excluded community members faced when they entered the library served as one of the major barriers to their continued use of public library services.

Negative Previous Library Staff Experiences – Changing Staff Attitudes

Each of the four Working Together sites was located in a local library branch. While many of the library staff who worked in these library branches also lived in the same communities, there was a disassociation with some segments of the community. Since most library staff functioned from the perspective of primarily working with existing library users who entered the branch, or had contact with the community outside the branch through outreach activities where library staff controlled the conversation, there was relatively little interaction with socially excluded community members. This lack of interaction led to a number of misconceptions about socially excluded communities:

> Staff attitudes toward members of marginalized communities was of particular concern to a number of interviewees, even in branches where the majority of staff live in the communities they serve. For example, one interviewee noted that 'I think barriers can be staff not understanding where people are coming from, past history, education level, struggling in different areas of life. A lot of branch staff know the community here because they live here but we don't always understand the whole picture.' (Atkey 2008: 129)

Consequently, the perceptions and assumptions which library staff members hold about socially excluded community members directly impacts staff behaviours and treatment of the excluded. Some community members discussed the 'perceived attitudes and norms of library staff' (Atkey 2008: 239) and the disrespectful treatment by staff because of physical appearance (ibid.: 215). However, as Working Together staff worked with branch staff to begin building sustainability of project learnings, one site focused on having a series of all-staff meetings which offered library staff the opportunity to reflect on their perceptions of the community. The session began by Working Together staff facilitating:

> ... questions [which] centred on staff descriptions of the community, staff perceptions of barriers and the services they provide, and how they see branch

services evolving in the future. Working Together staff found that their responses were fairly similar to the first staff training workshop held at the —— Library. Participants were reluctant to talk about issues such as poverty, race and racism, all of which impact the community. (Atkey 2008: 41)

It should be noted that, although library staff were initially hesitant to discuss issues such as the impact of poverty and racism on the community, Working Together staff at this location purposively spent a lot of time and energy on introducing and building relationships between socially excluded community members and branch staff. The development of relationships between all library staff and community members is essential, not just to ensure the sustainability of community-led approaches, but also to provide library staff with a better understanding of the life circumstances of people entering the branch.

Unfortunately, not all library staff are open to embracing community-led approaches to their work. This can lead to detrimental consequences for library branches and systems trying to implement a community-led approach.

Staff at other branches have typically functioned through an outreach model and feel 'threatened' by community development approaches and 'territorial' about their existing work. One interviewee summarized the challenge this way: 'I think that any staff is a function of its time. Most of the staff who would be intimately involved in this have been here a long time and they have a certain way of doing things. They were hired for a set of skills that doesn't necessarily match with what it takes to do community development work.' A general reluctance to develop new skills speaks to the discomfort many librarians feel about working in the community. (Atkey 2008: 91)

Not Represented

Many existing library users often feel and see themselves as part of public library services. They tend to be literate, comfortable approaching library staff with concerns or suggestions, and literally see themselves represented in the library in services, staffing and collections. The image and purpose of public libraries is clearly delineated for these library users.

While public libraries have a number of existing programmes, collections and other services, CDLs heard from the community that many of these simply do not reflect their existing realities or needs, nor do they see themselves reflected in them. For instance, in one library system when librarians began consultations with Aboriginal[2] community members:

---

2   In Canada, the term 'Aboriginals' comprises a number of indigenous first peoples in Canada, including First Nations, Métis and Inuit.

> The lack of Aboriginal specific programming for children and youth was also identified through the focus groups. The CDL could do little to address this issue specifically due to age-based funding restrictions. However, the information was passed from the CDL to the Branch Head who obtained a grant from the Provincial Government. The funds have allowed the —— Library to develop Aboriginal programming through a series of six workshops related to costume and dance and to develop satellite collections at various community organizations in North Central. (Atkey 2008: 204)

Library programmes need to move to locations where the community can access them. The image of the library does not make it an inviting place to approach or use. Many existing library services do not reflect community needs or the everyday realities of socially excluded people.

Impact of the Community-Led Approach on Library Image and Identity

The rigid nature of public libraries is an outcome, in part, of the size of library systems and the organization of library management. These factors should not be confused with the ability or inability of a library system to address the image that libraries portray to socially excluded individuals. By implementing community-led principles, approaches and learnings discussed in other chapters in this book, the perception and identity of public libraries can be dramatically shifted. This is not a public relations-based shift, but a true shift in the way in which library staff work with communities and build sustained relationships. As discovered through the Working Together Project, when libraries work with community members in the community and from a community-led perspective, there can be a shift in attitude:

> 'Reluctant' to use the library prior to partnering with Working Together, some clients viewed the library as 'another institution' or as a representation of 'conventional society that they do not have the right to access'. Others felt 'intimidated' or 'not wanted' and worried about being 'put down' for having late fees or not having the right identification. Working Together has helped to shift these perceptions to the extent that some of the youth participants now understand that the library is 'not a stuffy place'. Other participants have also 'broken down their stereotypes' and now realize that they 'don't need to be educated to go and they've gained a greater sense of acceptance'. One group rejected the notion of having a book drop at their halfway house because they were worried about the books being damaged. More importantly, however, 'they didn't want to lose a reason to go to the library.' (Atkey 2008: 212)

Another partner agency also discussed the impact of community-led approaches on increasing access and awareness of library services in the community.

[They] were unanimous in believing that their clients have a broadened perception of the library and what it has to offer as a result of the partnerships. Client perceptions have changed, with more participants now understanding that library services extend beyond children's programming. Another partner noted that her clients now feel more comfortable assisting their children with homework because of the computer training and are more comfortable with their children using the internet because they can now monitor their access.' (Atkey 2008: 172)

Approaches to work as minor as the way in which library staff display information to community members can break down barriers. There are numerous approaches which library staff can take both within the library and outside the confines of library branches that will both increase the relevance of library services for socially excluded community members, and will also more importantly change the perceptions and identity that community members hold of public library services. Finally, there was a very simple example of a CDL who went to a youth facility and did not tell people what the library had to offer. Instead, '"He [laid] things out and he [waited] for questions – it's very informal and casual rather than the normal stuffy and starchy perception of the library." The informal approach allowed the project to gain an initial sense of participant interests and develop more formal programming from there' (Atkey 2008: 219).

Helpful Hints

#1: Ask library staff in your branch to identify library language which they find is confusing or they would not expect members of the general community to understand. Ask staff in the library system to expand on this list. Circulate the list to all library staff and title it: 'Words Banned for use with the Public'!

#2: Ask library staff to identify interactions they are having with the public where there is confusion. These could be conversations at the checkout, at the information desk, etc. Ask staff to identify if this confusion is centred on specific policies, procedures or language that library staff are either explaining or using.

#3: One activity which library staff can do, and was tried through Working Together, is to have non-library users take library staff on a silent tour of the library (silence is only required of library staff). This is a great activity to do with larger groups which do not regularly use the library space because it allows them to tell library staff:

- how they navigate the library
- what their perceptions are of the library collection and space, and
- to point out issues and perceptions of the library which staff and regular

library users do not see, since they are using it every day.

#4: The image and identity of libraries need to be changed so that they do not appear as municipal, bureaucratic, unwelcoming and passive state institutions. This can be achieved according to local circumstances, by measures such as renaming libraries (for example, Idea Stores), or rebranding the traditional library name so that the new image is one of a proactive, friendly, relevant and easily accessible environment.

#5: Library practices and processes need to be challenged to ensure that they do not create barriers to usage. Joining procedures should not be over-bureaucratic and mechanisms should be created to overcome problems with bureaucracy for groups such as homeless people.

#6: The physical appearance of libraries needs to be audited to check that they are not forbidding from the outside and that the internal layout is easy to understand. Better signing, more self-help public access terminals and the removal of enquiry desks can all help overcome barriers to use experienced by some excluded people.

#7: The geographical location of libraries should be a prime factor in resource allocation. Priority should be given to those libraries serving communities in greatest need. This may result in the need to consider the existing location of libraries. Relocation and co-location (with community centres, schools, pubs, shops, leisure centres and other places used by the socially excluded) can both improve the impact of libraries in tackling social exclusion.

#8: Where appropriate, public libraries also need to work with neighbouring authorities to deliver services to socially excluded communities, such as refugees and travellers, who may be transient or who may span local authority boundaries, or where a service can be more effectively provided by the pooling of resources.

Chapter 5
Outreach, Community Development and Partnerships

In this chapter we consider the differences between outreach and community development in the context of traditional and community-led service planning. There is a critical differentiation to be made between outreach activities which are planned, designed, delivered and evaluated by library staff in non-library settings and community development which is based on creating meaningful and sustainable relationships with community members. This relationship-building is at the very heart of a community-led library service and is the start of a process which can both identify community needs and enable the co-production of services by library staff and local communities working in partnership.

Open to All? (Muddiman et al. 2000b) recognized that social exclusion strategies need to encompass proactive librarianship based not only on outreach, advocacy and intervention but also on community development through grassroots, community-based approaches and partnerships with those in the public, voluntary and private sectors. Public libraries had to offer relevant services in a variety of community settings and support a range of community initiatives, groups and organizations. Community information was an important resource which could be provided in partnership with the Citizens Advice Bureau and other agencies. Partnerships could also be formed with public health and education providers.

The Working Together Project recognized that while outreach had its place in the range of services provided by a public library, it tended to focus on the end product in terms of the delivery of the service to the community. The key question posed by Working Together when entering a community was to ask if a service or programme had already been determined for that community. If it had, then this was outreach rather than community-led service planning. Working Together shifted the focus from the end product (the programme or service being delivered) to how library staff engage with the community to build relationships and begin to hear community needs.

From Outreach to Co-Production

When *Open to All?* was published in 2000 it was the first public library report in the UK to recommend that outreach needed to be complemented by community development and partnership working. Up until this point the focus of community librarianship had been on outreach – taking library services out of the library building and delivering them directly to the community in a wide variety of locations, from parks and open spaces to playgroups and pubs. The services being delivered in these settings were very similar to the services available in libraries. With some notable exceptions (in particular, Lambeth Library Service), they were planned, designed, delivered and evaluated by library staff with little or no input from the local community. *Open to All?* argued that outreach alone would not meet the needs of socially excluded people and that what was required was community development through grassroots, community-based approaches. This meant that the library service shared power and resources with the local community and library workers became enablers rather than experts.

Outreach, community development and partnerships can be considered as a spectrum of activity, with outreach at the lowest end and co-production at the highest:

Outreach	Partnerships	Community development	Co-production
Library services are planned, designed, delivered and evaluated by library staff	Library services are delivered in cooperation with partner organizations	Library services are devised after developing relationships with local communities	Library services are co-produced by library workers and local communities

Figure 5.1   From outreach to co-production

Community-led library services can use a mixture of these approaches but community needs are best identified, prioritized and met through community development and co-production.

Outreach

The Modernisation Review of Public Libraries (DCMS 2010a) points out that outreach still has a role to play in delivering library services to socially excluded communities. Some people, such as the elderly, disabled and those with mobility problems, rely on the Home Library Service to meet their needs.

In Essex, the Home Library Service visits people who are unable to reach the library because of disability, age or long-term illness. Volunteers deliver books, CDs, DVDs and information to people in their homes, and talk to them about reading. When asked what they got out of the Home Library Service, people mentioned the benefits of social contact, stimulation and meeting new people. One person said, 'Without it, life wouldn't be so interesting. I'd miss out on a good friend. I look forward to her visits' and another 'I'd miss it greatly, his chats – it's a lifeline' (ibid.: 46).

In Birmingham the Home Library Service visits 2,000 people in their homes each month, as well as calling at 230 residential care homes and sheltered accommodation units. As well as lending books, music and DVDs, the library promotes the Stay Well 65 scheme. This is a partnership between Health Exchange CEC Limited, a social enterprise, and Birmingham City Council which assesses older people's needs and puts them in touch with the benefits and services they are entitled to. Library staff raise awareness of this scheme among the people they visit and take laptops out with them to help older people fill in the online forms.

It is important to recognize that some library authorities did not even get to 'first base' when it came to outreach services. It is also important to recognize that some library authorities went beyond the passive model of outreach which was entirely dictated by library staff. In Lambeth, for example, the Outreach Service took library materials to people, with two aims:

- that people might then find all they need (or ask for specific things) without having to go to a library building, and
- that some people could then be 'fed back' into libraries.

It can be argued that what Lambeth called 'outreach' in the 1970s and 1980s we would regard today as 'community development'.

Community Development

In more recent years community development has become a key concept in public service delivery and reform. The UK government's White Paper *Communities in Control: Real People, Real Power* (DCLG 2009) aimed to pass power into the hands of local communities:

> We want to generate vibrant local democracy in every part of the country, and to give real control over local decisions and services to a wider pool of active citizens.
>
> We want to shift power, influence and responsibility away from existing centres of power into the hands of communities and individual citizens. This is because we believe that they can take difficult decisions and solve complex problems for themselves. The state's role should be to set national priorities and minimum standards, while providing support and a fair distribution of resources.' (Ibid.: 1)

The White Paper addressed a number of key issues from the perspective of local communities, including being active in the community, access to information, having an influence and ownership, and control. The White Paper also recognized the importance of community development: 'Community development workers can help citizens to shape their own areas. We are keen to encourage other frontline workers to do community building' (ibid.: 3).

There are a number of complex social problems facing individuals and communities and these have been compounded by the worldwide economic recession and financial crisis which began in 2008. Neither public libraries nor local communities have access to all the necessary resources to tackle these problems on their own:

Local community resources	Public library resources
Knowledge, skill and understanding	Money
Energy, time and effort	Rules and regulation
Willpower and personal agency	Expert knowledge and skills
Motivations and aspirations	Energy, time and labour of public library professionals and workers
Social relationships within families and communities	Leadership, expectations and aspirations

Figure 5.2   Community and library resources

The resources needed to tackle social problems are distributed between public libraries and other agencies and local communities. Currently, local communities have little control over the resources that public libraries provide and are rarely encouraged to contribute their own resources. Solutions to these problems require a new relationship between local communities and public libraries that mobilizes more of the resources necessary to meet community needs.

Bringing these resources together in partnership through community development represents a distinct approach from traditional responses to social problems: voluntarism, paternalism or managerialism:

Voluntarism	Managerialism	Paternalism	Community development
Achieved by rolling back the state: reducing entitlements, cutting public libraries and encouraging families, local communities and the third sector (charities and voluntary groups) to fill the vacuum	Achieved using a carrot and stick approach via incentives for both service providers and local communities: discouraging and rewarding different behaviours; for example, setting targets for libraries to involve service users	Achieved through the 'professional gift' model of services. Library professionals treat local communities as recipients of services by handing down knowledge and expertise in a top-down way rather than by building partnerships	Establishing a partnership between local communities and library services to meet community needs. Local communities contribute their resources, share responsibility and manage risk in return for much greater control over resources and decisions

Figure 5.3   From voluntarism to community development

Community development is a partnership between local communities and library services to meet community needs. The most effective partnerships are based on four clear values:

1. Everyone has something to contribute, even though some have more resources than others. Local communities have resources which the library service cannot substitute. These contributions are recognized and fostered.
2. Reciprocity is important. Two-way mutual relationships, where responsibility, risk and power are shared and decisions are negotiated. The rights and responsibilities of both local communities and library services are recognized.
3. Social relationships matter. Social networks, especially families and local communities, are vital for achieving some types of change. Community support networks encourage support and sharing of expertise and grow capacity.
4. Social contributions are encouraged. There is recognition of the unpriced and often unvalued work of families and local communities, not just people's financial contributions. The commitment and energy of people who improve their local communities is recognized.

An EU survey (Löffler et al. 2008) indicated that 77 per cent of people in the UK believe that they can make a difference in improving community safety, the local environment and health. Of the UK population, 56 per cent often get involved in public services and there are some innovative projects that exemplify good examples of community development in practice. However, they are limited in scope and number, and there are very few examples of community development being used as a mainstream approach in the delivery of public library services.

Community development should be central to the public library agenda for meeting community needs. Public libraries should build on existing good practice in terms of outreach and make strengthening partnerships between libraries and local communities a more central part of their strategy, structures, systems and organizational culture. There are four reasons why community development should have a more significant role in the delivery of mainstream public library services:

- Community development often improves library and community outcomes – evidence shows that interventions that adopt a community development approach have a big impact on library outcomes and community needs.
- The community want to be partners – the local community want to be more involved when library services relate directly to them and their family. People's willingness to help others should not be underestimated.
- The value the community contributes is significant – the scale and value of the resources that the local community can contribute is enormous. Families and communities have a huge amount to offer that is currently unmeasured and unrecognized by library services.

- Community development can make best use of library and community resources – evidence shows that the benefits of community development approaches far outweigh the costs.

Across a number of sectors in the UK (including health and education) there is robust evidence that enabling local communities to work in partnership with professionals and to do more for themselves can meet community needs. In the health sector, for example, a high proportion of patients want to be treated as partners and want to do more for themselves. A significant number of people are willing to spend more time each week and month improving their neighbourhood: 28 per cent are willing to spend a few hours more per week, 43 per cent are prepared to spend a few more hours per month and only 29 per cent indicate that they are not willing to spend any time at all.

There are relatively high levels of participation in groups and organizations that encourage a partnership between local communities and public services in the UK. Particularly encouraging is the higher than average participation in health-focused civic groups such as exercise groups, Weightwatchers, Alcoholics Anonymous and community safety groups including residents' associations, tenants' groups and Neighbourhood Watch. According to research carried out by Ipsos MORI (Ipsos MORI 2009b) local communities want increased choice, control and involvement in public services. Of the survey respondents, 81 per cent agreed with the statement 'I like to make choices myself' but only 5 per cent of people thought that 'I like to have experts make choices for me'. Local communities also want public services to be different from normal retail/ supermarket experiences. When people were asked, 'Which aspects of service are most important in each of the following situations?' the answer was:

	Public services (%)	Supermarket (%)
Quality of advice/knowledge of staff	64	34
Respect and professionalism	39	13
Speed of service	30	60
Friendliness of service	30	60

Figure 5.4   Aspects of service

High-quality relationships in public services are premised on everyone having something to contribute and enhancing local community choice and control. The aim is not to mimic a 'supermarket'-style experience. Community development requires some fundamental changes to relationships, professional roles and management of library services.

The Importance of Getting Politicians on Board (and What Happens when They are Not)

John Vincent

Local councillors are critical to the success or failure of community-led approaches – and, indeed, any other initiatives – taken by public libraries. They have been elected to represent the views of their locality within the local authority, and, of course, also have a wider political brief, depending on their party allegiance.

Sadly, it is also true to say that very few will want to maintain a public library portfolio for long – it is not 'political' enough or strong enough a stepping-stone to greater political power. That said, however, across the UK there are superb local councillors working hard on behalf of their constituents and also strong advocates of public library services, supporting staff and putting their political weight behind all sorts of exciting initiatives.

Local authorities are political (of course), and councillors need to balance local needs and demands against their political 'brief'. When the two run together, this leads to the sorts of initiatives mentioned above – but what happens when they do not?

A good example is where a politician, keen to retain their council seat, tries to keep the support of strong political groupings within the community – and these may well be lobbyists on behalf of elite, exclusive services. This happened in Lambeth in the 1990s, for example, where lobby groups wanted to stop the development of community librarianship approaches (and outreach) and put a halt to the provision of community-related materials (books in community languages, material to support people with poor essential skills, 'positive image' materials about black or LGBT people, for example), in favour of a return to what they perceived as 'traditional' library values with traditional library stock.

It is absolutely critical, therefore, that libraries build and maintain two 'bridges' for support. Firstly, and this almost does not need saying in this book, they need to build and maintain strong links with their communities, recognizing and understanding how to deal with the different (and often competing) demands on library resources. To use a Lambeth example again, when the council was forced into a position of considering cuts and closures in the late 1980s, it was the strength of opposition from local people, who saw the vital provision that public libraries were making, that won the day. (In contrast, by the early 1990s, a combination of cuts to local community groups, and weakened relationships between libraries and community meant that support for libraries when the call for cuts came again was very much diminished.)

Secondly, libraries must build a strong 'bridge' to local politicians. It is all too common for library staff not to understand how a local authority functions, and to assume, for example, that the decision to close a library or reduce staff numbers has been made by senior managers at whim, without any grasp of why those decisions have been made and by whom. People still talk about public libraries being 'neutral' and 'non-political'. Libraries must think about the political messages they convey through their stock, their displays, what they choose to support in the community and what they do not – and also ensure that staff at all levels completely understand the political environment in which they are working.

This is hard work, but the results can be wonderful – or dire!

Choice and Control

It is essential to give local communities greater control over resources. Delegation of service budgets to the local community (for example, stock selection) will improve service responsiveness, drive professional culture change and enhance community control and sense of responsibility

Delegated budgets change the old professional 'gift' model of services, where professionals assess community needs, determine eligibility, ration resources and control services. Community development strengthens relationships between professionals and local communities and provides opportunities for the community to contribute knowledge and understanding of what will work.

Community Support

Helping local communities to support themselves and creating new rights for community groups will enable local people to participate more fully in public libraries, leading to increased confidence, self-efficacy and well-being. It will also offer practical advice and emotional support that only other members of the community can provide. In addition, self-support develops social capital in isolated or vulnerable groups.

The capacity-building support offered to local communities by library services can include providing meeting rooms and facilities, help with applying for grants, publicity and awareness-raising and official recognition of community groups.

Professional Culture

Community development requires a culture change whereby professionals consistently encourage community engagement and seek partnerships with local communities that share responsibility. For this to happen, the library service needs to support and enable those community members who are not usually engaged or involved in service planning, design, evaluation and delivery. Library staff with high levels of political awareness have a key role in fostering this engagement and involvement. The key questions to be considered here are:

- How will whole communities get involved and not just those who shout loudest, or who know their councillors?
- When communities plan, who is it? Everyone? A chosen group? How are they chosen?

Shifting power and sharing resources with local communities has big implications for professionals. It fundamentally changes the power dynamic between the community and professionals that may have been in place for decades. Culture change within the library profession requires visionary leadership and changes to professional training, recruitment and performance management. The local community should be involved in all aspects of library service planning, design, delivery and evaluation. Partnerships between the community and public libraries place greater value on new skills such as advice, brokerage, advocacy and support. New staff roles, such as that of Community Development Worker, should be created which embody these skills.

These proposals would need to be part of wider reforms to build community capacity, foster a new professionalism and create a more strategic role for public libraries:

- Involving local communities in policy-making – the leading examples of community development in practice did not originate from policy-makers, think tanks or governments but came from local communities. Systematically involving local people in the policy-making process – defining the problem, generating ideas and implementing solutions – is likely to lead to much greater community development in public libraries.
- Supporting community decision-making with better information – building community capacity requires not only greater access to information but the power to use it and re-use it in ways that professionals do not control and officials could not imagine.
- Commissioning long-term outcomes – public library service commissioning that is able to truly commission long-term outcomes rather than short-term outputs or service activity is much more likely to incentivize professionals to work in partnership with communities and co-produce better outcomes to chronic, complex and contested issues.
- A strategy for incubating local innovation – working in partnership with communities and enabling them to contribute more of their own resources is often incompatible with a top-down approach to reforming public library services. Local innovation that involves citizens in the way services are planned, designed, delivered and evaluated is much more likely to generate community development in practice.

Incentivizing Partnership Working

Partnerships between local communities and public libraries ensure that service providers are more accountable to communities and increase the commitment of community resources to achieving shared outcomes. These partnerships should be:

- reciprocal – give and take on both sides, a sense of mutuality and shared objectives
- negotiated – shared recognition of what both partners have to offer, and joint negotiation of goals and plans
- trust-based – trust is both a product of good relationships and essential for their maintenance.

Greater weight should be given to the quality of partnerships between public libraries and local communities in performance management frameworks. It is preferable to adopt a principles-based approach to measuring the quality of relationships between public libraries and the local community rather than a compliance model. The former would involve library workers reporting against high-level principles, such as trust, dignity and respect, rather than just shallow indicators of service user satisfaction. Benchmark perception data should be gathered relating to local communities' real and recent library experiences, to drive service improvement. Development of self-evaluation tools is necessary to measure the quality of relationships between library workers and the local community.

Partnerships

The importance of making connections to other local service providers and policy priorities was recognized by *The Modernisation Review of Public Libraries* (2010): 'Modern library services do not operate independently. They collaborate locally with a broad range of public, private and third sector partners because they work best when integrated with these services' (DCMS 2010a: 45).

There are opportunities for the library to be a 'shop window' for the council in every community and the best local leaders are already well aware of the opportunities offered by the library service for delivering on local priorities. Partnerships are also useful in shaping initiatives for targeting particular audiences, engaging with hard-to-reach groups and accessing funding streams to meet community needs.

An example of this is the Reading Agency's Six Book Challenge which encourages less-confident adults to read for pleasure by providing incentives and recognizing their achievement with certificates if they read six books. In 2009 the scheme was delivered by 121 library authorities in England in partnership with further education colleges, prisons and trade unions and more than 9,000 people took part. The scheme was found to increase learner confidence in reading, raise literacy rates and increase use of the library service.

There are a multitude of policy priorities where libraries can play a part – lifelong learning and literacy, online access, health services, links to services for children, families, schools and the curriculum, services for the unemployed and benefits services, work on community safety and with local police, links to local travel and transport services, green initiatives and rural outreach work. Figure 5.5 indicates how libraries can work in partnership with a wide range of organizations to build stronger communities.

There are a number of national partnerships already highlighting the library role. One is a partnership between libraries and NHS Choices (the comprehensive online information service about the NHS). Libraries' collections of printed material on a wide variety of health and lifestyle topics and the availability of free or low-cost Internet access make them an ideal place for people to research their condition, dispense their information prescriptions or to book their health appointments online.

Local need	Potential outcomes
• Increase access to public services • Improve mobile and housebound services • Engage community in service design and activities • Reach deprived communities • Create meaningful interactions • Increase volunteering opportunities	• Improvement and extension of services • Community engagement and management of assets • Stronger and more cohesive communities • User involvement in design and delivery of services • Improved co-working across community-focused organizations • Support tailored to people's individual needs
Where is it happening?	**Potential models**
• Leeds – libraries hosting community groups and sharing space and resources with youth service, housing and advice, information and guidance teams • Suffolk's mobile library service has longer stops for community activities, allowing other advisers and services to use the mobile to reach rural communities	• Libraries act as anchor services for a number of shared functions and services • Multi-agency delivery, including mobile services across rural areas and to housebound • Community and voluntary meeting spaces and services • Libraries as community forums

Figure 5.5   Partnership working

The valuable impact libraries can have on health was recognized via a campaign promoting public libraries in doctors' surgeries and other health outlets. The Department of Health has developed free online training for library staff around helping people to use the NHS Choices website to get advice about lifestyle issues like smoking, drinking and exercise or to find and use health services in England.

Another national partnership is the libraries' role in informal adult learning. Public libraries were recognized as playing a key role in supporting individuals, families and communities to learn throughout life in *The Learning Revolution* White Paper published in March 2009 (DIUS 2009). The White Paper identified the wider benefits of informal adult learning in building cohesive and confident communities, promoting health and well-being and supporting an increasingly ageing population to stay active, independent and fulfilled. Public libraries are engaging local spaces that offer access to a wide range of free resources that encourage people to continue learning throughout their lives. They play a significant role in supporting people who would not otherwise be able to participate in online learning opportunities by offering a largely free, community Internet service. They are ideally placed to support a thriving culture of lifelong learning in becoming established in communities. Local authorities can commission a broader range of learning opportunities for their local communities linked to local priorities. Public libraries, in partnership with other public and third sector bodies, can play a clear role in adult learning plans and strategies by opening up access to a wide range of learning opportunities.

Co-Production

An advanced form of community development which has started to emerge as a policy priority in the UK is co-production, which has been defined as: 'Delivering public services in an equal and reciprocal relationship between professionals, people using services, their families and their neighbours. Where activities are co-produced in this way, both services and neighbourhoods become far more effective agents of change' (Boyle and Harris 2009: 11).

Co-production suggests that the conscious or unconscious maintenance of library service users as passive recipients is not just a waste of their skills and time; it is also the reason why systemic change does not happen. When people are never asked to give anything back, and when the assets they represent are ignored or deliberately side-lined, they atrophy. The fact that social needs continue to rise is not due to a failure to consult or conduct opinion research, or even a failure to find enough resources. It is due to a failure to ask people for their help and to use the skills they have. The central idea in co-production is that local communities are hidden resources, not drains on the system, and that no library service that ignores this resource can be efficient. The local people who are currently defined as service users or potential users provide the vital ingredients which allow library service professionals to be effective.

Families and communities are the basic building blocks of the operating system, or core economy, which underpin economic activity as well as social development. The consequences of failing to recognize and support this core economy are all around us: isolation, time poverty, low levels of trust, engagement or social infrastructure. Co-production suggests ways we can rebuild and reinvigorate this core economy and realize its potential.

Co-production also suggests that library services need to be turned inside out, so that they can rediscover the human resources and remake the social networks that reduce demand on professionals and support public service interventions to succeed. This means that we must unleash the huge wasted resource represented by the recipients of services, and their families and neighbours. Co-production shifts the balance of power, responsibility and resources from professionals more to individuals, by involving people in the delivery of their own services. It recognizes that people are not merely repositories of need or recipients of services but are the very resource that can turn public services around.

Co-production means unleashing a wave of innovation about how library services are designed and delivered and how public goods are achieved, by expecting professionals to work alongside their communities. Co-production goes well beyond the idea of 'citizen engagement' or 'service user involvement' to foster the principle of equal partnership. It offers to transform the dynamic between the community and library service workers, putting an end to 'them' and 'us'. Instead, people pool different types of knowledge and skills, based on lived experience and professional learning. The effect of this, where it happens, is a huge shift of focus for public libraries, no longer obsessively looking inwards to targets and procedures, but increasingly looking outwards to local neighbourhoods to create supportive social networks, seeking out local energy where it exists to help deliver and broaden services, and seeing communities for what they can do, not just what they need. The idea is that, by working alongside the people they are supporting, public libraries can dramatically increase their resources, extend their reach, radically transform the way they operate, and be much more effective. Co-production makes strengthening the core economy of neighbourhood and family the central task of all public libraries, by:

- recognizing people as assets, because people themselves are the real wealth of society
- valuing work differently, to recognize everything as work that people do to raise families, look after people, maintain healthy communities, social justice and good governance
- promoting reciprocity, giving and receiving, because it builds trust between people and fosters mutual respect
- building social networks, because people's physical and mental well-being depends on strong, enduring relationships (Boyle and Harris 2009: 14).[1]

Co-production is the model by which public libraries can begin to prevent social problems like illiteracy and unemployment, understanding that this is only possible by providing a catalyst for communities to broaden the range of what they already do or can do in the future. It means public libraries:

- building mutual support systems that can tackle problems before they become acute
- encouraging behaviour that will prevent these problems happening in the first place, and building the social networks that can make this possible
- reshaping themselves to build the supportive relationships that can help people or families in crisis carry on coping when they no longer qualify for all-round professional support.

Co-production has the capacity to transform public libraries   Co-production has to be potentially *transformative*, not just for the individuals involved, but also for the professionals who are struggling to put it into practice and for the system as a whole. Public library workers will need to change the way they think about their role and how they operate and the people they have come to know as 'users', 'lapsed users' or 'non-users' who will now become their equal

---

1   In turn, taking this from Cahn 2001.

partners; they need to change their attitudes, priorities and training. They need to move from fixers to facilitators. Public library services that are delivered in this way are likely to be more participative, by definition, as well as more equitable, responsive and creatively designed and delivered. And, because the people who are supposed to benefit from them will have a strong and tangible stake in them, they are more likely to command wider public support.

Co-production promotes equal participation.   Co-production has to have *equality* at its heart. It can only be true to its principles if it is backed by measures to make sure that everyone has the capacity to participate on equal terms. This is partly because it fosters equal partnership between 'providers' and 'users' of library services, and affords equal value to different kinds of knowledge and skills, acknowledging that everyone has something of value to contribute. It is also because, in order to be effective, it must enable everyone to participate, not just those who are already more able, articulate and socially advantaged. Hence developing co-production forces us to think about the underlying causes of inequality and how these can be tackled, and embrace very different ways of framing participation. This is going to mean changing the perceptions and the approach of many public library professionals.

Co-production is essential to building sustainable public libraries.   Co-production has to be about *sustainability*. It is a method by which public libraries tap into the abundance of human assets, enabling them to flourish and expand, and then bringing them into play – complementing and augmenting the publicly funded resources of the state, which will be scarcer over the next few years. By helping to prevent harm and constrain demand, co-production can help to safeguard public resources for meeting needs that cannot be prevented. In this way, it helps to guarantee the long-term viability of public libraries.

Co-production must have a key role to play in commissioning library services.   Co-production can play a significant role in developing service innovations when library services are commissioned in the right way. This is the antidote to narrowing down public libraries to inputs and outputs, which does not just impoverish the service which is delivered, but can often impoverish the neighbourhood in which they are delivered. Narrow deliverables leave out the real value that public libraries can provide. When commissioners build co-production into the commissioning cycle, and try to procure co-produced library services, they enable providers and local communities to play a much more important role in designing and delivering services that work. As a result, they keep the most important ingredient of any public library – people – at their heart. Their model of delivery includes direct beneficiaries, their families and the wider community, as real resources built into the service design, making the service not just better value for money, but better for those involved. For these reasons it is clear that co-production cannot be a bolt-on innovation. It fundamentally changes the way library services are delivered, with the objectives of reducing need, rebuilding the social infrastructure and shifting the balance of power.

Working Together

> Librarians are not the experts on what our communities need or want in terms
> of library services – the community is the expert. It is our job to ensure that we
> develop a library service that reflects the community's needs and vision. We do
> this with them, not for them (Annette DeFaveri, quoted in Working Together
> Project 2008a: 28).

In North American libraries, outreach has become synonymous with library staff
taking a programme or service outside the branch and into a community. Regardless
of the approach used by library staff, if the event or activity occurs outside of the
physical branch, people automatically associate it with outreach. As was learned
through Working Together, not all approaches to working within communities are
interpreted by individual community members in the same way. Outreach is a
fundamentally different approach to community-led service planning.

Outreach

The major defining characteristic of outreach is that it is a process where library
programmes and services are internally defined and developed *by library staff.*
Library staff members are the people who are central to the formulation and
creation of outreach. In order to achieve this, community-based information gaps
and needs are identified by library staff. Additionally, since there is a recognition
that many members of the community 'choose' not to come to the library to access
information, outreach is viewed as the primary way in which community-based
information gaps and needs can be addressed; by taking the programme or service
into the community. During outreach a number of activities occur, including
library staff delivering a programme, delivering messages important to convey
to the public (such as marketing existing programmes or items they can come
and get at the library branch), or delivering existing services. In many instances,
existing in-house programmes and services are slightly adapted and taken into the
community.

WTP librarians identified the three core components to outreach. They are that:

1. planning is completed in the library
2. library activities are used multiple times in the community, and
3. library staff talk with people about the library.

The content used in each of these three core components is created by library
staff before they enter a community. As a result, internally predetermined
services are created for the community, which often leaves very little room for
the community to provide input. This results in a lack of control, variation or

change which local individuals, and librarians, can make to meet the particular information needs within communities.

Additionally, another key characteristic of outreach is that the process primarily consists of library staff giving out information. Communities are commonly viewed as lacking information, or in need of a service that the library can provide them. In response, the library enters the community to provide an activity, service or information which is currently lacking. Consequently, when library staff enter the local community they assume the role of an educator, and that is how they are perceived.

During the first two years of the WTP, there was some significant disagreement about the role that outreach should play when CDLs (community development librarians) were entering the community. Due in part to pre-existing experiences which CDLs brought with them from working in communities, they came to the project with pre-established understandings of how to work with and within the community. Part of this included recognition that there are a number of advantages to implementing outreach activities, including:

- It is a comfortable technique for staff to use when entering a community, since there is little need for critical adjustments to be made. Instead, library staff make centralized programme or service development decisions. Once these decisions are made, they may not 'need' to be adjusted for a long period of time. This gave staff the opportunity to become the deliverers of services or messages.
- It is the community's expectation that librarians serve them from an outreach perspective. Librarians working in communities have used outreach activities so often that it is hard for service agencies or individual community members to envision any other approach or role which librarians could play outside of a library branch. As discussed in the national evaluation:

> At one site it was really difficult for the CDL to gain access to community members at a local agency – [the main] issue was staff could understand library staff coming in to deliver a program or promote library service – but could not understand the value in library staff coming in without materials or engaging in discussion with community members about barriers to services. (Atkey 2008: 47)

When a process has been constructed which seems to work for the community and library staff, there may be little incentive to change it. However, two important issues must be addressed: why challenge and change it?; and if a library system is going to change the way in which they work with the community outside of the library branch, what approach(es) should be taken?

Issues with Outreach: Is there still a Role for Outreach?

WTP staff quickly recognized that various forms of outreach can create unequal power dynamics between library staff and community members, which are exacerbated in socially excluded communities. This power differential occurs when planning initially takes place within the confines of the library. Since library staff regularly predetermine the topic and content of the outreach event, the topic chosen by library staff and its relevance in addressing community need has to be questioned. This approach does not work for socially excluded communities, because it is premised on needs identification and service development from a frame of reference outside the lived experiences of individuals within local communities.

Based on librarian decisions about community need, *information is given out to the community*. The community member is viewed as the learner or receiver of information, while the librarian is the expert, bringing in and delivering information. This primarily one-way flow of information maintains the same hierarchical authority which disenfranchises the community. Once these dynamics are created, and these roles have been established, it can be hard for both library staff and the community to shift and create equitable relationships.

In addition to creating a power differential, outreach also plays another role by providing an opportunity for the library to market existing programmes and services. Many times it is believed that socially excluded individuals choose not to use the library because they do not know about existing services. From this perspective the commonly held view is that 'if the community only knew what the library had to offer them, they would be more likely to come to us and use library information'. From this perspective, librarians are very determined to justify that existing library services in their current form are relevant. By using outreach as a tool to increase knowledge of libraries so that all people start using their services, librarians fail to acknowledge, or provide an opportunity for active engagement with the community. Without this engagement they are not able to discover the barriers which people face when trying access library services and the reasons why people have chosen not to use library services (such as distrust of formal organizations, previous bad experiences, fines, transportation, etc.). For more information on these barriers to library use please see Chapter 4 on Library Image and Identity.

Two years into the Working Together Project it became essential for the CDLs to develop a clear differentiation between outreach and community development approaches. In fact, it created a sense of paralysis for librarians, since:

> [The CDL] is inclined to use outreach as an initial offering but we're trying not to do that. It might seem partially artificial but we're trying to shake librarians out of their comfort zone, because [starting with outreach] sets up the wrong dynamic and it doesn't force them to grow beyond that. (Atkey 2008: 216)

In response to this situation, in November 2006 CDLs began to view outreach not as an ends to working with the community but as a means to start engaging with socially excluded community members. Outreach is not a highly desirable community entry technique, but at times it may be necessary.

By taking a slight shift in the way in which outreach is delivered – changing from using outreach as a way to get a message out to the community to an approach which provides an opportunity to connect with community members to begin to build relationships – outreach activities can be used as a conduit, leading to community-led service development. For instance, at one library site a CDL was having trouble gaining access to socially excluded mothers because the agency staff could not see a role for the library service, beyond bringing in existing programmes or books. Working with the agency officials,

> … CDL entered a community agency to work with a group of single mothers with a load of clay rather than library materials. Working together with clay inspired a broader range of discussion with participants than would typically be seen in traditional outreach activities. According to one interviewee, 'the conversation went from "it feels empowering to do something creative," to "what other creative things we could do," to "it feels great to get together with other adults out in the community," to "let's get together and do things more often."' What started out being perceived as an outreach strategy, with a slight shift, grew into a strong example of collaborative service planning with the development of a not-for-profit arts society. (Atkey 2008: 25)

By recognizing a community's interests and strengths, an outreach response eventually led to the librarian and community members building trusting relationships and a service response which met the need of the community.

Community-Led Approaches Developed through Working Together

Most of the staff training was focused on community development, but not from a library perspective, because it had never been done before. It was not possible to predetermine the nature of this community development training because the project was approved on the condition that experimentation would occur. It was not desirable to create a predefined definition of community development because this would then have driven the approaches used by staff.

Retrospectively, the application of community-led approaches to working with the community can easily be understood once a person has grounding in service planning from a community-led perspective. The major premise of community-led approaches is that the reason for initial interactions with community members is to establish relationships, which eventually lead to trust, between socially excluded community members and library staff. Without the development of relationships, which occurs through sustained interactions between people over time, community-led approaches will not work:

> We couldn't just do traditional outreach with a new segment of the population, or in a new location. We had to do something that created a meaningful dialogue between the library and the communities who weren't coming in the door. Relationship building was the key to this. It allowed us, or more appropriately forced us, to approach the community on their terms, and on their turf. Instead of us holding all the cards, which is what we do when we passively expect the community to come to us, they had to be holding all the cards, and we had to have the humility to approach them, build relationships, and create the comfort level for them to reveal the cards to us. (Williment et al. 2011a)

Once relationships are established, it is important to not develop a programme or service quickly. The process of working with the community is more important, which will eventually lead to the devising of programmes or services for the community. The central focus of working in communities needs to switch focus from what 'we' the library has to offer, to how library staff engage with the community.

From a community-led perspective, working with the community shifts from outreach to a process whereby:

1. Library staff listen to people talk about their needs (based on life experiences, and put into the context of library services).
2. Based on community-identified needs, programmes and service planning are completed collaboratively with the community.
3. The collaborative community activity is changed or modified based on community input.

A community-led approach shifts the role of the librarian from a person who gives information out to the community, to someone who actively listens to the community and learns about their needs. Desirable community-based outcomes from working in the community should include sustainability and skills development.

It is inherently implied in a community-led approach that it is non-prescriptive. The techniques used by library staff to enter a community or to explore need may be similar in different communities, library branches or library systems. However, because community need drives the library response, the programme or service will always be different. Also, while the techniques used to engage with the community are exportable from community to community, the community-led programmes and services which are developed are rarely transferable from one community to another. For example:

A local library assistant was 'hanging out' at the local food bank, which served over 200 low-income families every two weeks. She saw that a great deal of fresh produce, especially 'exotic' food such as leeks and beans, were going bad. After talking with socially excluded volunteers at the food banks, she soon discovered that the food was rotting because people in the community were hesitant to take it as they had no history of eating it and did not know how to prepare it. In collaboration with community members, they decided to affix mailing labels with the local library branches phone number printed on them to the food. Local community members would then phone down to the local branch to get simple recipes which were identified by library staff. Upon visiting another food bank in another community about 50 miles away, the local librarian thought that he had a great service suggestion for the food bank, only to discover that this food bank had no issues with food spoiling, since they were already handing out recipes with the food they were providing to socially excluded community members.

Put simply, the way relationship building works is that we approach the community outside the library, in their spaces, with no set agenda, but simply with an earnest desire to get to know them and learn from them. Essentially, when we go somewhere, we don't deliver a program, or conduct a community survey, but instead we hang out, and get to know people. What this does is it levels the power imbalance between the library and the socially excluded community, and creates a comfort level where genuine collaboration can unfold. Once a relationship has been established, then it becomes possible to collaboratively explore a community's library service needs. The one thing we always have to be careful about though, is not to have preconceived notions of what that community's service needs are. They may not always, or even often, be for programming. (Williment et al. 2011a)

Helpful Hints

#1: Outreach activities tend to focus on the end product, the delivery of the service to the community. When entering a community, ask yourself if a service or programme has already been determined for that community. If it has, this is not community-led service planning; it is outreach. Shift the focus from the end product (the programme or service which will be delivered to a community) to how library staff will engage with the community to build relationships, and begin to hear community-based needs.

#2: Social exclusion strategies need to encompass the following: proactive community librarianship based on outreach, advocacy and intervention; community development through grassroots, community-based approaches; and partnerships with those in the public, voluntary and private sectors.

#3: Public libraries need to ensure that they are offering relevant services where they are best used by socially excluded people. Locations should not be limited to library buildings, but include 'outreach' locations and services of all kinds.

#4: Public libraries should support community-based initiatives, groups and organizations through outreach staff, materials and other resources.

#5: Public libraries should develop community information services, in partnership with other providers such as Citizens Advice Bureaux, which help socially excluded people deal with their daily problems, including health, education, housing, family and legal matters.

#6: Learning centres, literacy centres and other lifelong learning activities should be developed by public libraries on a much wider scale than at present. Often, joint provision with education services, the not-for-profit sector and local community groups will offer real advantages in terms of pooling of skills and funding and community involvement.

Chapter 6
Information and Communication Technologies and Social Exclusion

In this chapter we consider the role of new technology in tackling social exclusion. Whilst recognizing that ICT has a very important part to play in the delivery of modern public library services, we must also guard against the tendency to make a fetish out of technology or believe that it can be a panacea or 'silver bullet' which can solve all of the library's problems. The implementation of the People's Network (PN) in UK public libraries gave a massive boost to a flagging service which had seen year-on-year decreases in both visits and book issues. In the wake of the PN usage went up substantially but book issues continued to decline, indicating that new library users were taking advantage of free Internet access rather than borrowing books. There was also a professional complacency which suggested that the provision of public access terminals would automatically make the library more inclusive.

This complacency was challenged by *Open to All?* (Muddiman et al. 2000b) which recommended that public libraries should draw up ICT plans that included a strategy outlining how the needs of socially excluded communities could be prioritized. ICT should be used as a means to tackle social exclusion, rather than as an end in itself. ICT should be free at the point of need and ICT initiatives should be targeted at excluded groups in a proactive way via skilled staffing and support mechanisms. Libraries should also support community ICT initiatives.

In Canada the Working Together Project (WTP) placed a strong emphasis on supporting staff in the use of ICT to meet community needs. It was recognized that many library staff might be unsure of their own skills in using technology and have varying levels of comfort delivering IT training outside a scripted training course. Delivering community-led ICT instruction means that the content and approaches used will need to be adapted to best meet each individual's needs.

The People's Network

£100 million of National Lottery funding was invested in the People's Network (PN) programme which was launched in 2000. Delivered by the MLA (Museums, Libraries and Archives Council), the PN supported the development of ICT learning in public libraries through the provision of 30,000 Internet-enabled computers. It linked every public library in the UK to the Internet by the end of 2002. The expansion in hardware capacity, coupled with increased opening hours in many libraries, meant that over 68.5 million hours of potential Internet use were being provided by libraries across the UK every year. Monitoring data collected from all public libraries in England showed 11.7 million user sessions on the PN in 2003.

From 1999 a related £20 million ICT training programme equipped public library staff with skills, knowledge and confidence to use ICT effectively in their day-to-day work supporting users of the PN. A survey by MORI for the National Audit Office in March 2004 found that 16 per cent of the public aged 16 and over have used the Internet at a public library.

Despite this significant progress in equipping libraries with digital capability there are weaknesses in the public library digital infrastructure offer. There are barriers to access, in terms of charging and filtering. The PN is now often run down although some local authorities have invested in new computers and training. Broadband speeds are variable and local authority IT networks often hamper the digital offer. Most significantly, there has been a lack of targeting in terms of how the network is used.

Charges are a Barrier to Access

Open to All? recommended that ICT should be free at the point of access and this was certainly the case when the PN was first rolled out. There was a strong stipulation attached to the government funding of this network that it would be provided free of charge. Failure to do so could lead to the government asking for its money back. Over time, however, some library authorities decided to start charging for the PN. This was long before the more recent draconian cuts in public sector spending and so the initial impetus to charge was not related to the need to save money. Rather, the PN was seen as another potential income stream which could be used to augment or replace library expenditure.

A similar situation had arisen when public libraries first started to loan out audio and visual (AV) items such as records and videos. The 1964 Public Libraries Act stated that books should be loaned for free and this created a gap in the legislation which enabled local authorities to charge for non-book loans. The criteria for charging was purely one of format – because an audio book would have the same content as its written version, but could be charged for under the 1964 Act. Despite some weak protests from library professionals, charging for AV items became the norm and developed into a significant income stream, second only to fines for the late return of books (another technicality which worked around the 1964 Act). By the advent of CDs and DVDs every library authority was charging for AV items and this service was geared around maximizing income rather than meeting community needs. Indeed, socially excluded people were effectively barred from using this service because they did not have the financial means to pay for AV loans. As well as being a barrier to access, AV charges also became a hostage to fortune as library services became increasingly dependent on this income. When digital downloads of music and films became available the bottom fell out of the library AV market. This created a huge hole in library budgets which could only be filled by cuts in expenditure, usually from the book fund. This raised the profile of an unhelpful 'books versus AV' debate which continues to this day.

A similar situation has arisen around the PN and access to ICT. Given freely to local councils as a gift from central government to help close the digital divide in society, it has been turned into a 'cash cow'. To prevent the government claiming its investment money back and to meet the letter of the PN agreement (but certainly not the spirit), those councils which introduced charges also allowed 30 minutes or one hour free access. This enabled them to argue that there were no barriers to access and that the PN was open to all. In fact, anyone who uses the Internet knows that 30/60 minutes is barely enough time to check emails, let alone carry out a sophisticated online search or research.

Filtering is a Form of Censorship

Charging is not the only barrier to access. Censorship, or (to use a more polite and professional description) filtering, also creates a two-tier system: those who have full and unimpeded access to the Internet at home and those who have to rely solely on the PN. The filtering mechanisms used by public libraries are aimed primarily at 'protecting' children and young people from 'inappropriate' websites. This is at the behest of council ICT and legal departments who do not want the organization to be put at risk by providing unfettered access to the Internet. But the filtering systems affect adults as well and are both clumsy and ineffective. They block access to legitimate websites such as searches for place names like Sussex and Scunthorpe. If a website gets caught in the council's filter, the library user can request that the site be unblocked. But few people make this request, mostly because they do not want to reveal which sites they are visiting, which is completely valid and understandable.

Filtering is aimed in particular at pornographic websites but the owners of these sites, which are very lucrative, find ways to get around the filter and are always one step ahead. Their profit motive and resources are much stronger than the council's ability to 'protect the public'. This is an echo of our Victorian forefathers who invented public libraries to ensure that the working classes were only exposed to 'healthy literature' rather than the 'penny dreadfuls' and seditious political literature which was circulating around public houses. Similar attempts are being made now to limit access to or control the use of social websites such as Facebook and Youtube, particularly by young people. There is also an aversion to young people being able to play online games via library computers. This is viewed as a 'waste of public resources'. If public libraries are to stay modern and relevant to the needs of their communities, particularly their future potential users, they need to be less risk-averse and more embracing of new technology and social media.

The Internet is impossible to control and manage. Its great strength is that it is governed and led by its users, many of who supply the content, Wikipedia being a case in point. All attempts to manage the Internet and how it is used are doomed to fail. Public libraries should not be positioned as Internet policemen or information gatekeepers. Libraries should be a place where anyone can go to get their information needs met unimpeded by barriers of finance or censorship.

This debate erupted into the public domain in the UK in April 2012 when MPs warned that it was too easy for children to watch online pornography. But could the Internet be regulated to protect children? And should it? Internet freedom campaigner Jim Killock, from the Open Rights Group, was firmly of the opinion that default filtering is a form of censorship, is not simple and will not work technically:

> If ISPs and the state decide what children can see, by default – automatically generated lists based on key words – an eight-year-old would probably still be able to find highly unsuitable, upsetting non-adult material. And default filters might block lots of things adults want to see – such as political blogs or anti-censorship sites – and the government should not be given powers to censor adults. For example, the BBC wouldn't get banned for using the word 'sex' three times on a page, but a blog or small independent site – that is reasonable but not as well-known – might be.

> So the default filter would have to be pretty weak, otherwise too many adults would get annoyed as they wouldn't be able to access things and would switch the filter off anyway. Practically speaking, lots of sites are beginning to turn to encrypting as a way to get around filters. Also, filtering already happens on mobile phones and people can still find pornography. So the nanny state approach will make parents feel safer, will make them think that the problem is taken care of, but default blocking is actually deeply irresponsible because it will fail to protect the most vulnerable children. (BBC News, 2012)

Hardware and Software must be Updated

When the government invested in the PN, local councils were grateful recipients of this opportunity to modernize and transform public library services. But they have failed to make optimum use of this free gift. Few councils made financial provision within their capital budgets to replace or refresh computer terminals and software. Public access PCs are quickly worn out by use and abuse and monitors, keyboards and mice need replacing on a regular basis. Similarly, software needs to be upgraded to be able to manage the latest applications. Internet cafés do this as a matter of course but in many public libraries the PN quickly became out of date. Corporate funding from ICT departments was made available in a handful of places, but in general any resources to update the PN had to come from the library budget and this usually meant frequent and deep raids on the book fund. This led to charges from some users and commentators that public libraries were replacing books with computers, which is, to a large extent, true. This has triggered an unhealthy ICT versus books argument when, of course, these two formats should complement rather than compete with each other.

ICT must be Targeted at the Socially Excluded

But the biggest failure of the PN was that there were very few attempts made to implement the most important *Open to All?* recommendations: ICT initiatives should be targeted more closely at excluded groups and communities in a proactive way. Appropriate levels of skilled staffing and support should be offered to users; libraries should enthusiastically commit funding and support to neighbourhood ICT initiatives.

The PN was seen as an end in itself rather than a means to an end. It was viewed as a panacea which would automatically make public libraries more socially inclusive without any effort required beyond providing the public access terminals. No attempt was made to target the network at excluded groups and communities in a proactive way. Few programmes were devised which aimed to meet the needs of the socially excluded. Where these programmes did exist, they were planned, designed, delivered and assessed by professional library staff with no input from excluded communities.

Most frontline staff have been trained in providing help to library users to get them online, but there is very little specific training around how ICT could be used to support and engage excluded communities. Few attempts were made to link public libraries to neighbourhood community ICT initiatives. Indeed, these initiatives were often seen as a competitor to the PN and a threat to its ability to drive more people through the library doors.

Digital access to UK public libraries has increased but there is still a significant amount of untapped potential take-up. According to the *Taking Part* (DCMS 2011a) survey in 2008/09 the proportion of library users who accessed public libraries via digital technology stood at 2.4 per cent. By 2010/11 this had grown to 3.6 per cent, but was still considerably less than digital access to other cultural sectors such as sports (11.6 per cent) and archives (7.6 per cent). With regards to gender there is more digital access to libraries by men (4.2 per cent) than women (3.1 per cent). These figures could have been considerably higher if library authorities had followed the *Open to All?* recommendations as part of their PN strategies.

Access to Digital Skills and Services including E-Government

Framework for the Future: Libraries, Learning and Information in the Next Decade (DCMS 2003) identified three key activities which should be at the heart of public libraries' modern mission:

- the promotion of reading and informal learning
- access to digital skills and services including e-government
- measures to tackle social exclusion, build community identity and develop citizenship.

Framework for the Future (*F4F*) was an attempt to define what a 'comprehensive and efficient' (Public Libraries and Museums Act 1964) public library service should look like. The aim was to create a consensus among public library authorities that the prime focus of library services should be on books and learning, digital skills and services and tackling social exclusion. The three key objectives listed above were intended to be equally important, relevant and mutually supporting and reinforcing key objectives of any library service in the UK.

In reality much more focus was placed on reading and ICT than on tackling social exclusion. A wide range of national, regional and local initiatives were launched around the reading and informal learning programme. Books and reading were regarded as the core purpose of public libraries – a book service rather than a people service. Libraries were focused on those whose needs revolved around books and reading. Wider social needs were the responsibility of other council services and agencies. Books and reading were located well within the comfort zone of library managers and workers who greeted the *F4F* focus with professional relish. They worked with local schools to provide planned programmes of reader development to enrich and enhance the curriculum. They created a national network of homework clubs. They used the national Summer Reading Challenge to help children to continue to learn during the summer vacation and so help minimize the 'summer learning dip'. We will examine some of these initiatives in more detail in Chapter 7 which focuses on materials provision and the development of holistic collections policies to ensure that library stock reflects the needs of local communities.

Similar attempts were made to maximize digital citizenship among existing library users. Lottery funding from the New Opportunities Fund enabled almost all public libraries in England to establish UK online learning centres. A related £50 million programme created online content. *F4F* encouraged library services to develop the PN through:

- Communities online – public libraries could offer to create, host and manage websites for local community groups.
- Culture online – to create new online content and interactive services. Libraries have a role in providing access and in generating content, including national content.
- Alliances with broadcasters – libraries could be an important physical point of contact for people learning through broadcasters' online services.
- Information – the scope for a national service to answer queries online (Ask a Librarian), building on similar services already offered by some library authorities.

There were a host of conferences, seminars and professional events to promote these strands of *F4F* but there was much less activity when it came to tackling social exclusion. Much of this effort was left to the Network ('tackling social exclusion in libraries, museums and galleries') which had been formed as a direct legacy of the *Open to All?* research project. The Network did the job of government and local authorities by linking together the three key strands of *F4F*; for example, by showing how digital citizenship was an essential element in building strong and cohesive communities. We will examine the community and civic values strand of *F4F* in our chapter on mainstreaming and resourcing for social exclusion and how to place community needs at the heart of public library strategy, structures, systems and organizational culture.

The Digital Divide

The scope for digital technologies in meeting many of the needs of vulnerable social groups is extensive. In an age of often widening social inequalities in education, health and living standards (among other areas), digital inclusion has the capacity to help close the gap. In this way, not only are the problems of digital and social exclusion inextricably linked, but so too are their solutions. The key findings from *Understanding Digital Exclusion* (DCLG 2008) were that:

- ICT ownership has broadly increased across all traditional platforms. Most noticeably, the Internet witnessed a growth in use with 84 per cent of household connections using broadband technology.
- Those without access to the Internet are typically those who are also socially disadvantaged. They tend to be elderly, working class, are likely to live by themselves and have few professional qualifications. The relative isolation of these groups indicates that digital exclusion cannot be solved in isolation from other policy areas.
- Access is still not enough. Nearly two fifths of non-users fail to see the need or benefit of using the Internet and other ICTs or they feel that they are not the right kind of person to use them. The greatest share of the population who hold this view are the elderly and those on low incomes. These groups were also the most likely to not use the Internet, even if they had a connection at home.
- Skills, confidence and trust are linked. A lack of skills leads to a lack of confidence, which in turn leads to a lack of trust of technologies. There is a correlation between lack of confidence and reluctance to use personal information over the Internet.
- The digital divide is deepening. The persistent lack of motivation and perceived need from those who do not use the Internet means those that are still not included are at risk of being left further and further behind.
- Wider digital technologies are a key part of the answer, particularly for those who are vulnerable or disadvantaged. Wider technologies affect these different groups in different ways and that is why a targeted approach is required. Technologies that provide direct benefits tend to have a deeper impact on smaller, more focused segments of the population. However,

the indirect benefits of digital technologies can be vast and affect a wider number of people.

These findings indicate that some fundamental changes in public library approaches to ICT are required if community needs are to be met.

Race Online 2012

Another important initiative was launched by Culture Minister Ed Vaizey on 1 July 2010. Mr Vaizey announced – in collaboration with the Society of Chief Librarians – a public library promise to Race Online 2012, the campaign led by UK digital champion Martha Lane Fox, that the library network will help half a million people gain digital skills by the end of 2012. Martha Lane Fox added:

> Libraries are fantastic sources of information, advice and support for the communities they serve. They provide Internet access for anyone, in an environment that feels safe and secure. I am delighted that the Society of Chief Librarians has pledged that the library network will help half a million people gain digital skills by the end of 2012. That's a major step on the road to getting all 10 million people in the UK who've never used the Internet online, and I hope it will inspire more people to pledge to help people get online through raceonline2012.org. Thank you!

The Internet – Don't Need It, Can't Afford It

According to the Office for National Statistics (2012), 50 per cent of people who do not have an Internet connection claim they do not have one because they 'don't need the Internet'. Interestingly, this attitude also seems to be reflected in other nations. The recent Pew report in the US, for example, revealed that 48 per cent of non-Internet users do not think that the Internet is 'relevant to them'. Either there has been a problem articulating the benefits that come with possessing an Internet connection, or people are aware of the benefits but do not think they are a sufficient reason to connect. This is an area where libraries can play a bigger role in getting the unconnected connected.

Another key statistic is the cost factor. Of non-users, 32 per cent said that they did not have household Internet because either the equipment or connection costs were prohibitive. This is not surprising given the statistical relationship between non-use and income. These non-users would benefit from free Internet access at their local library. Paying in an Internet café or alternative establishment would not be a feasible option. It is the local library with free access or no connection at all.

Furthermore, around 20 per cent of non-users claim that a lack of skills is preventing them from accessing the Internet. This underlines the need for skilled support to be provided for those that are not connected. The provision of skilled support can have a substantial impact on an individual's confidence. Where once they were scared of trying to learn how to use the Internet on their own, they can become confident users taking full advantage of the access available to them. But they *must* have the skilled support there in order for them to do so. Without the initial support it is unlikely that many of those who believe they lack the skills will *ever* get connected. Considering the extent to which non-users are unconnected due to financial or confidence reasons, the public library has an important role in getting people online and helping them to navigate the Internet.

The dismissive attitude toward ICT by some excluded people is a key barrier that needs to be overcome in order to motivate these groups. It is important to note that neither the needs of the different disadvantaged groups nor the respective benefits for each group are necessarily the same. What is crucial, and most successful, is that programmes focus on the individual needs of participants – the actual applications and their benefits rather than the ICT. Focus must lie on specific targeted benefits, rather than a 'one solution for all' approach.

Non-users of the Internet were reported to be the most interested in sending emails, transferring digital photos to computers, making purchases and finding out hospital information. Targeted campaigns focusing on such functions could be used to activate non-users. For example, public library programmes could provide ICT training for the unemployed, linked to job searching and writing CVs.

One way of converting attitudes could be to link ICT with social interactions:
- Public libraries working with schools to enable children to take their parents or grandparents to school in order to teach them how to use computers and the Internet.
- Public libraries working with 'silver surfers' so that ICT-literate seniors can tutor fellow library members. The similar age and life experiences between tutor and pupil reinforce confidence in the training and support provided and also improve the social inclusion of members.

The Income Divide and Its Impact on Digital Exclusion

The Internet has massively changed the information landscape. Its development has led to an explosion in the availability of information. There is more information available to the average citizen now than there has ever been. However, whilst it is accessible for many, there is still a significant proportion of people who either do not have the equipment or the skills required to take advantage of this development.

Take, for example, the Office for National Statistics (2012) report regarding Internet access statistics in relation to age, gender, disability and earnings. The statistics in relation to earnings particularly demonstrate the extent of the divide between those that can be defined as 'information rich' and 'information poor'. There is a stark difference between higher and lower wage earners. As you move up the scale from low to high earners, the proportion of those who have never *used* the Internet (not just do not have access at home, but have never even *used* the Internet) drops dramatically.

There is a *very* substantial divide between the rich and poor when it comes to Internet access. Those with higher incomes can afford the equipment and connection charges. It is particularly easy for higher earners to assume that everyone has access to the Internet or has at least *used* it. After all, if everyone around you is connected, why should you believe that there are people out there who are not? This may help to explain why it is always middle-class commentators who argue that libraries are irrelevant in the age of the Internet. Their friends all have a connection so of course that means *everyone* has.

For those on low incomes there are a multitude of concerns that take priority over the ownership of a computer and an Internet connection, not least putting food on the table. As long as their gross income remains so low, it is highly unlikely that they are going to invest in the technology required to connect to the Internet. Furthermore, given their restrictive budgets, it is highly unlikely that they would be prepared to spend any of their money on making use of high street Internet facilities if doing so requires payment, no matter how seemingly insignificant the fee. For people on such a restrictive budget, the local public library is their best and most feasible means of connecting to the Internet.

The challenge for public libraries is to ensure that they do not have policies and practices which further exclude entire communities. Given that many low earners have *never* used the Internet, public libraries have been unsuccessful in getting this particular section of the community connected. Despite the intentions of the People's Network to connect the socially and digitally excluded, it is clear that many remain excluded. More effort should be put into public libraries reaching the 'information poor'. Sophisticated social networking marketing will clearly not have any impact on this section of society.

The link between social and digital exclusion means that active and targeted public library intervention will be required to support disadvantaged groups in accessing the more direct benefits of digital technologies. For example, the benefits of online employment support for job seekers can only be realized by those who have easy access to the Internet, and this is what the PN can provide. Public libraries can reach out to those without access, skills or motivation to become otherwise digitally included.

Age, Disability and the Digital Divide

It is not just the low-paid who are victims of the digital divide, it also impacts upon disabled people and those over 65. The latest statistics from the Office for National Statistics (2012) reveals that 71 per cent of the over-75s and 40 per cent of the 65–74 age group have never used the Internet. This drops dramatically when you hit the 55–64 age group (18.7 per cent). Clearly, a substantial proportion of the population aged over 65 have never used the Internet.

Public libraries have an important role to play in getting older people connected and teaching them the skills they need. 'Silver surfer' sessions have been successful in bringing the Internet to the over-65s, getting them connected and showing them how to complete basic tasks like sending an email or watching a video. Elderly people who are housebound should have the same degree of access and support as those that are able to visit their local public library. A recent pilot involving Birmingham City and Devon libraries demonstrated the extent to which public libraries can assist the housebound in connecting to the Internet. The evaluation report (Pask and Wilkie 2011) referred to a number of case studies which demonstrated the impact that these opportunities had on individuals. Ivor, for example, initially wished he had not signed up for the project as he did not want to 'look like a fool if [he] couldn't get the hang of it'. However, after receiving support he found:

> I could search the web for anything I want, I can transfer anything into Favourites, I've spoken to me friend on Skype … I can email, I can answer emails, I can research Google Earth … First thing I do when I come in is switch it on … I've gone from wishing I hadn't signed up to loving every minute. I use it all the time! I just want to keep exploring. I don't want to run before I can walk and I would like a printer I think.

Without the support provided by trained library staff it is unlikely that Ivor would have gained the skills and confidence that the pilot clearly gave him. Initiatives such as this can play a key role in ensuring that housebound people are not excluded and left behind by the connected. Similar schemes can also produce significant benefits for disabled people. According to the most recent Office of National Statistics (2012) report, 34.5 per cent of those classed as disabled have never accessed the Internet. This includes anyone affected by sensory impairments, learning difficulties or anyone suffering impairments with recurring effects (epilepsy, depression, rheumatoid arthritis). As with the over-65s, home visits by library staff can help to close the digital divide for disabled people.

Skills breed confidence which in turn breeds trust. The Oxford Internet Institute (Dutton and Helsper 2007) has found that the more basic activities a user undertakes on the Internet, the more likely they are to undertake intermediate and advanced activities. It is therefore necessary to implant basic skills among those who lack general ICT skills and provide continuous support to all levels of ability.

It is important to remember that computers may seem alien or inaccessible to those who have little or no experience with them. The People's Network can be used to reduce such barriers. For example, public libraries can work with the Royal National Institute for the Blind to provide training in ICT for blind or partially sighted people via screen magnification and speech software. Three out of four of those with sight problems in the UK remain unemployed.

Digital Inclusion, E-Books and Digital Content

The Modernisation Review of Public Libraries (2010) considered three key aspects of ICT: putting libraries at the heart of digital inclusion; the role of e-books and e-lending; and digital content and engagement.

> Libraries' traditional role has been providing books, learning and information and it is critical that this role is transposed into the digital world where a vast quantity of information is online and communities, more than ever, need support in navigating through it. Embracing the digital revolution is essential for libraries to remain relevant. (DCMS 2010a: 38)

Changes in the market – such as the mass digitization of content by Google and others, Web 2.0 technology and the advent of e-books – are changing how people want to receive and engage with information. In 2006/07 there were 180 million visits to local authority websites in England and 48 million of them were to public library sites. Visits to public library websites in 2007/08 grew to 57 million. Consumption of digital information has been transforming the library's role as an information provider over the last ten years. Digital media offer new opportunities to libraries. They can help the service to:

- be more accessible more of the time
- bridge the digital divide for those people without online access or skills
- offer a broader range of content and resources and new ways of accessing, manipulating and comparing information
- attract new users to library services as research suggests that online usage has a positive effect on in-person visits to libraries
- be more efficient and cost-effective, both directly for the public and the back of house operation.

Public libraries are embracing digital opportunities at very different rates. For instance, all public libraries have an online presence but relatively few currently offer e-book loans.

Libraries at the Heart of Digital Inclusion

> At a time when around 80 per cent of the population is online, communities now see access to the Internet as a right rather than a 'nice to have'. Libraries have a central role to play in providing access to the Internet and helping people get online. There are 12.5 million adults in the UK who do not use the Internet today and this group will rely heavily on libraries to reach online information, including public services which will increasingly be delivered online. (DCMS 2010a: 38)

Silver Surfers' Day, coordinated by Digital Unite, provides an opportunity to positively encourage older people to take the first step to get online by participating in IT taster events in May each year. Older people are a significant proportion of the current 12.5 million digitally excluded and make up 39 per cent of the six million socially and digitally excluded adults. Public libraries have an important role in reducing this digital divide. Forty-four per cent of libraries offer regular one-to-one support or group sessions specifically aimed at supporting older people to get online. Of the 1,000 Silver Surfers' Day events in 2009, 400 took place in public libraries.

Get Online Day, run by UKOnline Centres, is an annual campaign to communicate the benefit of getting online and offering support through UKOnline Centres to develop digital skills. In October 2009 some 700 events took place, which included 29 per cent of library services.

E-Books and E-Lending

> There are new and exciting opportunities around digital lending. With the launch of a number of different e-reading devices, digital reading is growing in the public consciousness where downloadable audio books are already fully established. Libraries must have the freedom to experiment with these new services and test out the market for new and established library users. Currently 14 library services offer e-book services in England with more planning to launch shortly. All lend for free.

> Although media commentators are fond of setting up an opposition between printed and digital books, there is no suggestion that e-books will drive out our nation's passion for printed books or that libraries will be delivered only in the online space. E-books will enable library services to remain relevant in a market where people are using mobile devices to access information and entertainment and will provide a new opportunity to reach people who may not visit their local library building regularly, but who would like to borrow e-books from home. It is important to extend to e-book loans the principle of 'free at the point of demand'. The Government believes that e-book lending is likely to form a key 24/7 public service in the future with public library services being accessed from home and on the move as well as in library buildings. (DCMS 2010a: 41–2)

It is difficult to share this view of the benefits of e-books to public libraries and local communities as the analysis is both naive and flawed. Nottinghamshire County Council became the first public library service to charge for e-books and many others will follow their lead. The barriers to access created by charges for AV and PN will be replicated by e-books, but with a bigger knock-on effect when book funds are increasingly diverted (and reduced) to pay for e-books (which are much cheaper to buy than print versions). These charging mechanisms will prevent people on low incomes from accessing books in e-format, which will significantly undermine the requirement to provide books for loan free of charge under the 1964 Public Libraries Act.

E-books will act as a Trojan Horse by legitimizing the concept of paying for public library book loans; it will then be just a small step to enable charges for all book loans. Also, the cost of e-book readers is prohibitive for socially excluded people and the whole e-book agenda is aimed at the usual core library user market of predominantly white, middle-class, middle-aged people. In addition, if people can download books from home, why should they go to the library and why should local councils pay for library buildings and staff?

Without wishing to sound like a Luddite, e-books could become the final nail in the public library coffin. Library staff are being replaced by RFID (self-service) technology and if books are replaced by e-books then the rationale for providing public libraries will disappear. Publishers have identified the threat to their business model which e-book loans from public libraries pose and have started to cut off or limit the supply by insisting that downloads must take place on library premises or that only one copy of an e-book can be borrowed at a time. Alternatively it could be that legal complications around copyright and digital lending spike the e-book revolution before it causes any lasting damage to public libraries.

Digital Content and Management

'Digital content and networks bring with them new ways to communicate and engage with customers. All library services already have a web presence and libraries should publish information about their services in a free, open and re-useable form including their location, opening hours and catalogues' (DCMS 2010a: 43).

Despite great potential and customers' high expectations, local authorities and library services are rarely early adopters of new technologies. Libraries should be using Web 2.0 but local authority network security policies often restrict their ability to do so. This may be because authorities are cautious about investing in resources to develop relatively new and untested services, but it is more likely that IT departments want to manage and control the flow of information.

There is a need for greater shared awareness about emerging technologies, testing and learning lessons about implementation and ensuring that they meet community needs. Success will depend on the ability of library services to talk constructively with local IT and legal departments, to make the case for change.

And there are huge opportunities for libraries to consider – many libraries already use email and text alerts, library applications and innovative web content (like links to reading materials) are achievable and inexpensive opportunities. For instance, in Leicester the desktop of all the libraries' public computers is used to showcase library or local partner initiatives, which significantly increases attendance. The service sends 14,000 emails a month to library members about events and book reviews and also partner promotions. They also send texts for requests and overdue reminders instead of posting letters whenever possible. The service uses Youtube to advertise events and has used Web 2.0 technology to develop an events calendar for libraries using free Google tools.

At a time when public services are encouraging citizens to engage with online content and services it is important that libraries provide a compelling offer to their users, especially in attracting young people and the socially excluded to use libraries.

Community-Led Information Technology Instruction

When working with socially excluded individuals it is important to understand the many socially constructed barriers and individual life circumstances which people experience which directly impact their ability to access ICT. This sensitivity to the barriers imposed on socially excluded individuals provides a foundation for library systems to begin to discover their role(s) in addressing the digital divide. Community development librarians (CDLs) recognized a number of barriers experienced by socially excluded individuals because of their socioeconomic status and the impact these barriers have on accessing technology, including:

- little disposable income to be able to afford 'newer' or emerging technologies
- a limited use of older technology (for example, people having access to dial-up connections with computers with older operating systems such as Windows 95) and
- relatively few free public access points in communal gathering locations (for example, there were a limited number of service providers who offer IT and computer access. Most community-based locations only provide the service within their physical space, so individuals wanting to access computers may also feel obliged to access additional services outside of IT).

Additionally, there were a number of individual characteristics which acted as barriers to accessing technology. For instance, a number of people had ongoing visual and mobility conditions that severely impacted their ability to access existing technology. Many of these issues could be addressed through adaptive technology, but usually with additional costs or expenses to purchase computer hardware or software.

Steps for Developing Community-Led ICT

The Working Together *Toolkit* lays out five important steps which need to be taken into consideration and applied in order to truly create community-led computer or ICT training (Working Together 2008a: 95–104). These include:

1. development of comfortable relationships

2. library staff identifying needs and interests with community members
3. library staff actively collaborating with community members to define the format and content of ICT delivery
4. library staff being able to provide flexible instruction, and
5. library staff continuously evaluating the planning process and programme with community members.

This process follows the community-led service planning model and has been adapted in its application to ICT. In the toolkit, CDLs provide a number of examples of how they collaboratively walked though this process with individual community members, groups of community members and service providers to ensure that library-supported ICT services were meeting the needs of the community. By taking this approach when developing services, the focus shifts from library staff members' perceptions of community computer training needs, to discovering and responding to the community and their self-identified needs.

Computer instruction should be viewed as a means of creating relationships and as a potential entry point for building more inclusive library services. ICT instruction should not be viewed as the end point. As discussed by the national evaluator: 'Having computers present may give a focal point for conversations, but it can place limitations on what participants identify in terms of their needs because the computers are [or can become] the focal point' (Atkey 2008: 82).

Barriers to ICT and Computer 'Training'

There is an inherent power dynamic created when individuals come into libraries to receive computer instruction. There are a number of concepts and loaded terminology which can make the interaction between the library staff and community member uncomfortable. For instance, the community member is automatically viewed as the 'learner', is receiving 'training' from someone they will view as an 'expert', and may be exposed to computers or other technology for the first time. Additionally, people may be entering a space (the library where the training is taking place) which they are not familiar with and which can be viewed as intimidating.

In order to mitigate both the power differential traditionally created by the ICT 'instructor/teacher' and to minimize the barrier created by entering a new space, a number of approaches to ICT training were piloted through Working Together. The first and most important approach was the development of relationships. By establishing relationships with individuals first, trust is built and library staff are able to discover if information technology is an interest or concern for community members. While library staff may believe that ICT is a community need, relationships lead to discussions which can confirm or deny this assumption.

Community Entry: Getting the Word Out to the Community

As has been previously expressed, socially excluded individuals are under-represented in 'traditional' library use, and this includes use of ICT. In order to ensure that ICT is not overrun by existing library users, it is important to specifically target messaging through methods which work within each respective community. Many of the community entry techniques which have previously been discussed were used when targeting ICT services towards socially excluded community members. For instance, a number of library systems ensured that traditional 'marketing' techniques used by their respective systems to let users know about ICT services were not applied during the WTP. When services are 'marketed' using traditional means, existing library users will become aware of the service and overwhelm it. Instead, a much slower but more effective technique was 'word of mouth'. Participants in the programme would tell of their experiences with library staff to friends and other family members.

Also, like other community-led activities, it is important for library staff to be proactive in the community. Library staff cannot sit within the confines of the library waiting for socially excluded community members to come to them. In order to resolve this issue, CDLs used the asset mapping process to identify established ICT service points or areas which had potential in the respective targeted communities. Some of these included service providers who welcomed library staff into their physical locations, with an understanding that WTP staff would be coming into their spaces with technology. These interactions took a number of different forms, including:

- WTP staff having designated hours at formalized computer stations set up in other service provider locations in the community
- incorporating ICT into other activities already occurring at sites in the community (for example, during a community kitchen where library staff had 'dropped in' to assist in making meals)
- formal classroom training with content provided by community agency staff, or supplied by WTP staff. Eventually, once relationships became better established and community-led approaches were shared with partners and members of the community, more individualized ICT 'training' was developed.

Additionally, it was important that ICT hardware was portable. A number of portable laptop labs were purchased which allowed CDLs to take the technology out of the branch and into the community. Keeping this in mind, there were a number of major learnings which should be considered when developing ICT services.

Relationship-Building Comes First

It may be tempting to take technology into the community and ask to deliver a programme. However, as previously mentioned, it is important to view ICT as a means to develop relationships which can extend the breadth of library services in the community beyond technology. As discussed by the national evaluator, one CDL recognized that when computers were brought into the community it was important not to push the technology onto community members, but to focus on building relationships and allow community members to observe the use of the computers and to be able to begin using them at their own speed:

> As a means of getting to know community members at the agency, the CDL suggested to agency staff that she bring in laptop computers and have coffee with community members. During the first few visits, only agency staff and volunteers expressed interest in the computers, but within a few weeks there was growing interest on the part of community members who expressed an interest in learning more about computers. This community entry strategy has proven effective in developing relationships, according to one interviewee, and community members appear to appreciate that there is no set program and no registration. (Atkey 2008: 81)

At another location a CDL discovered that a traditional approach to computer instruction at a community agency had stalled. However,

> By providing instruction in the common area where agency clients had their coffee rather than in a separate room, there was an increased uptake in participation and the CDL was able to participate in 'coffee talk' and hear about the goings-on in the community. The relationships developed in this informal setting were stronger than those developed through previous methods and can be credited to a slight shift in approach. (Atkey 2008: 25)

By moving the location, and adjusting the approach to computer instruction from a formalized setting to an informal location where people were already having discussions, it became relevant to potential participants. By removing the formality and focusing on relationship-building, trust was built between WTP staff and community members. Also, by making computers available but not the central focus of the interaction, there was an increased likelihood that people would be more willing to try and explore computer use.

Delivery Methods: Group and Individual Instruction

One of the major benefits of doing group computer instruction is that it allows for a larger number of people to be exposed to the sessions at one time. In addition, different people learn better in different types of environments. As discussed in the Working Together *Toolkit* (2008a), librarians need to take into account the individual needs of people participating in group instruction. While delivering the instruction in a group session, library staff need to respond to requests by:

- asking each individual about their computer experience
- asking what each person would like to learn and why
- speaking with each person if they do not identify their needs to the group
- working with the group and the staff to schedule the session
- deciding with the group if the session should be hands-on or presentation style, and
- developing a lesson plan that touches on all the areas identified by the participants. (Working Together 2008a: 102)

Ultimately, although computer training may be taking place within the context of a large group, the individual needs of each of the participants should be taken into account and incorporated throughout the training session. Group instruction did not work for some individuals. While this delivery method may initially be perceived by library staff as being less staff-intensive, there are relatively few people who have the same ICT needs, abilities, interests and previous experiences with technology. A number of people taking group-based ICT instruction were experiencing difficulty keeping up with others and a significant amount of time was being spent reviewing and repeating tasks.

In response, a number of WTP sites began delivering one-to-one computer training. This type of training gives library staff and community members the opportunity to co-create and tailor ICT instruction to meet the individualized needs of socially excluded community members. At one WTP site CDLs developed and implemented an intake interview which took place during the initial meeting between the computer trainer and community members. This intake process focused on asking questions to clarify:

- their interests in ICT instruction
- previous ICT experience
- what they hoped to accomplish
- what time works best for them to have the instruction, and
- it provided an opportunity to link with other library services.

As discovered by the national project evaluator, the intake process

> ... identified the interests and goals of the participants to the greatest extent possible. It also allowed participants to self-identify any learning difficulties they may have had in the past, and allowed staff to identify any other potential learning impediments (e.g. hearing impairments). That the assessment process is iterative is important because one of the learnings from the approach has been

the tendency for people to 'under-evaluate' their actual skills or to 'report only what they learned in a class'. That the conversation on needs and abilities is ongoing helps to correct for the under-evaluation. ... Once the relationship and a sense of rapport has been built between the instructor and participant, this information emerges more organically and the instructor documents what other types of services could be offered. (Atkey 2008: 46–7)

Partnering

Partnering with community agencies[1] is another community entry technique which provided Working Together CDLs with direct contact with groups of socially excluded individuals. Community agency staff were excited that 'the library' was interested in delivering computer 'training' and instruction to socially excluded participants in their programmes. However, due to many of these agencies' mandates and funding requirements, the content and/or curriculum they wanted library staff to deliver to their participants was predetermined. Thus it was important to have discussions and clarify at the beginning of the partnership what the role was that individual community members could play in driving the content delivered and approach used. As discussed by one CDL:

At one site, in order to develop a stronger and trusting relationship with the service provider, ICT training initially focused on the content which the partnering organization had created for their participants. However, over the course of a number of years, library staff entered into discussions with the partnering organization staff to share community-led approaches. By the third year of the relationships, Working Together IT staff were able to adjust the ICT sessions so they started with individual intake assessments with each person and asked participants what types of computer training they wanted to learn. The content shifted from Microsoft Office applications to computer skill development which helped them with daily activities such as assisting their children with doing homework assignments, accessing online banking etc. (Author's personal experience, unpublished)

At another community agency, as the relationship became more established, the CDL began discussions regarding the possibility of extending the computer training to involve other members of the community – beyond the socially excluded patrons who were receiving services from the community agency. While there was initially hesitation,

Because [the agency] had a mandate to de-stigmatize mental health issues in the broader community, a decision was collectively made to continue offering the

1   A community agency is a formal institution which provides services to a particular targeted group of people (for example, the Salvation Army). Some may be large national institutions with local offices, while others may be more regional or local in nature.

classes within [the agency] but to open the classes to other community members
… the members were enthusiastic about being able to maintain programming in
a place where they felt comfortable but where they could also interact with other
community members. (Atkey 2008: 98–9)

This example displays how library staff can work with community partners
to create truly inclusive ICT services, which reach community members who
may be hesitant about entering library spaces, while at the same time assisting
community agencies meet their mandate. The impact of these relationships
and the delivery of ICT training with community partners are potentially quite
profound:

Project partners were generally agreed that they benefit by gaining opportunities
to provide services for which they do not have the capacity, particularly in the
area of computer training and resource information. One partner suggested that
clients at their facility are able to develop 'tangible' and 'softer' skills such as
social interaction and expanding comfort zones. The nature of fiscal constraints
within not-for-profit organizations suggests that the development of these skills
are often not the focus of programming. As a result, one partner noted that the
computer training offered through the project has helped people to 'move on to
educational opportunities' or 'reception jobs'. (Atkey 2008: 211)

Helpful Hints

#1: Many library staff may be unsure of their own skills using technology and
have varying levels of comfort delivering ICT training outside a scripted training
course. Delivering community-led ICT instruction means that the content and
approaches used to deliver the instruction will need to be adapted to best meet
each individual's needs.

#2: Libraries should to draw up ICT plans which include a strategy outlining how
the needs of socially excluded communities are to be prioritized. ICT should be
used as a means to tackle social exclusion rather than as an end in itself.

#3: ICT provision should be free at the point of access.

#4: ICT initiatives should be targeted more closely at excluded groups and
communities in a proactive way. Appropriate levels of skilled staffing and support
should be offered to users.

#5: Libraries should enthusiastically commit funding and support to neighbourhood
ICT initiatives.

Chapter 7
Materials Provision

In this chapter we consider the development of holistic collections policies to ensure that library stock reflects the needs of local communities. Also we continue a big debate about stock selection which has been going on since public libraries were established in the UK 150 years ago and, more recently, in Canada. This debate can be summarized as social control versus social change or 'reads versus needs'. One school of thought argues that public libraries were introduced as an agent of social change, to enable the 'deserving poor' to obtain work and other opportunities through access to free books and informal learning. We argue that public libraries were, and still are to some extent at least, agents of social control by providing what the Victorians called 'healthy' literature which would keep workers out of the pubs where they were exposed to 'seditious' literature. The modern equivalent of this debate is focused on whether libraries should provide access to materials in alternative formats, CDs, DVDs, computer games, etc.

Open to All? (Muddiman et al. 2000a) was strongly of the view that for libraries to become agents of social change they had to urgently develop materials selection policies to meet the needs of socially excluded people. Library stock had to be relevant to local communities and reflect a wide range of interests and formats. Stock selection could not be the sole preserve of the librarian who made decisions based on professional judgement and personal values. The local community should be actively engaged in the selection process.

The Working Together Project (WTP) also found that it was important to include both the library systems collection development/access team and the community in the selection process. While librarians traditionally view themselves as being experts in selecting relevant and high-quality information sources, community also plays a role in the selection process. By actively engaging the community and allowing its members to express their needs, and involving them in the selection of materials, libraries will ensure that collections will be relevant and reflect the needs of the local people using them.

'Reads Versus Needs'

Library stock – books, CDs, DVDs, video games and other materials – are the lifeblood of a public library service. Community needs cannot be met unless the public library offers a wide range of materials in a variety of formats. Library collection development must be directly informed by the needs of the local community. For many years in the UK library materials were exclusively selected by professional library staff with little or no input from local people. At best, the needs of local people would be determined by recourse to official data such as census returns and community profiles. At worst, the needs of local communities would be assumed by library staff based on their own knowledge and perceptions of those communities. For example, when Polish migrant workers moved into one local area, it was assumed that they would require books in Polish, when in fact their greatest need was to learn English so that they could get a job and start to assimilate into the local community. Much time and many resources were wasted on buying books in languages that librarians did not understand and the target audience did not want or need. These problems can be overcome if librarians are willing to share their power and resources with local communities and take a cooperative approach to stock purchase.

There has been an ongoing debate in UK public libraries about the type of materials which should be stocked, and this debate dates back to the origin and purpose of the library service itself. There are two broad schools of thought, one based on notions of social control and the other focused more on social change. Until quite recently the school of social control has had the upper hand.

Social Control

The speeches made by eminent Victorians such as Charles Dickens at the opening of public libraries in the mid-nineteenth century make it clear that, for the ruling class, these libraries were to be agents of social control. The industrial revolution was at its height and workers had flooded into cities from the surrounding countryside seeking work. They worked long hours in poorly paid and dangerous jobs and they lived in damp and unsanitary housing. They spent the little spare time they were given in public houses and gin palaces where they drank away their sorrows. There was no formal education system and many workers could not read or write but some of the better-off workers did make use of the Mechanics Institutes which were run by workers and provided reading materials. Literature was also circulated around the pubs and gin houses in the form of 'penny dreadfuls' (melodramatic stories of murder and romance) and seditious political tracts (such as the *Communist Manifesto*, 1848) which were read out loud to the assembled masses. The ruling class was alarmed by these developments because, as Mark and Engels had pointed out: 'A spectre is haunting Europe – the spectre of Communism. All the Powers of old Europe have entered into a holy alliance to exorcise this spectre'.

Part of the ruling class's response to this spectre in the UK was the creation of a number of institutions – libraries, museums, parks – which would control the idle time of working men and divert them from thoughts and actions of dissent and revolution. It was proposed that a national system of public libraries be established, paid for by adding a penny to the rates. The Earl of Shaftesbury described the public library as 'an antidote to mischiefs' that arise in 'these days of pursuit and excitement'. Edward Bulwer-Lytton (1st Baron) believed that public libraries were 'healthful stimulants' that would 'replace the old English excitements of the ale house and the gin palace'. When Manchester Public Library was opened in 1852, its aim was to teach the working man 'that capital and labour are not opposed, but are mutually dependent and supporting'. In other words, public libraries were to be an antidote to the rising power of the trade union movement. This may all sound like a strange conspiracy theory but the evidence gathered by Philip Corrigan and Val Gillespie (1978) conclusively demonstrated that public libraries were a powerful weapon in the context of *Class Struggle, Social Literacy and Idle Time*:

> We question first the far too general depiction of State or philanthropic provision as a kind of donation into a vacuum. Such provisions are more accurately to be linked to a range of coercive actions and legal prohibitions which reveal a parallel or preparatory suppression of pre-existing alternatives. Secondly, these provisions are seen as means of changing the organizational form, the overall objectives, and thus the politics of cultural collective practices. (Corrigan and Gillespie 1978: 6)

Public libraries were to replace other forms of working class self-organization such as Mechanics Institutes. Public libraries were to lure workers away from the collective reading of 'penny dreadfuls' and seditious political tracts and replace them with repositories of 'healthful' literature. Public libraries were part of a wider social control movement to manage and control the idle time of industrial workers, to head off the kind of uprisings and revolutions which had been witnessed in other parts of Europe, most notably in France and Germany. This social control movement encompassed the development of municipal museums, open free to the workers, to manage their idle time at the weekends. Public parks were also provided where the workers could meet, walk and talk under the watchful eyes and ears of the local constabulary. It is no coincidence that these parks were often linked by wide carriageways to the local army barracks so that troops could be dispatched at a moment's notice if the workers got out of hand. Similarly, street lights were installed so that the workers could be kept under observation when they stepped out of their dirty and crowded slums.

Public libraries were aimed at what the Victorians called the 'deserving poor'. These were the better-off workers who had aspirations to improve themselves and their families. Public libraries were not intended for the 'undeserving poor' – what we would today call the socially excluded – who had to look to other Victorian institutions such as the workhouse (or poorhouse in North America), the prison and the asylum to meet their needs.

It is necessary to understand the early history of public libraries because this heritage was absolutely fundamental to the development of professional attitudes and values which still shape modern library services. There is an enduring professional belief that only qualified staff should select stock, as they alone know best what the 'deserving poor' want and need. For example, Bob Usherwood (2007) argues passionately that quality, excellence and ethical standards should not be compromised by a library service that prioritizes equity and social inclusion. The 'undeserving poor' still have no place in the public library:

> Britain is now subject to the behaviour of the members of an amoral and apolitical section in society who are neither deserving nor poor. Their attitudes are contrary to all the public library stands for and the profession must be prepared to confront them. In times of limited resources we need to ask if the profession should attempt to provide specifically for people who choose to exclude themselves. They should be given every chance to engage with the service but not at the expense of people who can and want to benefit from what a library provides. (Usherwood 2007: 99)

Usherwood argues that stock selection should effectively be the professional preserve of a small clique of white, middle-aged, middle-class librarians. Any attempt to share this power with local people – especially the socially excluded – is seen as a form of 'populism' or 'dumbing down'. Public libraries should be stocked with healthy literature which reflects solid middle-class values, and not trashy novels or computer games. In this context excellence becomes elitism and public libraries remain agents of social control. It is little wonder then that public libraries are used more by middle-class than working-class people. According to the 2011 *Taking Part Survey*, 44 per cent of middle-class people (who make up 40 per cent of the population) used a public library in 2010/11 compared to just 33 per cent of working-class people (who make up 60 per cent of the population). The *Taking Part Survey* also revealed that:

- Library use continues to be significantly higher among those in the least deprived areas of England.
- As educational attainment increases, so too does the propensity to visit and use libraries. People with fewer qualifications than five or more GCSE/O Levels grade A*–C were 12 per cent less likely to have used a library in the last 12 months. Those with A levels or equivalent were 13 per cent more likely and those with a higher education or equivalent were 23 per cent more likely to have used a library in the same period.
- Readers of *The Daily Telegraph*, *The Guardian*, *The Independent* and *The Times* all had a highly significant and positive association with library participation. But the readers of the *Daily Express* and *The Sun* had a lower frequency of library use.

In summary, the social control tendency is alive and well in UK public libraries but it has been challenged strongly in recent years by an alternative view which positions libraries as agents of social change.

Social Change

This agenda first emerged in the 1970s in London and other metropolitan areas when the Community Librarianship movement started to develop outreach programmes for ethnic minorities and other excluded groups. This was an important period in terms of stock collections as local people were given some say for the first time regarding which books to purchase and how these could be promoted and displayed. Special collections for black and minority ethnic (BME) communities were developed, in consultation with black communities. Lesbian, gay, bisexual and transgendered (LGBT) collections were created, with associated events and programmes. Women's collections also emerged at this time, aided by specialist publishing houses aimed at women (such as Virago). A fierce professional debate broke out over the value – and values – of the Dewey Decimal Scheme, and some library services switched from Dewey to categorization schemes which made more sense to library users. These developments mirrored wider social struggles for equal rights for BME, LGBT and women. In time, as some of these struggles were advanced, the special library collections were disbanded and the books were integrated with the general stock. Some of the reasons for this were complaints from people from these groups that they continued to be marginalized by being in separate areas.

Under the dark years of Margaret Thatcher and her right-wing Conservative government which came to power in 1979, many of these moves to make public libraries more open and accessible were dismissed as 'political correctness'. But libraries had discovered their political power and were not afraid to use it. During the Wapping dispute, for example, when hundreds of print workers were sacked just because they belonged to a trade union, some public libraries refused to stock any newspapers published by Rupert Murdoch, who was in cahoots with Thatcher to destroy the trade union movement. Some libraries also stood up to Thatcher when she introduced Section 28 to make it illegal for schools and councils to 'promote homosexuality'. While some brave library services continued to stock *Gay News* and the *Pink Paper* many others abandoned their LGBT collections, fearful of prosecution, or maybe just relieved that they could drop the pretence of being interested in this community in the first place.

The election of New Labour in 1997 created space for the discussion of issues such as social exclusion, and the topic of libraries as agents of social change rose up the professional agenda. It is likely that this was more to do with the need to comply with the new government and the attendant possibility of acquiring additional funding, rather than a real shift in professional attitudes towards a pro-poor library service. New national policy guidance on social exclusion was provided via *Libraries for All: Social Inclusion in Public Libraries* (DCMS 1999), which noted that one of the barriers to library use was 'book stock policies which do not reflect the needs of the community or are not in suitable formats' (ibid.: 12).

Books, Learning and Reading

Framework for the Future (2003), a ten-year national strategy for public libraries, positioned books, learning and reading at the heart of libraries' modern mission, and noted that:

> Some libraries can be proud of the range and comprehensiveness of their book stock. But only 59 per cent of users find the book they come to borrow or use, an under-supply in some types of book particularly those of appeal to younger readers, and a reduction in book buying. (DCMS 2003: 7)

Framework also promoted the role that libraries can play in supporting adults with basic literacy problems: 'Seven million adults in England have levels of attainment in reading and writing lower than that expected for children aged eleven. Libraries are ideally placed to recognize and support people who might benefit from tuition' (ibid.: 8).

Literacy and Emerging Readers

This theme was explored by Viv Bird and Rodie Akerman in *Literacy and Social Inclusion: The Handbook* (2005). Libraries can play an important role in offering exciting learning opportunities that motivate children, young people and adults at risk of social exclusion to engage in literacy learning. Some libraries have successfully recruited and re-engaged adult basic skills learners, especially those from hard-to-reach communities. Key success factors include the informal learning environment, the quality of the tutors and their one-to-one relationship with learners. Libraries have been shown to affect individuals by facilitating skills acquisition and new experiences and by supporting informal learning opportunities: 'Libraries in particular had a learning and empowerment role, through provision of information, Internet access, books and other leisure and learning opportunities. Libraries were seen as promoting individual awareness of history and culture and, therefore, also promoting both individual and group identity' (Bird and Akerman 2005: 28).

A more in-depth study was carried out by The Vital Link and published in *Confidence All Round: The Impact on Emergent Adult Readers of Reading for Pleasure through Libraries* (2005). This report explored the individual and societal outcomes for emergent readers from libraries' reader development activity. The research collected evidence about how libraries can make a difference for adult learners by connecting:

- an enjoyment of reading
- improved skills
- motivation to continue reading and learning.

Emergent readers reported that they were either reading for pleasure for the first time or reading more frequently. Those who had not used libraries before had a more positive view of their role and value, and most respondents reported new or increased library use and use of a wider range of library services. Their literacy, thinking and learning skills were improved and these skills were reinforced by learning how to select books and how to use a library. Participants noted significant increases in self-confidence, arising from a greater ability for self-expression, enhanced self-esteem, a sense of achievement and improved self-worth. They had a sense of greater independence and increased control over their own lives, leading to empowerment and self-motivation. As one emergent reader described it: 'I used to get shouted down but now I can stand up more for myself. Now I can say "I believe it is this way". I think it gives me confidence all round' (Vital Link 2005: 5).

This improved self-confidence, sense of independence and empowerment provided a platform for greater social inclusion, including increased social interaction and feeling more respected by others. At a societal level this contributed to greater social connectedness and community cohesion. According to *Confidence All Round* (Vital Link 2005) the critical success factors for libraries that want to tackle social exclusion through reader development programmes are:

- Positioning – reader development is purposefully positioned to encourage people to read for pleasure through libraries as an enhancement to formal learning.
- Egalitarian ethos – the ethos behind reader development, which is presented simply as a group of people sharing books with the support of library and adult learning workers, makes it accessible for emergent readers and enhances their sense of social inclusion.
- Self-motivated and independent activity – emergent readers choose to engage with this activity and are responsible for their own reading.
- The range of activities involved – choosing and finding appealing books, reading, analysing and discussing them with others, recommending and writing about them and visiting and using libraries – all require emergent readers to develop and use a variety of skills, both learning and personal.
- Effective resources – the range of books employed with associated promotional and display materials need to be pitched exactly at the right level and presented in the right way.
- Partnership working – the delivery partnership between libraries and adult learning creates added value for both sectors. Libraries gain access to emergent readers and non-users in a context in which they are open to the library offer. For the adult learning sector, libraries' use of reader development extends and embeds emerging literacy skills. The enjoyment and achievement arising from reading for pleasure contributes to increased learning motivation.

While libraries' use of reader development is clearly contributing to significant outcomes for individuals, there are ways in which the impact can be enhanced, through interventions at both strategic and delivery levels, as listed below.

Strategic Level

- Embedding reader development at a strategic level within the library and adult learning sectors to ensure inclusion in core delivery plans and continued funding to aid sustainability.
- Extending and promoting the full range of resources to ensure that both tutors and emergent readers are aware of what is available, including fiction, non-fiction, poetry, books for parents to share with children at different ages and books in multi-media formats.
- Developing an evaluation framework to measure the impact of reader development at a strategic policy level, at delivery level with libraries and the adult learning sector, and for emergent readers as the target users. This should include the development of generic and specific outcome measures which are co-produced by reader development workers and emergent readers.
- Undertaking longitudinal evaluation with individual emergent readers from the start of their learning journey, through their engagement with reader development and into the medium and longer term so that the full impact of the outcomes, especially in terms of economic and social impact, can be identified.

Delivery Level

- Ensuring that for libraries and the adult learning sector sufficient resources are allocated to partnership development, planning, delivery, monitoring and evaluation.
- Training all library workers, not just those involved in delivery of the reader development programme, in the personal and curriculum needs of adult learners and emergent readers.
- Raising awareness that some emergent readers need a significant amount of encouragement and support to engage fully with libraries. This could include providing a wide range of resources in non-library locations through library outreach and partnership working as a stepping stone to library use.
- Encouraging multiple library visits for adult learners and making engagement with the library as interactive as possible in order to build awareness and knowledge and create a sense of belonging and ownership. This engagement should include involving emergent readers in stock selection, display and development of promotional materials.
- Stepping up the promotion of what the library has to offer which, for new

users, can change their perceptions of libraries. This will require changes to library systems and procedures including being able to experiment with book choices, ease of renewals, lack of fines and libraries' increasing role as social community spaces welcoming to all, including families.

Not all socially excluded people are emergent readers but reader development provides public libraries with a unique opportunity to tackle social exclusion by enabling people to gain the essential skills which they need to grow as individuals and as communities.

The Library Offer

A small but vocal lobby group, led in the UK by Tim Coates (formerly a managing director of Waterstones bookshops), support a clear vision of libraries as singly a book loaning service with a mantra of 'If you buy the books they will come'. In other words, public libraries should go back to basics and focus solely on their book-lending function. They should not be in the business of community development or tackling social exclusion, which is the job of social workers. *The Modernisation Review of Public Libraries* (2010) took a more balanced view:

Book stock, of course, is vital, and as the recent DCMS Omnibus survey confirms, books are the main reason why people go to the library. But which books and what other library services? As all the best Heads of Service know, libraries cannot passively sit back and wait for people to borrow books – however good the stock is. The library workforce and policy makers must actively engage with local people, finding out what they want and need from their service, and respond to those needs. And in a 24/7 culture, that is not about a stagnant book stock. (DCMS 2010a: 35)

The review recommended that the community should be at the heart of the public library service and all library authorities should introduce a Library Offer to the public This Library Offer will be made up of a 'core offer' of services which all library services should deliver and a 'local offer' of services, shaped and delivered at local level:

Core Offer

This should comprise:

- library membership from birth
- an opportunity for people to have their say and get involved in shaping the service
- free access to a range and quality of book stock to browse and borrow and online resources and information that meet local needs
- access to the national book collection – any book from anywhere

- free Internet access for all
- help to get online via support for people using the Internet for the first time or searching for information
- links to other public services and opportunities through connections to health, education and learning or employment opportunities
- a community of readers, connecting people to other readers through reading groups, activities and recommendations
- flexible opening hours to suit the needs of local people
- commitment to customer service and expert, helpful staff
- a safe local space which is accessible and convenient for the community
- 24-hour access through the library online catalogue, online reference and other services
- services which reach out and attract local people, including 'at home' services to housebound people
- an opportunity to be a member of all libraries in England.

Local Offer

This should comprise:

- commitments on book stock variety, investment and procurement
- opportunities and activities for young people as part of the local provision of positive activities
- provisions for learning such as improving reading and writing skills, and partnerships with local schools, early years settings and children's centres
- an events programme, including training events or activities for readers and author visits
- family activities, including family reading and learning activities, homework clubs, links to family information services, holiday reading challenges
- programmes of engagement with the community, including outreach initiatives and ways of encouraging wider usage, including families
- details of how to get involved with user groups, supporting or influencing the library service
- spaces for community use
- childcare or crèche
- additional services like CD and DVD borrowing, book delivery service, coffee shops, etc.

The original intention was that the government would review the Library Offer after two years and consider whether to legislate or make it a statutory obligation. But two months after the modernization review was published, a new Conservative-Liberal Democrat Coalition government came into power. Most of the commitments in the modernization review were dropped on the grounds that they were not affordable at a time when the government had to make substantial public service cuts in order to reduce the national deficit created by the financial crisis of 2008.

The result is a postcode lottery of public library services with some facing severe cuts. In 2011 revenue expenditure was cut by up to 35 per cent, while cuts to material budgets of up to 90 per cent were reported in some authorities. There have also been a number of more positive developments, including:

- the impact of reading as a new major group activity as evidenced by the massive growth of reading groups, and the emergence of the Reader Organisation and specific groups for visually impaired people, etc.
- the impact of the National Year of Reading
- the changing role of library staff to inspire reading and use of materials, for example with children and young people
- the role of libraries to draw to communities' attention to materials that they would otherwise never know about.

Working Together

As described above, historically the selection of materials within library systems has primarily been left to qualified librarians to use their professional judgement when choosing library materials. The professional selection of materials is often based on assessing the 'quality' and legitimacy of materials for the community, regardless of community interests and needs. Both the purchasing and accession of library materials have traditionally been highly controlled by library staff, resulting in

> ... the ongoing challenge of shifting the perceptions of the role of the library, from one of protecting collections to one of facilitating unfettered access to information [and] library staff [being] stuck on fines as a way to protect the library's collection and ... it's hard for the library culture to see past that. (Atkey 2008: 129)

A full day pre-conference session during Ontario Library 2008 focused on disseminating Working Together learnings. Over the course of this interactive session, a number of participants who worked with diverse community members were convinced that 'their' collections were representative of the communities they served. However, a number of simple questions were posed, including:

- How did they know what materials the community wanted?
- How had the community been involved in the material provision process?
- If library staff were selecting materials, did their perceptions as librarians accurately reflect the perceptions and needs of socially excluded community members, non-library users, or even regular library users?

Since collections are viewed as the 'bread and butter' of library services, most people equate libraries with the materials which are circulated or made available for public consumption. Shifting material provision from a traditional information-out approach (where library staff determine and let the community know about the collection after it has been developed) to an active community engagement approach (where community members and librarians collaboratively select materials) can result in huge rewards for progressive library systems. This is a relatively easy process to undertake by library systems, with fairly immediate and significant rewards. The rewards can benefit both underserved individuals and traditional library users who are actively included in the decision-making process by:

- Identifying gaps and providing information regarding localized community-based information needs.
- Having tangible outcomes which can be displayed by community members who have influenced the purchasing and selection decisions. Since this process is usually reserved for someone without localized or intimate knowledge of socially excluded or culturally diverse communities, the shift to involving the community will most likely result in community members:
  - inquiring about the addition of materials to a library collection
  - actively showing and displaying materials to other people within their networks. By letting others in the community know about the materials which 'they' have chosen, the community voice becomes a powerful marketing tool. Word of mouth within socially excluded and underserved communities is more effective than traditional marketing methods.

During the WTP, once relationships were built with socially excluded community members, a number of different collections-based activities were undertaken. These included, but were not limited to, the following.

Moving Collections

Probably one of the easiest small changes which had a significant impact on people's perceptions of library materials, was changing the location of existing stock based on community feedback.

- In many instances, the findings enabled branch staff to make small changes at the branch; for example, by giving certain collections increased visibility (Atkey 2008: 10).
- In one case, branch staff [at a participating] Library moved foreign language materials from the back corner to the front of the branch to better respond to the needs of their community (Atkey 2008: 129).

By moving to higher-profile locations those materials the community has identified as being important, socially excluded community members may enter the space for the first time and immediately see themselves reflected in the collection. Something this simple can immediately create a sense of belonging.

Developing Satellite Collections

One library system was partnered with agencies in the community who provided services to youth, and moved duplicate collections into the community. This provided the library system with the opportunity to offer a service in a space which was safe and familiar to youth, and library staff were able to begin to explore which parts of the collection were relevant to them. As written by the national evaluator:

One project site established satellite collections at five partner agencies … One interviewee noted that the collection is well used by youth at [the partner site], and thought that the reason for this is that its 'lack of structure and organization makes it user friendly'. In the interviewee's perception, the youth that access the agency are intimidated by the library because of its institutional nature, whereas at the agency 'kids will lie there and read the books and nobody walks through that area so they can get some quiet time'. The agency does not concern itself with whether or not the books are returned, because if 'there are books laying around the house, then people will read them but they have to be there because people won't go looking for them'. Interestingly, the youth at the agency have started to show ownership of the collection by organizing and maintaining the bookshelves on their own … there are several agencies with satellite collections that are not well utilized and the CDL began to work with those agencies to determine how they could encourage better use of the collections. *Although librarians have an obvious expertise in information management and collections development, a balance must be struck between a library's desire for a community to utilize the resources available to it and the community's own determination of whether or not those particular resources are meaningful.* The collections are currently high quality, but are largely comprised of the branch's duplicates, and the needs for the collections are determined by identifying 'what kinds of books people are taking home'. (Atkey 2008: 84)

The development of satellite collections, which will and are occurring with or without public library support, provides opportunities to work with underserved individuals in locations where individual community members feel comfortable. By determining the potential role that public libraries can play in supporting these community-based collections, through consultation with the community, the power differential is shifted so that community members are treated as equals, while relationships can also be developed.

Assisting in the Development of Local Community Information Resources

Through existing relationships which the CDLs had with volunteers in the community, they were able to link those volunteers to an organization which needed information translated from English to other languages. This demonstrates the role that the library can play in facilitating the creation of information materials which are needed by community members:

> The Food Bank undertook a Healthy Heart Campaign, an idea that emerged from the coordinator at the agency, and the CDL participated in developing materials for the campaign … Translation of the materials into the community's main languages was seen as critical to the success of the campaign, and the CDL was able to identify volunteers who could use the library's computers to assist with translation. While the translation work was being completed by the volunteers, the CDL engaged them in conversation about their information needs. Although the Food Bank program itself was not collaboratively designed with Food Bank clients, the program allowed the CDL an opportunity to support the service … [and develop] knowledge of community members [which] allowed her to engage Working Together's target group about their needs from the library. (Atkey 2008: 66)

Also, during this process the CDL created stronger relationships with individuals and learnt about additional needs.

Using Collections as an Approach to Discovering Community Interest/Need

The following example provides an interesting approach commonly undertaken by CDLs, where they enter a space and introduce a collection in a non-obtrusive manner:

> A Working Together instructor takes material to display at the youth facility. One interviewee described the approach this way: 'He lays things out and he waits for questions – it's very informal and casual rather than the normal stuffy and starchy perception of the library.' The informal approach allowed the project to gain an initial sense of participant interests and develop more formal programming from there. (Atkey 2008: 219)

In this example, the librarian did not take charge of the interaction and impose their own values on the collection, nor did he/she presume community interest in a specific subject. By letting the community lead the discussion around the collection brought into the community, a range of possible areas of interest were raised by the community which the library could follow up on. Furthermore,

> Based on the interest of several participants, a program about tarot card readings was developed by Working Together staff. The Tarot Card Art Project involves activities related to planning and designing a deck of tarot cards 'as a basis for users to explore the range of library resources in the area of esoterica'. The project is also used to raise awareness about the range of resources available through

[the library system]. The Working Together instructor facilitates the sessions, but 'participant interests guide the program's evolution', so that the deck design may become secondary to other interests related to tarot. The program utilizes a 'softer' approach to programming in the hopes of 'paving the way for harder programming in the area of literacy skills development'. Although evaluation forms were not completed by program participants, interest in the program is evidenced by youth continuing to participate voluntarily. (Atkey 2008: 220)

Collaborative Collections Development

The most powerful examples of how collections can be developed by involving the community occurred through collaborative processes. One of the first times this occurred was through the:

> ... development of an Aboriginal collection [in one library system], made possible through the leveraging of funding based on the learnings of Working Together. When approached by a foundation to develop an Aboriginal collection for the [participating] branch, [the library system] outlined a collaborative collection development strategy to the funder. Impressed by the innovative ideas, the funder wanted to see the community involved in the process and the CDL began strengthening existing relationships with Aboriginal communities and building new ones. (Atkey 2008: 27)

While the funder wanted money to be directed towards materials which originated with Aboriginal authors, library staff soon discovered that community perception of collection needs was slightly different. During one of the first conversations CDLs had with a member of the community it was discovered that they were looking for materials which were of interest to other Aboriginal community members. The library system worked with the community to help select materials and to ensure that the collection developed within the branch reflected both the funders' requirements and the community's needs.

Collaborative collection development has also been piloted and used with youth, who have become actively involved in the selection, purchasing (through shopping trips with the librarian!) and launching of materials in branches. In some systems this has become fairly common practice. Consequently, library staff have also discovered that youth are contacting the library branch within days of the shopping trips, to see if their books are available.

After the conclusion of Working Together, one library system branch began to

> ... engage with the Painters using the branch. Library staff saw that many of them were placing holds on art books (using other Branches' collections) during their session, and then checking them back in, during which the materials returned to the originating Branches. Library staff mentioned this to the Painters in a non-obtrusive way, and the artists explained that the Art collection at the

Branch really did not support them or the Artist community, which was fairly significant in the area.

Coordinating with the collections department, the Painters and library staff met during one of their library sessions to talk about the collection. The community and library staff decided on an amount to spend which was satisfactory to both groups. With their knowledge of the Painters community as well as their particular information needs, together library staff and members of the community discussed the gaps/material types needed. (Library staff knew nothing about painting!). They described how an artist begins to create, then progresses, then completes and the library needed to cover all these areas in the collection. With this collaboration, the library now have a well-used and well-thought, pertinent collection that reflects the needs of the painters in this particular community. (Personal correspondence, Denise Somers, 20 October 2011, unpublished)

Final Thoughts

Each of these examples highlights the importance of having existing relationships and beginning the engagement process first; then the collection development aspect became a natural and logical outgrowth of that.

From a traditional library approach, librarians can continue to select what they view as being the 'best' materials. However, it quickly becomes apparent when working with socially excluded and other underserved communities that the perceptions of librarians and community members can differ significantly with regard to the selection of relevant materials. If the material is not of interest, or reflective of community needs, then it will not be used or borrowed – or communities may come to view their local public library as a space which does not serve their information needs. There is no point in a librarian selecting 'good' materials if they are irrelevant or exclude a large segment of the community.

Helpful Hints

1: *It is important to include the library systems collection development/access team in the process.* In one case, a CDL discovered a library staff member in the collection department was selectively 'weeding out' materials that youth had purchased. The collections librarian objected to the theme being added to the collection – only to discover within the next year that it was one of the 'hottest' trends in Hollywood and youth services.

#2: Public libraries need to urgently develop materials selection policies to cover the requirements of socially excluded people. Existing library stock selection policies – and the stock on the shelves – need to be critically examined to ensure that they are relevant to the community which they serve.

#3: Public libraries should systematically acquire underground and alternative material in all forms (including orature) which are created by, and are of interest to, those excluded from the public library system.

#4: Public libraries need to continue to raise with materials suppliers (writers, illustrators, publishers, booksellers, library suppliers) the range of materials available for socially excluded people and gaps in that provision.

Chapter 8
Staffing, Recruitment, Training and Education

In this chapter we consider the skills and competencies that library workers must have to build relationships with excluded communities. Staff skills and, even more importantly attitude and empathy, are critical to the development of needs-based and community-led library services. Library schools in the UK and Canada tend to focus on the technical skills needed by a professional librarian, rather than the people skills which are required to work with local communities. We believe the way forward is to retrain library staff with community development skills as a first step to shifting mindsets, attitudes and behaviours. In the longer term we need to start recruiting a different kind of library worker who seamlessly combines library and information skills with a capacity to focus on building community relationships and facilitating the development of library responses collaboratively with community.

Open to All? (Muddiman et al. 2000a) suggested that public libraries need to reassess their recruitment and selection policies to attract more staff from socially excluded communities. Staff training programmes should link equal opportunities, anti-racism, anti-sexism and cultural and social exclusion awareness. Positive action would ensure that the workforce reflected the demography of local communities. Most importantly, staff and organizational attitudes, behaviour, values and culture should be challenged through a competency-based approach to staff recruitment and appraisal.

Those conducting the Working Together Project (WTP) in Canada understood that the most important elements in library training programmes included providing library staff with an opportunity to express their perceptions or pre-conceived notions of the community. Staff should be given an overview of community-led service planning and tools and interactive activities which enabled staff to practice these skills. These non-prescriptive activities can then be adapted by staff to fit the specific context of the local community. Opportunities should also be provided for staff to be constantly exposed to socially excluded or underserved communities either inside the library or in the community. Relationships can only be established and sustained through continuous interactions.

A People Service

Staffing structures should be aligned with social exclusion strategies. This will require new job titles, job descriptions, person profiles and competencies which recognize the importance of outreach, partnerships, community development and proactive ways of working.

Public libraries are, at heart, a people service and they need the right people with the right skills in the right jobs if community needs are to be met. The common perception of public libraries is that they are quiet oases of intellectual and academic endeavour where those with brains and a love of books can seek sanctuary from the hurly-burly of everyday life. The stereotypical image of a librarian is of a shy and retiring, rather dusty-looking character, who dresses conservatively and wears thick glasses (if a man) or pearl necklace (if a woman). Librarians are deemed to have high levels of book-related skills but they are not very good at relating to other people. While this is a stereotype, there are many library workers who fit this mould and who place more value on their love of books than their commitment to identify, prioritize and meet community needs.

The attitude, behaviour and values of library staff are a large component of organizational culture – 'the way we do things around here'. That is why it is essential that libraries employ the right 'man' for the job. Kerry Wilson and Briony Birdi (2008) investigated public library staff attitudes towards the concept of social inclusion and the role of empathy in community librarianship. They identified three different qualities of empathy:

- *knowing* what another person is feeling
- *feeling* what another is feeling and
- *responding compassionately* to another person's [distress].

Wilson and Birdi suggested that:

> It would be difficult to 'teach empathy', to train staff to develop an emotional response that is informed and influenced by personality, belief systems and other individual characteristics. However, the development of certain empathic skills can be encouraged by providing public library staff with the right knowledge and circumstantial information, involving them in decision-making processes, and facilitating the development of appropriate skills. (Wilson and Birdi 2008: 111)

As a result of such interventions, staff can be enabled to show higher levels of empathy towards members of all communities, provided that they are willing – and have some natural capacity – to do so. This is a significant finding in supporting library staff at all levels to communicate with library users from all cultural backgrounds and, in the longer term, to deliver a more effective service.

As such, the future recruitment of the right 'man' for the job will be intrinsic to the effectiveness of public libraries' contribution to the social inclusion agenda, and should be an absolute priority for the future of community librarianship.

Skills, Partnerships and Professional Identity

Wilson and Birdi suggest that there is a predominant generic skills base when seeking to audit the required skills and competencies for staff working with socially excluded groups. Generic and interpersonal skills are the most frequently asked for in job descriptions and person specifications:

- Generic skills account for 50 per cent of the skills required – these skills could be associated with a wide range of posts and sectors, such as time management, organizational skills, creativity, customer care skills, ICT skills, previous experience of managing staff.
- Interpersonal skills make up a further 29 per cent of the required skills – these include communication skills, or behavioural skills linked to personality traits such as enthusiasm and having an 'outgoing' personality.
- Library specific skills only account for 15 per cent of the total skill set – these are skills, knowledge or experience explicitly/specifically linked to library work.
- Social inclusion and community-based skills come bottom of the list at just 6 per cent – these skills include community development, outreach, prior experience of working in a community setting, or of working with socially excluded groups.

With respect to staff skills, there is evidence of role strain and a lack of confidence amongst some public library staff working with some of the more challenging excluded target groups, including disaffected teenagers, and adults with mental health and substance abuse problems. Staff do not feel that they have the necessary skills and experience to work with these groups, or feel that they should not be expected to do so within their roles as public library staff.

There are many benefits to working on a partnership basis with relevant external agencies. The ability to draw upon the skills, knowledge and experiences of professionals from other sectors and services, and to use networks to effectively target new user groups and communities, is invaluable within the social inclusion context.

The use of volunteers from community groups themselves is also important in facilitating genuinely empathic library services that are relevant and responsive to actual community and user needs. For example, Merton Libraries won the 2001 CILIP Libraries Change Lives Award 'in recognition of excellence and good practice for library and information services' to refugees and asylum seekers. Merton is an outer London borough, close to one of the UK centres for 'processing' refugees and asylum seekers. These groups have needs ranging from housing and health to education and employment. English is often not their first language and they face a number of barriers to integrating with the local community. Back in 2001 there were no agencies in Merton who had the skills to work with asylum seekers and refugees. The library service responded by redirecting funding from mainstream services to recruit a team who had the skills to identify, prioritize and meet community needs. This service was staffed by two full-time library workers who went out into the community and developed relationships with asylum seekers and refugees. Some members of these groups then started to do voluntary work in branch libraries which created a win-win situation: the asylum seekers and refugees gained valuable work experience which they could use to seek paid employment; and the library service had a direct link into these communities to assist with the needs assessment process.

A similar situation occurred in Lincolnshire when the county experienced mass inward migration by workers, initially from Portugal and later from EU accession countries, especially Poland and Romania. Lincolnshire is a huge rural county (the same size as a small country like Northern Ireland) with a largely static and homogeneous population, unused to the demands of assimilating new cultures. Without interventions to ensure community cohesion, tensions developed and erupted into a full race riot in Boston when England played Portugal in the Euro 2004 football tournament. While broken glass was being swept up off the streets the next day, the first agency to respond was the Lincolnshire library service which had developed links with the migrant community. The Multicultural Development Service (MDS) had recruited its workers directly from migrant worker communities and included staff who had the language and cultural skills to understand the needs of these communities. The MDS included workers from Portugal, Romania, Poland, Russia, Jamaica, the Sudan and English Romany. This mini 'United Nations' of library workers had a major impact on the whole library service which won the 2005 CILIP Diversity Award 'for outstanding achievement in the promotion of the principles of diversity, equal opportunities and social inclusion through the provision and promotion of library and information services'.

The value accorded to generic skills and the benefits of working with partners and community volunteers have raised some debate over the role and value of accredited library qualifications and 'professional' status for library staff working in community-based and social inclusion roles. There is already evidence of growing recruitment from alternative sectors and a certain level of acceptance that a library qualification is not a prerequisite for effective community-based library services.

Those who wish to preserve professional status at all levels of public library service, and within all aspects of service provision, feel that within a social inclusion context, libraries are starting to provide too many non-library services and that the service is going too far in destabilizing traditional roles and concepts of the profession. Such perceptions could be very damaging to the social inclusion offer from public libraries within modern society and mitigating strategies should be developed to guard against this happening.

While the entrenched views of some qualified staff are not helpful and can be damaging, there are also dangers if professional library staff are replaced by unqualified workers or volunteers. The debate about the need for 'proper librarians' has been hijacked by those who are using the Big Society agenda to make paid staff redundant and substitute them with untrained volunteers.

Empathy and Cultural Representation

Wilson and Birdi found that public library staff in England are culturally homogeneous, with the dominant profile being predominantly female, white British, middle-aged and middle class.

The gender ratio of library staff in England is 80 per cent female and 20 per cent male. The predominant age group is 46–55, with 43 per cent of staff falling into this category. A further 15 per cent of staff are aged 56–65. Only 17 per cent of staff are aged 35 or less, with just 3 per cent of staff in the 16–25 age group.

The largest ethnic grouping is 'White British', with 90 per cent of library staff falling into this category. The second largest ethnic grouping is 'White Other', who make up 2 per cent of staff. A range of ethnic groups are represented, including 'Indian', 'Black Caribbean' and 'Chinese', but only in very small numbers.

The most frequent gender/age/ethnicity grouping is 'female + 46–55 + White British', with 32 per cent of staff falling into this category.

Library staff are a highly qualified occupational grouping: more than a third of staff (37 per cent) are educated to postgraduate level. A further 30 per cent are educated to degree level.

The social class of library staff can be gauged by their school background. Seventy-seven per cent of library staff describe the pupil and staff profile of their school(s) as *culturally homogeneous* (that is, groups of people with similar ethnic, social, cultural and religious backgrounds). Seventeen per cent of staff describe the same profile as *culturally diverse* (that is, groups of people with differing ethnic, social, cultural and religious backgrounds). Educational denomination is a little more varied, with 48 per cent of staff describing their secondary education experience as *dominated by one faith*, and 44 per cent as *largely secular*. Fifty per cent of staff describe their school's educational performance as 'good' and 26 per cent as 'excellent', suggesting that the majority of staff attended achieving schools.

The most frequent secondary education experience grouping is 'culturally homogeneous + dominated by one faith + good', suggesting that 20 per cent of staff had a culturally and socially homogeneous and academically successful formative educational experience.

When asked to discuss cultural representation, library staff instinctively refer to ethnicity in the first instance, rather than age, gender and social class, cultural characteristics that are arguably of equal (if not greater in the case of the latter variable) importance when describing cultural representation in a social inclusion context. This infers a lack of clarity and understanding of the multi-faceted nature of social exclusion, and how those affected may feel under-represented in public services and civic life.

Some library staff believe that within the empathy dynamic, staff cultural profiles are irrelevant, and that they themselves as public library staff have sufficient cognitive empathy skills, and are therefore able to provide responsive and sensitive library services for a wide range of users and social groups. Others, however, feel that traditionally disadvantaged groups place a greater degree of trust and confidence in people they can recognize as familiar, relate to and understand, such as people of a similar age or people from the same neighbourhoods. A direct correlation is similarly made between effective staff performance and the concept of living and working in the same communities. That is why the recruitment of workers from local communities by Merton and Lincolnshire library services was so important. When refugees and asylum seekers go into Merton libraries they see staff who reflect their communities. And when migrant workers go into Lincolnshire libraries they interact with staff who understand their needs.

It is possible to differentiate between staff members with a natural aptitude (which can be described as intuitive empathy) for working with excluded groups, and those without. Survey results suggest high levels of cognitive empathy within a culturally homogeneous workforce sample. Qualitative data, however, strongly challenge this assumption, as anecdotal evidence suggests strong resistance to cultural change in libraries, to certain traditionally excluded groups, and to the social inclusion agenda as a whole amongst public library staff.

Within this context, there are clear distinctions between 'older' and 'younger' members of staff, with the former group more likely to be resistant to cultural change and objecting towards the targeting of excluded groups and communities. At the same time, there are also some younger staff who hold poor attitudes. It is more about openness to change, to seeing the job as working with the community, not working in the library. This raises issues concerning this staff group's motivation in deciding to work for the public library service and, in particular, their reasons for remaining in public library service for long periods of time. There is a feeling that a certain 'nice little job' syndrome may still exist amongst some staff groups, particularly those in part-time posts, where staff do not want to feel challenged by their role. It is also the case that many people opt to work part-time for other reasons (for example, they may have caring responsibilities) and do not want a job that carries any emotional burden.

Staff Training and Development

Knowledge

Wilson and Birdi suggest that the priority for public library managers within the context of staff training is to address the apparent gap in staff knowledge and understanding of social inclusion policy and political drivers. Staff at all levels working within services and projects that are responsive to such drivers should be fully informed of relevant external and political influences, and be given the opportunity to question and discuss them further, and thus fully engage with the reasons for particular service developments and initiatives.

Similarly, greater effort should be made to provide *relevant* training and information on groups affected by social exclusion, in an attempt to significantly raise levels of awareness and cultural sensitivity amongst all staff.

Staff need the intellectual time and space to fully engage with and consider these issues, so the 'away day' method may be appropriate, particularly in reducing the risk of staff feeling additional pressure in having to absorb new information in their day-to-day work environment, and subsequently form a negative perception of inclusive approaches as 'add-on' responsibilities. This needs to be carefully planned and scheduled into all new projects and service developments as an important part of the process, particularly in overcoming the ever-present 'lack of time and money' barrier.

Skills

The skills required to work in socially inclusive services have been defined by Wilson and Birdi as 'advanced customer care' skills, and some public library authorities are already providing valuable training in this area. This should be prioritized within project and service development plans. The skills required to provide advanced customer care include:

- communication skills
- listening skills
- influencing relationships
- reflective practice
- improved confidence and assertiveness
- negotiation skills
- dealing with conflict.

There is encouraging evidence which indicates that these skills are being incorporated into CILIP's emerging Body of Professional Knowledge (BPK). The BPK is presented as a wheel at the hub of which are 'ethics and values' supported by 'professional expertise' and 'professional leadership and advocacy'. There are also 13 knowledge and skills sets, radiating out as spokes on the wheel, including:

- professional confidence
- marketing and customer focus
- literacies and learning.

Sitting behind these knowledge and skills sets is a further level of detail which outlines the knowledge and skills encompassed in each segment. It is here that the advanced customer care skills recommended by Wilson and Birdi can be found. In addition, John Vincent (2009) cites some good examples of practical approaches in staff training to tackle social exclusion.

Providing a Community-Focused Workforce

Library services need a flexible and user-responsive workforce if they are to successfully and consistently identify, prioritize and meet community needs. While some excellent best practices do exist, many services remain unable to meet this challenge. Most innovative library services have staff who can respond to change with speed and imagination and who can ensure local communities understand and use the library service. These staff can clearly articulate the benefits that libraries can deliver and can empower local communities by actively engaging them in the design, planning, delivery and assessment of library services.

Increasingly, new library staff will not have come up through the service itself. As well as having the right mix of people, the following competencies are also becoming increasingly vital: people and project management; community development; performance management and advocacy. Future library staff will need to have a proactive and community-focused approach, seeking continual service improvement and pursuing and making partnerships with the public, private and third sectors where they see the potential for community benefit and the delivery of shared priorities.

Nearly 75 per cent of library staff think that library schools do not have the relevant content or teach the right skills to equip the library workforce. The modern library workforce can and should be drawn from a wide range of skills and experience such as youth work, community development and adult education to fulfil the service's potential to flexibly respond to the needs and expectations of users. IT, marketing and community development skills and information-handling skills are considered essential now.

Workforce development was a key recommendation in *The Modernisation Review of Public Libraries* (2010): 'Providers of library and information sector courses should develop and implement a new framework for public library professional qualifications, founded on user-driven policy and practices including customer service and people skills, community outreach, working with children, marketing and leadership' (DCMS 2010a: 36).

Library services are best when staffed by a mixture of professionals, including librarians and people qualified for work in other fields. Figure 8.1 illustrates the mix of workforce skills necessary to deliver a modernized library service.

A broad range of generic skills and attributes underpins a successful contemporary service and these skills may be derived from different careers and training routes. Above all, the sector must be receptive to new ways of working to ensure that libraries satisfy community needs and deliver a modernized service.

To address unhelpful hierarchical structures, a whole workforce approach needs to be taken to training provision. Some library services already work in partnership with local training and skills providers, including library and information schools, to develop the training they need. Libraries should also work with early years settings, schools and youth workers to help library staff benefit from professional development in working with children and their families. Mentoring and work-shadowing opportunities should also be developed.

Personal attributes and behaviours:	Core library and information skills:
• Values and ethics • Reflective practice • Go-to people with a can-do approach • Flexibility • Positive and helpful attitude • Lateral thinking and creativity • Strategic vision and thinking • Political awareness	• Knowledge, understanding and enthusiasm for reading, learning and information literacy in the community • Managing, promoting, preserving and evaluating resources • Understand, facilitate and support community needs
Generic skills:	**Specific leadership and management skills:**
• Community engagement • Communication and marketing • Relationship management • Partnership working • Working with children, young people and vulnerable adults • Project management and outcome delivery • E-capable and e-confident • Advocacy	• Performance management • Financial management • Community development • Inspiring leadership • Governance and ethics • Managing and developing people • Political advocacy • Cultural expertise and understanding

Figure 8.1   The library worker skill set

Volunteers

Volunteers play an important role in supporting key activities by building bridges to local communities and supporting staff in the library team. Volunteers often have skills which complement (but do not replace) staff expertise. For example, the *Welcome to Your Library* (ADP 2004) project encouraged asylum seekers and refugees to engage with the library service as volunteers. Most of the participants went on to find jobs, some of them in the library service and, at their suggestion, new informal learning programmes have been developed that continue to attract black and minority ethnic (BME) audiences. Recruiting socially excluded people as library workers can have a strong effect on organizational culture. As well as giving insights into the culture and lifestyle of excluded groups, the very presence of an alternative viewpoint can have a powerful influence on staff attitude and behaviour. For example, in Merton there was often much discussion by library staff and users about the large numbers of asylum seekers and refugees who had moved into the local area. When members of these communities were recruited onto the library staff they were able to inform these discussions because refugees and asylum seekers were no longer 'them' but part of 'us'. Library staff and users were able to discover at first hand (and not via the hostile media, or hearsay) what it was actually like to be a refugee or asylum seeker. And what they discovered was that these people had the same ambitions and aspirations as indigenous library workers – jobs, good housing and schools for their children, healthcare and a good quality of life. By creating this direct contact between library staff and users and asylum seekers and refugees, barriers were broken down, myths and misunderstandings were dispelled and mutual needs and wants were identified via a shared and common humanity. The power of direct contact in tackling prejudice and discrimination was explored by Stonewall in *Profiles of Prejudice* (2003), which found that:

- 64 per cent of people admitted to be prejudiced against at least one minority group.
- Most prejudice was expressed against refugees/asylum seekers, travellers/ gypsies, people from minority ethnic communities, and gay or lesbian people.
- Personal contact with minority groups decreases the likelihood of prejudice, while lack of contact with minority groups increases the likelihood of prejudice.
- Knowing someone from a minority group significantly reduces the likelihood of prejudice towards that particular group and other minority groups. (Stonewall 2003: 12–13)

Public libraries can play a key role in tackling prejudice and discrimination and helping communities to understand each other. Public libraries provide free, democratic public space where different communities can meet and interact. With the right skills, attitudes and behaviours library staff can be powerful agents of community cohesion.

Without radical change in the workforce, library services will not be able to modernize or meet community needs. Real change needs partnership working, leadership within the library sector and a readiness and willingness from all library staff to embrace a new role.

Working Together

Librarians are a barrier because we are mired in a culture of comfort. Like most people we remain where we are comfortable: comfortable with the programs we offer, comfortable with the services we provide, and comfortable with the people we serve. Even our challenges are comfortable: to do more of what we always do for the people we always serve. As a result we often fail to serve communities that do not look, feel, or think like us … we must shed our culture of comfort. We need to emphasize ideas over tasks, and processes over solutions. We need to insist that experiences and effects are as significant a measure of our success as counting heads at a library program. Collectively we can debunk the myth that the current definition of the library and librarian is complete and needs only to be reproduced to be successful. This is not a 'them or us' or an 'old versus new' split in our profession. It is simply the recognition that if we are indeed society's most egalitarian institution we must become egalitarian. (DeFaveri 2005b)

Unfortunately, for the library profession the hiring of staff has become a cyclical process. Most public libraries are looking for staff who have the skills, knowledge and expertise which reflect many of the attributes that current library staff hold. This is mirrored in the hiring process, such as interview questions, where potential new staff are compared to existing library-based knowledge. The existing skills, knowledge, and attributes which libraries have traditionally sought are beneficial for serving current library users. The knowledge, skills and attributes of socially excluded and underserved communities need to be reflected in the hiring process, if library systems are to expand their range of library users and to reflect the true characteristics of a local community. Only by expanding this to professional roles within the library system will libraries attract professionals who are committed to ensuring that programmes and services reflect a wide range of community needs.

Initially, stepping outside of our comfort zone can be an intimidating experience. As library systems begin to envision the application of community-led service planning into respective workplaces, each system will need to determine the skill sets which are required to meet community needs. The initial apprehension experienced by existing library staff can be overcome, with proper support, training, and authorization from senior library staff. While there may be debates which ensue on whether essential skill sets for conducting community-based work can be taught or if they are inherent traits that individuals hold, there are a number of benefits to be gained by starting the process of developing staff training, recruitment and education programmes which focus on community-based work.

Skills and Attributes of Staff

Over four years there were a number of library staff who were either directly or indirectly involved with the WTP. Based on the lived experiences of library staff who worked continuously in the community and who developed deep relationships with socially excluded community members, a number of skills and attributes were identified as being beneficial to either possess or continuously develop. If someone gets to the point where they feel they posses all these skills and attributes, it would be good to step back and self-reflect. Instead of believing that staff can attain all of these and be fully competent, it is more important that workers are able to be self-critical.

As discussed in the Working Together *Toolkit* (2008a), it is essential that library staff have and continuously strive to develop:

- *Humility* – Leaving behind the 'expert' mentality and approaching the community on an equitable level will help the community to see us as equals. Acknowledging that community members are the experts on their own needs is the first step in this approach. Our position is that of a learner – working with the community to discover how the library might meet community needs (ibid.: 74).

- *Empathy* – Empathy can help us see the library through the community's eyes and experiences. Empathy involves taking a perspective that is different from our own, imagining how an interaction might feel or be interpreted by someone else, and being able to see how another person's life circumstances impact their ability to access library services. Empathy lets us transcend our assumptions about the community and what we usually believe to be appropriate (ibid.: 119).

- *Confidence* – Your confidence will increase as you develop a solid understanding of community-based library work. The more you think and work outside the traditional library model, the more comfortable and self-confident you will become in applying equitable service principles (ibid.: 119). Only once a library staff is confident can they *surrender expertise*: for many librarians, this will be the first time they enter into the community's space as learners and not as experts. In outreach scenarios, staff are always positioned as the expert or authority. Becoming the learner is the challenge. Be watchful that you do not revert to the familiar outreach and service paradigm (ibid.: 48).

- *Curiosity* – Being genuinely curious about the lives of community members and the conditions in the community helps build valuable insight into how the library can meet community needs. Developing a sense of curiosity helps you move past the expected norms or status quo of your institution and culture and helps reinforce your role as a learner (ibid.: 120).

- *Critical thinking* – In the context of the Community-Led Service Planning Model, critical thinking means understanding, assessing and, where necessary, changing library policies and methods so they are more responsive to the community's needs and wants. At the same time, in order to effectively assess our institutions, we need to continuously examine ourselves. We all have cultural beliefs, and we all make assumptions about people (ibid.: 116).

- *Self-awareness* – Be sensitive to how you may appear to socially excluded community members. Words and actions might be misunderstood or have a more profound impact than intended (ibid.: 116).

When working with and in the community there are a number of different techniques which library workers should constantly be checking. By following each of these points, library staff will be more likely to influence appropriate changes, both from the perspective of community-identified need and expanding the definition and the role the library can play in community-based information-seeking. In addition, since library staff working from a community-led perspective are inherently change agents for libraries, and they will be exposed to community members with a high level of need, it is important for library staff to constantly check and seek assistance in managing their own well-being.

- *Listening (active)* – The focus of active listening is the same as being a learner: we are trying to receive information and build understanding. A number of additional helpful hints are highlighted in the *Toolkit*. We all know that it is possible to hear what people are saying without understanding what they mean. Listening for the nuance and subtleties of responses and reactions and then applying context to what is heard can provide depth to our understanding (ibid.: 118).
- *An open-minded attitude* – Being open to social, cultural, economic, political or any other differences in the community is essential when working with diverse community members. Practise your ability to remain open-minded when meeting people who may be extremely different from you. A non-judgemental attitude can help us move away from imposing traditionally rigid library procedures or imposing Western cultural traditions and values on community members. It can help us approach situations without any expectation of what should or should not happen (ibid.: 120).
- *Setting boundaries* – While it may be difficult at first to say 'no' to personal requests such as a ride to a meeting or invitations to family events, think about what is appropriate given your role. For example, it is probably not appropriate to attend a community member's birthday party if this is a party at a home, restaurant or other private location. But you could join in the birthday celebration, perhaps bringing a card, if there is cake for everyone at a service provider's space (ibid.: 73).
- *Stress management* – Working with socially excluded people means you may sometimes hear stories about personal hardships, poverty, illness, addictions and other difficult circumstances. Hearing these stories may become emotionally exhausting. It is helpful to be aware of this ahead of time and seek appropriate support for yourself when necessary. Always listen for opportunities to discover how the library, and not you as an individual, can be supportive (ibid.: 120).

Recruitment

A number of positions were created to complete the objectives of the WTP. It was quickly recognized that library systems needed to recruit employees who either possessed or had the potential to develop the skills and attributes discussed above. To do this:

Project libraries began modifying job postings. It was essential to ask for proficiencies and comfort levels for staff members who would be working directly with community members. The job postings emphasized that new recruits should feel comfortable in community spaces and meeting new people outside traditional library settings. New staff members should be willing and excited to plan services in collaboration with diverse communities. (Working Together 2008a: 136)

Furthermore, competencies needed to be adjusted to reflect these new skills and attributes. Examples included:

- ability to engage the community
- respect for diverse backgrounds, opinions and beliefs of library users and workers
- ability to consult with, respond to and reflect communities served by the branch
- ability to work in non-traditional environments
- thrive on engaging a wide and diverse range of users in an interactive environment (Working Together 2008a: 136)

These changes to the hiring process allowed library systems to:

- hire Working Together staff from within the partner branch [which was] anticipated to have a considerable impact on the project's sustainability at the branch level (Atkey 2008: 57)
- hire someone who was from the local community, who had existing relationships and family members living in the socially excluded community: this was an invaluable 'in' into a community which did not regularly use library services, and to
- hire a librarian from within the system to champion the approach with other co-workers within the library system: the intent was, if you could find an internal candidate with influence within the library system, he/she could then advocate for the approach with other library staff.

The success that participating libraries had in changing, and to some extent integrating, the hiring process into their library systems had an impact not only locally, but also nationally. This is a major testament to the legitimacy, need, and desire of library systems to adjust their hiring practices in order to become more reflective of a wide range of underserved communities. As discussed in the national evaluation (Atkey 2008),

One of the project tasks was to learn how to recruit for community development work, and the results of this are evidenced in new job descriptions and job postings in each of the four library systems. That several city library systems outside of the project have contacted Working Together administrators for guidance on how to hire into their own newly created CDL positions, indicates that the learning in this area has been exceptional. The detailed articulation of the 'soft skills' required for this type of work, found in the Community-Led Libraries Toolkit, not only assists with recruitment, it provides a useful framework for ongoing training of library workers. This is one of the project's most valuable contributions to libraries in Canada. (Atkey 2008: 13)

Training and the Role of Library Programmes

The vast majority of librarians working in public libraries have attained credentials from accredited institutions. This accreditation process is supposed to ensure that the content covered in library school is relevant to the practical application within library environments. In order to ensure that library schools were aware of the WTP, and the potential impact they could have on preparing future librarians to work within a truly inclusive environment, two major activities occurred:

- the Working Together *Toolkit* was sent to each of the MLIS programmes in Canada
- as one of the ten major deliverables for the WTP, course content was developed in 2008 for a stand-alone course to be used in a library programme (see Appendix below).

As of the spring of 2012, there have been relatively few attempts by library schools to fully integrate coursework which solely focuses on either social exclusion and the role of libraries or community-led work. As public libraries continue to move towards integrating community-led service planning approaches into programme and service development, there will be an increasing need to recruit library staff with the desired interpersonal skills and knowledge of community-led work. If gaps persist between library school programme content and the continuing evolution of community-based library practitioner approaches, public libraries will need to proactively engage and train new professionals entering the field upon hiring.

The Model Branch

Community development librarians (CDLs) were based out of library branches in each of the library systems. There were many discussions regarding the sustainability of CDL work in each library branch when the project ended in 2008. The development of a model branch provided a very important testing ground for trying to integrate community-led service planning within an existing branch, with many long-term employees. A number of different approaches were taken by the various participating library systems. In one, library staff skills were developed organically, where regular library branch staff were encouraged to observe and model community development librarian behaviours and were invited to come with CDLs into the community. Another library system began to internally engage with library staff through a series of progressive all-staff meetings, where learnings were progressively rolled out to all library staff. These staff meetings took the following formats:

- Gain an understanding of branch staffs' grasp of local communities and what their perceptions of community-led work is.
- Bring in outside community members who rarely or infrequently use library services to speak about their experiences and barriers they have encountered when trying to access library services.
- Ensure that library staff are provided with a safe environment in which to be exposed to diverse communities and to be asked tough questions that challenge their perceptions about how to serve communities and populations which don't 'look like them'.
- Provide an opportunity for library staff to learn about community-led concepts and approaches to engaging the community. This can be achieved via multiple training sessions and should be interactive, allowing library staff to try and seek solutions to identified approaches or issues as they arise.
- Involve senior staff in exercises to rethink branch staffing levels and potential changes to current activities, to free up time and resources to work with socially excluded community members.
- Provide library staff with opportunities to debrief and evaluate the process and their progress.

By providing library staff with opportunities to internally engage – as equals *regardless of their role within the library branch* – they were provided with a safe space to discuss their perceptions of the local community, social exclusion, and community-led services. Additionally, these staff engagement sessions provided library staff with an opportunity to learn *from* the community and build community-led skills.

Additional Ideal Characteristics

Since the conclusion of the WTP there have been a number of observations regarding the type of employee who is desired by library systems moving in this direction. Many of these skills and attributes reflect the findings developed through Working Together. As observed by Martinez and Williment (2012):

> The skill sets required for this type of library work are not customary to the library profession. The 'new' librarian needs excellent interpersonal skills, a high degree of flexibility and adaptability, superb facilitation and listening skills, a sense of humility, and above all, leadership – the ability to influence and navigate the change process in the library, so the library can shift to meet the needs of community where they are.

A number of other thoughts have also arisen regarding the type of library employee who can effectively influence change in a library system. This includes:

- A person who is able to be humble and move beyond their role as 'expert'. Becoming an expert in engaging, finding the appropriate role for facilitating the link between people and information (or maybe even people and people), and linking and visualizing the role which libraries can play in the community, is a different kind of expertise from being a spokesperson who informs people of information or existing programmes.
- Someone who can move beyond the perceived barriers to community-led work (resources, role of services, the unknown), and not allow these barriers to stop them from trying it.
- A willingness to seriously accept trial and error – and report on the learnings that occurred when trying new and innovative approaches to working with the community. Anyone who says they 'have got it' to working with the community needs to re-evaluate. When one person has always 'got' the answer for the community they need to review the concepts behind the engagement process.
- A willingness to shift library-based responses from 'No, it does not fit within our mandate' to 'How can we work with the community-based information needs to make them fit within the libraries' mandate?' If community members are saying that they see a link between the library and their need, we should be encouraging staff to find this linkage – otherwise it is another lost opportunity for library service development.
- An ability to think and act on our role in the information exchange and how we engage with the community outside the confines of the physical library branch.
- An acknowledgement that the penalization of the community and the concept of librarians as stewards (keepers and holders of information) are outdated concepts. Libraries once possessed warehouses of information which community members can now find on the click of an iPad or laptop. We are no longer entitled to create barriers which limit library use, when we should be developing new services which attract new users.

Helpful Hints

#1: Regardless of the approach taken by a library system, the most important elements in library staff training include the following actions:

- Provide library staff with an opportunity to express their perceptions or pre-conceived notions of the community.
- Provide library staff with training and an overview of community-led service planning and tools. Try to build in interactive activities, where

library staff can apply principles with the community.

- Provide opportunities for library staff to be constantly exposed to socially excluded or underserved communities, either inside the library or in the community. Relationships can only be established and sustained through continuous interactions.
- Display organizational support. Ensure messages are coming from senior management, so that all staff understand that the organization is advocating that library staff work from a community-led approach.

#2: Public libraries need to reassess their recruitment and selection policies (including reassessing the requirement for qualifications in librarianship) in order to attract more staff into the workforce from socially excluded backgrounds.

#3: Public libraries should urgently analyse the training needs of their staff, to ensure that they have the necessary knowledge and skills to provide the best services for socially excluded people. Training programmes to be developed for all services linking equal opportunities, anti-racism, anti-sexism, cultural and social exclusion awareness.

#4: Public libraries should adopt positive action programmes so that the library workforce incorporates socially excluded people more equitably than at present. All library authorities should aim to develop recruitment and selection statements outlining how this will be achieved.

#5: Public libraries should challenge staff and organizational attitudes, behaviour, values and culture through staff development and training and a competency-based approach to staff recruitment and appraisal.

Appendix: Proposed Community Development Course for Library Schools[1]

Rationale

Library schools in Canada offer some excellent elective courses which focus on inclusive library services for marginalized community members. However, the number of these courses is relatively small compared to the number of graduates who seek employment in a public library. Because the courses are electives, many students who would be interested in them may be unable to fit them into their timetables. Other students may not take these courses because they lack an awareness of the subject's relevance to library service planning.

In addition, the existing library school courses tend to focus on one target group, such as at-risk youth or immigrants, rather than on a comprehensive approach to

---

1   Working Together (2008b).

providing inclusive library services to all community members. Focusing on one group may result in a more prescriptive approach, while using a broader model tends to encourage flexibility, ongoing learning and critical evaluation.

A community development approach, as applied in the Community-Led Library Service Model, provides a comprehensive foundation to the philosophy, challenges and practical application of inclusive library services, with particular attention to the needs of socially excluded community members.

Course Goals

Students will become familiar with the philosophy, rationale, concepts and practices which form the foundation of inclusive community-led library services. Particular attention will be given to working in the community with socially excluded community members, and applying the Community-Led Library Service Model to traditional library work. Students will be expected to enter community spaces (in pairs or with public library staff mentors), interact with community members, and listen to them with the intent of identifying a need in the community which could potentially be addressed by the public library.

Course Objectives

Upon completion of this course, students will be able to:

- describe a variety of reasons why people may feel negative or indifferent toward libraries.
- explain and give examples of real and perceived systemic barriers
- explain the difference between equal treatment and equitable access
- explain the differences between outreach and community-led/community development approaches and practices
- critique library policies and practices for inclusiveness and/or barriers to equitable access
- evaluate solutions to a variety of day-to-day 'problem' situations encountered in traditional library settings as either library-centred or patron-centred and, where appropriate, suggest alternative and more inclusive ways of responding
- describe the main components of the Community-Led Library Service Model
- identify skills and abilities required to create or adapt programming to suit the needs of various communities and individuals
- develop skills and abilities required to create or adapt programming to suit the needs of various communities and individuals
- conduct a one-to-one or small group session using a community-led process: learners in this session may be other students or community members off-campus

- research and compile statistical data and profiles on a given neighbourhood, using electronic or print resources such as Statistics Canada and local directories
- walk through a neighbourhood and identify community service providers and community spaces and then identify how students' observations are consistent with, or differ from, community profiles from the traditional print or electronic resources used above
- evaluate a library activity using both qualitative and quantitative methods
- identify the differences between personal beliefs and values, and the core values of the public library
- self-evaluate personal soft skills, noting those which are already areas of strength and other skills which may need attention and development
- identify the role of the librarian in the community, as distinct from the role of volunteer, social worker, teacher, or other community workers and professionals.

Content

(Topics marked with an asterisk* indicate student-led seminar topics.)

- Systemic barriers
- Fair treatment versus equitable access
- The Community-Led Library Service Model

Community entry and community mapping

Relationship building
Partnerships
Programme planning
Collection development
Customer service
- Mission statements, mandates, values of public libraries*
- Inclusion and exclusion; outreach versus community development
- Search skills: identifying the many names for similar work*
- The UK experience (John Pateman)*
- Traditional methods for gathering community feedback and input; how these reinforce exclusion*
- Past and current definitions of literacy*
- Digital divide and its implications*
- Qualitative and quantitative evaluation

Format and Delivery

The class will meet once a week for 3 hours. Some sessions will take place in the community or the public library.

A student-led seminar model will be combined with the traditional format of instructor-led presentations and guest lecturers.

Service learning will be integrated into a portion of the course. The service learning component will not duplicate or replace the experience available to individual students through practical placements, or through other existing courses.

Suggested Outline of 13 Sessions

(Topics marked with an asterisk* indicate student-led seminars.)

Session 1

- Overview, expectations, discussion, assignments, reading lists, journals, assigning student-led seminar instructions
- Community-led service: what is it and why do it? Inclusion and exclusion. Outreach versus community-led and community development

Session 2

- Search skills: identifying the many names for similar work*
- Mission statements, mandates, values of public libraries*

Session 3

- Visit and tour a community service provider: if possible, hold the class in a community space
- Public libraries and persons with mental illness (or other focus suitable to the community)
- Community partnerships

Session 4

- Arrange for guest lecturer, perhaps a former Working Together librarian
- Systemic barriers
- Fair treatment versus equitable access

Session 5

- The UK experience (John Pateman)*
- Traditional methods for gathering community feedback and input; how these reinforce exclusion*

Session 6

- Visit an inner-city library or a library serving a sizeable socially excluded population: if possible, hold class in the branch and include branch staff
- Putting theory to practice: socially excluded community members and library services

Session 7

- Past and current definitions of literacy*
- Digital divide and its implications*
- Planning for service learning

Session 8

- Visits to various sites where a community-led library service is currently or has recently taken place

Sessions 9 and 10

- The Community-Led Library Service Model
- Qualitative evaluation

Sessions 11 and 12

- Service learning activities

Session 13

- Student sharing of community-led sessions and service learning experiences; compilation of learnings; summary and review
- Course evaluation: suggestions and directions for further activities, future directions for the course

Note that if experienced persons are not locally available as guest lecturers, some sessions could be conducted as teleconferences led by librarians from Working Together sites across Canada.

Chapter 9

Mainstreaming and Resourcing for Social Exclusion

In this chapter we consider how to place community needs at the centre of public library strategy, structures, systems and organizational culture. We argue that social exclusion needs to be placed at the heart of the public library service to ensure that adequate resources are provided to meet community needs. This can create some interesting and creative tensions with library managers, staff, boards and users who do not understand or support the redirection of resources away from 'core' users and towards those who need libraries the most but use them the least. A robust library strategy can ensure that staffing and service structures, systems and procedures and, most importantly, values, style and culture ('the way we do things around here') are all in alignment and able to meet community needs.

Mainstreaming of social exclusion was a key recommendation of *Open to All?* (Muddiman et al. 2000b) as this enabled a needs-led, as opposed to demand-led, approach to resourcing which was more equitable for disadvantaged groups. Everything should flow from the needs-based strategy, including management and organizational structures that worked for communities. Service targets, planning and monitoring should be shared with community members.

The Working Together Project (WTP) identified the importance of ensuring the staff member has the authority to create change. It was also important to create a network and informal support between those staff who largely work in isolation so that they could share their experiences and strategies. Community-led wording should be integrated into the library mission and vision statements. Senior management must be educated to ensure that their buy-in moves beyond 'speaking community-led'. The focus should be on actions and not adoption of language. System-wide and branch-based plans should ensure accountability, timelines and levels of authority and make tackling social exclusion a part of everyone's job.

Holistic and Systematic Approach

One of the major problems with social exclusion initiatives is that they nearly always tend to rely on extended funding and short-term timescales. This prevents the work from being embedded within the strategy, structures, systems and organizational culture of the organization. As a result:

- Social exclusion is not central to library strategies, plans and policies.
- Staff do not learn the skills required to work with socially excluded communities.
- Social exclusion is not reflected in library service and staffing structures.
- Library systems are not changed to remove or reduce barriers to participation by excluded communities.
- The organizational culture – 'the way we do things around here' – is not informed by community needs.

For a library service to be socially inclusive it needs to have mutually reinforcing strategies, structures, systems and cultures. This cannot be achieved from short-term projects which parachute in 'expert' or 'specialist' staff who then depart when the external funding runs out. This is damaging on two levels:

- It does not mainstream and embed social exclusion work into the library service. Indeed, it has the opposite effect – library staff do not feel part of the project initiative (they may even feel threatened by it) and they simply pass on all social exclusion work to the 'experts'.
- It raises hopes and expectations within socially excluded communities who then feel let down when the project comes to an end. Social exclusion is a long-term problem which requires long-term solutions and not short-term fixes. The project culture can breed cynicism and consultation fatigue within communities and undermine future efforts to tackle social exclusion.

The importance of mainstreaming social exclusion work was first recognized in *Libraries for All: Social Inclusion in Public Libraries* (1999):

Social inclusion should be mainstreamed as a policy priority for library and information services. Mainstreaming means putting principle at the heart of policy making and the development of services. Social inclusion issues should underpin all aspects of library provision. This applies both where services are being enhanced, and when there is pressure to reduce or cut library services. (DCMS 1999: 14)

The last point is very important and emphasizes why social exclusion work should be embedded and made sustainable. When the financial crisis hit the UK in 2008 it started to have an effect on public sector funding which fed through to public libraries in 2010. Local council budgets were reduced by 28 per cent and public libraries – which are not seen as an essential service like social care or education – bore the brunt of these cuts. In order to minimize the impact on frontline services and to limit the number of library closures, the cuts mostly affected backoffice staff and any services which were deemed to be specialist or peripheral. This made any library services to excluded communities which had not been embedded extremely vulnerable to cuts and closure. There are many instances of library community development services being decimated or wiped out altogether, because they were stand-alone services which could be easily deleted from the budget book. This failure to embed also meant that the value of these services was not recognized by policy-makers and decision-makers. Services which were aimed at 'minority groups' suddenly seemed very expensive, poor value for money and easy to close down because the communities they were targeted at did not have any political power. The lesson to be learned from this experience is that social exclusion should be mainstreamed when the going is good and resources are available, but it is even more important that these services become embedded when the going gets tough and there is intense competition for scarce resources.

The imperative to mainstream social exclusion was emphasized by Pateman (2003) in *Developing a Needs-Based Library Service*:

> Transforming a library service so that it can effectively tackle social exclusion is not an easy task. Equally challenging is the task of keeping the transformation going and sustaining the new services and initiatives. You must constantly review your social inclusion strategy, your staffing structure and your organizational culture to make sure that all three are in line with each other and that they are all still focused on combating social exclusion. (Pateman 2003: 29)

Strategy

The starting point for mainstreaming social exclusion is the library strategy because this in turn informs policies and resource allocation. If social exclusion is not central to the public library strategy, vision and mission statements, then it will not be possible to successfully identify, prioritize and meet community needs. The strategy development process should be open and transparent and should include all key stakeholders including the local community, staff, politicians, board members, suppliers and partners. By including all of these interests at the very beginning of the strategy development process it is possible to build a consensus around why tackling social exclusion is an important strategic objective and how this can be achieved. By getting key stakeholders to collectively sign up to a social exclusion strategy it is more likely that the value of this approach will be recognized and there will no departure from the long-term aims, objectives and resources required to tackle exclusion and build inclusive communities.

While the strategy should be grounded in local circumstances and, in particular, community needs, it should also be connected to higher-level strategies and policies at organizational and national level. In the UK, for example, *Framework for the Future* (DCMS 2003) provided a strategic framework for public libraries based on three key objectives:

- the promotion of reading and informal learning
- access to digital skills and services including e-government
- measures to tackle social exclusion, build community identity and develop citizenship.

It is interesting to note the order in which these objectives were presented. Although they were all intended to be equal in importance, experience since 2003 has shown that most effort has been put into reading and informal learning, some effort has been put into digital skills and services and relatively little effort has been put into tackling social exclusion. There has been a wide range of initiatives to boost reading and learning including the establishment of the Reading Agency and the commitment to the Summer Reading Challenge. There was massive investment in ICT via the People's Network and RFID self-issue systems. But there have been no similar initiatives around tackling social exclusion. In order to fill this gap, The Network – 'tackling social exclusion in libraries, museums, archives, galleries and other cultural and heritage organizations' – was set up as a legacy of *Open to All?* by members of the research team without external support or funding.

Framework for the Future recognized that libraries needed to 'reach lapsed and non-users ... People who find reading difficult and groups in the community most at risk of social exclusion may find libraries distant or even intimidating places rather than seeing them as symbols of community' (DCMS 2003: 40). Non-users could be engaged through closer collaboration with other public services and partner organizations and it was suggested that 'Libraries deliver on their potential as community catalysts when they actively and imaginatively seek out the views of users and crucially, non-users, and translate those views into new services' (ibid.: 41).

This is central to developing a needs-based social exclusion strategy. All members of the community – particularly those who are socially excluded or at risk of social exclusion – must be included in the strategy development process to ensure that their views are heard. They must be actively involved at every stage, from strategy development through to service planning, design, delivery and evaluation:

> All libraries need to ... engage groups and individuals that are hard to reach by identifying them and establishing what are their particular needs and then by re-designing services when necessary so that there are no barriers to inclusion. Those libraries which are already successful in this important work frequently involve the communities themselves in the design and implementation of services. (Ibid.: 41)

It was also suggested that library strategies should be subsumed within community strategies: 'It is important that the library planning process should be linked to community planning, so that the contribution of libraries to the broader priorities of local communities is identified and integrated with other service provision' (ibid.: 41).

Strategy development is one of the most important element of the mainstreaming process. But the strategy must be more than just a written document, it must be a living embodiment of community needs and the library service response to those needs. The strategy must be reviewed and updated on a regular basis to keep it fresh and relevant to community lifestyles and challenges. We will now explore how the strategy can be used to inform the development of inclusive library staffing and service structures, systems and organizational culture.

Structures

Structures are critical to the delivery of needs-based library services. If the staffing and service structures do not reflect the social exclusion strategy then it will not be possible to successfully engage with local communities and provide services which meet community needs.

The importance of having staffing structures which are fit for purpose and able to tackle social exclusion was recognized by the Local Government Association in *Extending the Role of Libraries* (2004):

> Within library services, management structures needed to be reviewed in light of the changing role of the service. A number of the library services visited had made changes to their management structures. In some cases they had strengthened their strategic management in order to ensure that appropriate services were delivered across the public library authority, rather than leaving project development to individual operational management teams that targeted specific areas and populations. (LGA 2004: 41)

Specialist Team Approach

This was an important recommendation because, to date, most library services had tried to tackle social exclusion by setting up specialist teams. These typically had names such as Special Services Team, Outreach Team or Community Development Team. Many of these teams had their genesis in external funding such as the Section 11 money provided by central government to deliver services to ethnic minorities. In some cases this service comprised just one member of staff (often from an ethnic minority) who was expected to meet all of the needs of the diverse communities in their catchment area without any support or resources. Despite the significant weaknesses of this approach, there were some advantages:

- These were vanguard services which provided a big leap forward and paved the way for a more mainstreamed approach.
- They enabled innovation, experimentation and change.
- They led to the development of new collections and services.
- They often recruited staff who had a knowledge of local communities and an appreciation of community development work.
- They were able to raise awareness among library staff and provide training and guidance.

But these advantages were outweighed by several substantial disadvantages:

- Their work was not mainstreamed and became isolated from the rest of the service.
- Two-tier services emerged, with one (first-class) service for the mainstream community and another (second-class) service for the special interest groups or minorities.
- There was no attempt to redirect resources away from mainstream users and towards those with the greatest needs in the community.
- Library staff were not engaged with the social exclusion agenda and just passed this work onto the 'experts'. In worst-case scenarios this work was seen as a distraction from or in competition with 'real library work'.
- Specialist staff and teams had little or no access to resources and their work was not embedded in service plans and priorities.
- There were no performance indicators to measure the outcomes and impact of this work.
- The value of this work was not recognized by decision-makers and these services were extremely vulnerable to budget cuts.

Whole Service Approach

To avoid these pitfalls it is important that a whole service approach is used to tackling social exclusion. In terms of staffing structures this means that social exclusion is reflected in job titles, job descriptions, person specifications and competency frameworks. For example, community development should be embedded in the job description of every library worker – from frontline assistant to service head – so that no member of staff can say that tackling social exclusion is 'not my job'. The benefits of this whole service approach are that:

- Staffing structures are aligned with the service strategy and able to deliver social exclusion objectives.
- Staff are clear about what is expected of them and can see the connection between their individual roles and broader organizational aims and objectives.
- Everyone is pulling in the same direction to ensure that community needs are met.
- Performance can be measured in terms of community impact and outcomes.
- There is a positive effect on the organizational culture as staff values, attitudes and behaviour are aligned with community needs.
- Services to excluded communities become embedded and not vulnerable to changes of policy or budget reductions.

Service structures should also be aligned with the social exclusion strategy to ensure that the right services are in the right places and at the right times to meet community needs.

There are many ways to deliver library services, particularly to excluded communities, ranging from mobile provision to deposit collections, outreach and community development. Services can also be delivered in partnership with other organizations and through co-location of services on multi-use sites. Resources should be diverted from building-based services to fund community-based initiatives. *Framework for the Future* concluded that for libraries to play a role in civic life they have to remain relevant to the needs of all within the community:

> Those needs cannot be assumed or taken for granted. Libraries must be adept at seeking, understanding and serving the needs of non-users, some of whom may be ill at ease in a library setting. Library authorities need to survey and review the needs of the communities they serve, focusing particularly on the needs of people who do not currently use libraries but might be attracted to do so and might benefit disproportionately from the services on offer. This should form part of the local authority community strategy. (DCMS 2003: 42)

Systems

Library systems should also be aligned with the social exclusion strategy to ensure that there are no barriers to access. These barriers include: unsuitable or unduly restrictive opening hours; lack of or negative signage; charging policies which disadvantage those on low incomes; and arbitrary book loan periods and borrowing limits.

Opening Hours

Static branch libraries are the backbone of most public library services and yet many of them are not open enough hours or at times when people want to use them. This represents a waste of resources – buildings account for a large proportion of the total library budget – and cuts to hours can trigger a downward spiral in use which eventually leads to library closures. The Local Government Association found that the impact of increasing opening hours included 'more use of ICT facilities, more visitors in total, more visits from target groups and more books lent' (LGA 2004: 24).

The Modernisation Review of Public Libraries (DCMS 2010a) noted that people's lives and expectations have changed and library opening hours need to respond to their communities' needs and wants including those of families. Library services should determine opening hours in consultation with the community. Libraries can consider using volunteers to help deliver longer opening hours. Of the respondents to the Department of Culture, Media and Sport's *Taking Part* survey (2011) who had not visited a public library, 15 per cent said they did not have time to go. The most innovative libraries are changing – opening later in the evening and opening on Sundays. For example, in Suffolk, Sunday opening was introduced across the whole library service and attracted 5,200 additional visitors per week. The *Modernisation Review* recommended that: 'Local authorities should review opening hours to assess whether they meet local need, including that of families. Opening hours should reflect customer demand' (DCMS 2010a: 26).

Fees and Fines

The fees and fines culture is still a significant barrier, fed by press stories of people who forget to renew their library books and accrue huge fines (though in most authorities there is an upper fines limit) and a staff attitude driven by a mistaken view of fairness. Library staff tend to like rules and want to apply them evenly so that, regardless of personal circumstances, fines are levied on rich and poor alike. Those who do not pay fines can have their library membership suspended and they may even be taken to court for recovery of outstanding books. A fines amnesty would produce the same outcome without stigmatizing whole families who feel that they cannot afford to use the library service. These stories spread by word of mouth like wildfire and contribute to the significant under-use of libraries by disadvantaged communities. Library fines have become a substantial source of income and it is unlikely that policy-makers will discontinue them, even though there is little evidence to show that they have the desired effect (to encourage people to return their books) and plenty of evidence to show that they have a negative impact on library usage.

Welcome to Your Library (2004) assessed the accessibility of library services for asylum seekers and refugees via mystery shopping visits to libraries. The following barriers to access were identified:

- External signage – premises hard to find; no external direction visible; not clear where it is until front door.
- Internal signage – unclear and no arrows indicating location of resources.
- Environment – insufficient seating; unwelcoming, especially for families.
- Stock and information – no evidence of books in other languages.
- Joining procedures – when enquirer asked how to join, staff member simply handed out a form, no particular sensitivity to possibility that person might be 'new to the system'.
- Customer care – staff not friendly at all, an asylum seeker or refugee would find it difficult to ask for information.
- Other – general perception that asylum seekers and refugees would not be welcome unless UK status was 'correct', i.e. sufficient to meet joining evidence requirements. (ADP 2004: 28–9)

Welcome to Your Library helped to shift the culture of many UK public libraries and made them more accessible and open to excluded communities. For example, some library authorities stopped asking for proof of identity and address when people joined the service as this was a particular barrier to people who were homeless or highly mobile.

Organizational Culture

Social exclusion strategy, structures and systems are vital but without an appropriate organizational culture it is not possible to meet community needs. Organizational change is the toughest challenge in developing needs-based and community-led library services – how to create a culture which can enable community needs to be identified, prioritized and met. For this to happen the strategy, structures and systems must be aligned with a set of values, attitudes and behaviours which are owned and consistently enacted by every member of staff. Such a process takes time and will not happen overnight. It has been suggested that culture change can take up to five, ten or even fifteen years. Failure to embed culture change will mean that staff may not buy into the social exclusion strategy and nothing will really change beyond cosmetic alterations. The norms and expectations of a community-led library service must be constantly reinforced to prevent a slow slide back to the status quo as the staff seek refuge in their comfort zones. This is much less likely to happen if the staff have been involved in the strategy development process and if they are working in job roles and with systems which have mainstreamed social exclusion.

The development of social exclusion strategy, structure and systems is the starting point of the culture change process, but it will still take some time for staff to adapt to the new ways of 'how we do things around here'. There are, however, a number of mechanisms which can be deployed to accelerate culture change, including service planning, performance measurement and workforce development.

Service Planning

The social exclusion strategy needs to be translated into operational policies and plans. This is a good opportunity to involve staff and local communities in the service planning process to identify shared outcomes for the library service and the local community. To ensure that this process is fully inclusive nothing should be committed to paper until staff and community have agreed key aims and objectives. In other words, staff should not come up with a draft plan which the community is then consulted on, because it is difficult to challenge the written word laid down in 'tablets of stone' by 'the experts'. The co-production of a service plan also paves the way for the community to be actively involved in service delivery and evaluation.

Achieving Inclusion (Leicester City Libraries 2000) is a good example of a library service plan which was co-produced by the staff of Leicester City libraries in partnership with some highly diverse local communities. The library plan included current performance levels, who was using the library service, and who was not using the service and why. Local performance was compared with national standards and targets for improvement were set, particularly with regard to engaging excluded communities. These targets covered every aspect of the service including access, books and reading, ICT, lifelong learning, services for children and young people and services to older people. There was a strong social inclusion focus on managing diversity and delivering equality.

Leicester City's three-year library service plan generated a wide range of recommendations (with timescale and budget) including:

> ... to change the staffing structure ... to reduce the distance between decision making and front line [and] to review all working and professional practices to eliminate those which can be considered to be institutionally racist and which have become barriers to achieving equality and diversity in both the workforce and service provision. (Leicester City Libraries 2000: 56)

These recommendations demonstrate how organizational culture can inform social exclusion strategy, structures and systems.

Performance Measures

Producing a service plan is one thing but delivering it is another and to ensure that targets are met and progress is on track it is necessary to devise a set of appropriate performance indicators. These should be developed at the same time as the service plan and be co-produced by library staff and the local community. The question for staff should be: 'How will you know if service plan objectives and targets have been achieved?' And the question for the community should be: 'How will you know when the library service has made a positive impact on your lives?'

Traditional ways of measuring library service performance (by counting book issues or visitors, for example) are of no use when measuring community impact and outcomes. Quantitative indicators need to be complemented with qualitative tools such as the *Social Impact Audit* devised by Bryson and Usherwood (2002) who identified five issues that need to be considered by public museums, libraries and archives:

- Library services must increase the regularity of two-way conversations with the public (such as regular social audits). There must be an asking, listening and acting on stakeholders' interests through outcome-based evaluations.
- There needs to be an awareness of the significance of initial conditions for programmes. In other words, social objectives must be clear, relevant, strategic (this means taking a long-term view, with a consideration of the ultimate consequences), and respecting of stakeholders' interests (including the staff who must provide the service).
- Social impact auditing must build trust through honest, open, and accessible execution. The relationship between social objectives and stakeholders'

interests are made visible through a system of outcome-based evaluative techniques, including the social impact audit.

- Library services must be willing to act and follow through, adjusting their objectives, and finding new and creative routes to producing their final services. Expectations are increased in the public when a dialogue is conducted rather than a monologue.
- An increase in financial and human resources is required to establish the capabilities to conduct outcome-based assessment.

This study concluded that libraries can:

> ... create opportunities for people to engage with others in a shared space, providing the raw materials for education and the crafting of social capital that can help bind communities together. The social audit process offers a tool for listening to stakeholders and informing policy makers. Qualitative data, obtained via social audits, are valid evidence and should be used by professionals and policy makers to inform and improve the management of cultural organizations. (Bryan and Usherwood 2002: 7–8)

Workforce Development

Workforce development can also be used to accelerate culture change. The changing role of staff in libraries is taking them out from behind desks and away from books to deal directly with a wide range of user groups. This has considerable implications, not just for the training and development of existing staff but for the recruitment of future staff and the structuring and deployment of the workforce:

- Sufficient funding and appropriate training need to be put in place to ensure that staff are fully supported and equipped to engage with socially excluded communities.
- Staffing structures need to reflect the changing roles of library staff and efforts must be made to match staff skills to appropriate types and levels of work.
- Policy-makers and library service managers need to address the issue of what kind of skills the library workers of the future need to have.

We consider this issue in more detail in our chapter on staffing, recruitment and education where we explore the skills and competencies that library workers must have to build relationships with excluded communities.

Community-Led Mainstreaming

> One of the major accomplishments around institutional change was the extent to which each of the four systems began talking about the needs of socially excluded populations: 'Before Working Together, this was not happening in

any of the four systems and the project put that on the map.' Library systems, including those outside of the project, are talking about non-users and how systems can be more cognizant of their needs. (Atkey 2008: 11)

Apply Findings or Learnings?

While WTP was considered a pilot project with a finite timeline, project funders, participating library systems and other library systems observing the project quickly became aware of the potential systemic impact that project learnings would have on library services. Accordingly, there were a number of fundamental principles which were discovered that need to be applied when mainstreaming community-led approaches into library services.

Since community-led work is fundamentally based on the premise that each community and library is different, this individual difference will result in programme and service development which will fit the specific needs and contexts of each community. The Working Together *Toolkit* properly highlights a number of these *findings*, while also, and more importantly, providing a non-prescriptive overview of the methods and approaches which library systems should use to incorporate the *learnings* of the project.

A library system which will consider incorporating and mainstreaming a community-led approach to library service development must differentiate the distinction between findings and learnings: 'Findings are the barriers and community needs identified through Working Together. Learnings, on the other hand, are the community development processes adapted to a library context that have been developed through the project' (Atkey 2008: 34).

While it is possible to generalize some 'findings' across various communities (such as barriers faced by socially excluded community members using library services), the vast majority are site- or context-specific. Just because one community identifies a particular need does not mean that another community will identify the same need. However, 'learnings' regarding the community development approaches and methodologies used within a library context are quite portable and can be adapted to fit within each library's specific context(s).

Whose Job Is It Anyway?

There are a number of different approaches which can be taken in applying community-led work to a library system. From the perspective of WTP staff and senior management, there was 'a stronger desire … to ensure that community-led service planning became an operating paradigm for library systems, rather than have it fall to one or several individuals within a system.' In order for this community-led approach to have the greatest impact, library systems should develop senior-level plans and messaging that support all staff to work with the community. There may be benefits in creating a few positions working with 'specific populations', or to act as a resource as other library staff learn and adopt community-led work.

However, there are a number of inherent risks in only allocating community-led work to a dedicated few people to complete, including:

- 'community work becoming [viewed as] "that person's job"' (Atkey 2008: 36)
- increased likelihood that special positions and programmes are eliminated when library budgets decrease, and
- '[challenges] creating specialized positions in unionized environments' (Atkey 2008: 77).

There are also risks to both the staff and the community if this 'specialist staff' approach is taken. The risk to 'specialist staff' is that their work may not be understood by other library staff who approach the community from a traditional service planning perspective. The risk to community members is that differing and specialized service delivery by a few staff can lead to inequitable service delivery. The type of service they receive from a library staff member will drastically vary based upon the service approach employed. The benefits of mainstreaming the 'specialist approach' across all positions in the library service outweigh the limited application of this approach by a few library staff members.

Barriers to Mainstreaming

As with any change process, there tend to be a significant number of systemic cultural-based barriers, which are either internally imposed by people working in libraries or more structural in nature and will impede the implementation of a mainstreaming process. The application of a new service model does not fundamentally change the work library staff carry out, but it does primarily change their approach to this work. As a result, many staff:

- … tend to perceive [the new service approach] as additional activities [or work]
- [feel] 'threatened' or 'territorial' when changes are suggested and may perceive new ways of working as a criticism of previous methods. (Atkey 2008: 36)

A number of other barriers were faced by the library systems involved in WTP which limited their ability to begin mainstreaming the approach. One of the most significant barriers, perhaps, given that this was a pilot project with a finite timeline, was that learnings and findings were constantly occurring throughout the four years. Consequently it was not feasible to expect that learnings would immediately generate fundamental systemic change. In addition, other issues arose when trying to mainstream community-led approaches, including but not limited to:

- In the case of the model branch (discussed in more detail below), staff commitment to the process and support for the model branch from senior management.
- Library managers did not have the authority, or felt they were not in a position to make changes – to alter staffing, to restructure staff schedules, to eliminate current programmes and services – to support community-led opportunities, without senior level management support.
- Staff who had bought into community-led approaches were hesitant to implement these approaches without senior and mid-level management displaying support.
- The need to determine how best to implement change within each individual library systems culture.

As tangible evidence and support for community-led library services has accumulated since the findings and learnings were disseminated to library systems at the conclusion of the project, and as library systems either begin or continue to adopt this approach (Prendergast 2011, Edmonton Public Library 2011, Williment et al. 2011b), the need for senior management to begin addressing identified barriers is vital.

Model Branches

Although it was not initially identified as a project deliverable, each of the four WTP library sites began exploring and testing approaches to mainstreaming community-led work within a branch context. The purpose of doing this was to determine 'what ... a branch look[s] like that uses a community development approach to work with and in the community' (Atkey 2008: 72).

One of the major advantages of focusing on a branch was that it created a more manageable and tangible process for WTP staff to address than 'creating wholesale systemic change in a short timeframe' (Atkey 2008: 11).

Given the short timeframe, and the number of different approaches which were tested, the outcomes were varied, in part due to 'drastically different starting points in branch staff understanding and acceptance of community development approaches. The variation was also attributed to different approaches taken by each of the sites, as well as the degree to which the development of a model branch was a focus of local Working Together initiatives' (Atkey 2008: 10).

Many of the sites were more easily able to action findings, as opposed to more systemic changes based on learnings. In many instances, the findings enabled branch staff to make small changes at the branch (for example, giving certain collections increased visibility or taking branch staff out into the community to observe community-led approaches).

While these may seem like relatively small steps taken by branch staff compared to the approaches taken by WTP staff, it provided an opportunity to begin involving library staff and to recognize that community-led approaches were not 'just project-based'.

Successful Mainstreaming

There are numerous examples of successful approaches taken during or at the end of Working Together that have assisted in mainstreaming community-led approaches within the participating library systems. For instance in Vancouver, a significant initiative was undertaken:

> [Steps to] identify policy barriers to library access for socially excluded populations have been undertaken in Vancouver ... The circulation, security and customer service manuals have been reviewed by teams consisting of both Working Together and system staff. The intent was to ensure that the manuals provided staff the flexibility required to make values-based decisions. Further, a report on circulation policy barriers was developed with extensive community involvement and recommendations shared with VPL staff and Board. Such initiatives begin to build awareness amongst many staff that barriers to library access do in fact exist for some individuals and communities. (Atkey 2008: 35)

In Halifax, a Community Development Manager was hired to assist in the systemic integration of this approach in branches and service areas (Williment et al. 2011b). This has also included creating library staff training sessions, and developing regional-based community-led service plans, which are multi-phased (see Figure 9.1) and look at service planning holistically, taking into account library and community capacity/assets (ibid.).

Multi-Phased Planning Process		
Phase I	**Phase II**	**Phase III**
Determine Baseline	**Engage**	**Change**
Internal Assets	Increase staff capacity	Branch/Systemic Change
External Assets	Work with individuals in the community	Change to services/ programs
Communicate and Evaluate		

Figure 9.1   Multi-phased planning process

In order to successfully integrate and adopt a community-led or needs-based approach (Pateman 2003), service planning requires a significant commitment from senior decision-makers within a library system. As learned through Working Together, library management – at both senior and mid-level – will need to be responsible for building broader support for systemic change. In part this will include:

- [adding] additional resources at least in the short term
- displaying support from the library system:
  - communicating support for change
  - targeted messaging to staff and the community
- clarification of the role of the existing service model and its continued application while implementing a community-led approach
- making commitments to adjusting staff structures
- addressing changes to job descriptions, including emphasis on working in communities, and non-traditional work environments
- [dedicating the] time necessary for training, and
- the restructuring and reprioritizing of activities. (Atkey 2008: 10)

By ensuring that a vision from senior management enables cultural adjustments, resource (re)allocation and accountability, public library systems will be well on their way to ensuring the development of needs-based and inclusive library services.

Helpful Hints

#1: The national evaluator identified the importance of ensuring the staff member has the authority to create change:

> The higher the CDL's level of authority, the more empowered the CDL was to create effective change both at the branch and within the system more broadly. While building this responsibility and authority into the position appeared to contribute to more meaningful systemic change at both the branch and system level, it may also have contributed to tension between the branch manager and CDL because there was no direct reporting responsibility between the two. (Atkey 2008: 12)

As identified through WTP, regardless of whether a library system systematically mainstreams community-led work or assigns the work to a few people, it will be important to both 'create a network and informal supports between those who largely work in isolation so that they could share their experiences and strategies [and ensure] the reporting out of project learnings is also happening within each ... system'.

#2: Community needs should be at the heart of your public library strategy, structures, systems and organizational culture:

- Develop community engagement or community-led statements to clarify to senior management, staff and the community the approach the library will be taking.
- Integrate community-led wording into the libraries' mission and vision statements.

#3: Educate senior management (without this there will not be buy-in):

- Explain the rationale and teach community-led language, while also ensuring that buy-in moves beyond 'speaking community-led'. The focus should be on actions not adoption of language.
- Determine and implement system-wide and branch-based plans, ensuring accountability, timelines and levels of authority.
- Make it a part of everyone's job.

#4: Social exclusion should be mainstreamed across all areas of library activity and management.

#5: Demand-led resourcing is generally not equitable for socially excluded groups and communities. Public library services may have to redistribute or redirect resources to meet the needs of the socially excluded.

#6: Guidelines should be developed to help library services move to a needs-based service. This should include information on management and organizational structures that work for communities.

#7: All library services should introduce local service targets as part of detailed library planning and monitoring.

Chapter 10
Standards and Monitoring
of Services

In this chapter we consider how to work with local people to create meaningful performance indicators and evaluation systems. Performance management of public libraries has gone almost full circle in the UK. At one time there was little or no meaningful performance measurement beyond the simplistic counting of library visits and book issues. Then, when public libraries entered the world of efficiency, effectiveness and 'value for money' they started to count everything while almost ignoring the value of what was being provided. The whole point and purpose of a library service could be summed up in the metric which measured cost per visit – the total cost of a library service divided by the number of times it was used. Today we are moving away from statistical quantitative indicators and towards those which measure quality, satisfaction, impact and outcomes. We argue that public libraries are public goods and should be measured by their relevance to the community rather than the number of transactions they perform.

Open to All? (Muddiman et al. 2000b) called for national service standards for public library activities related to social exclusion which were both quantitative and qualitative. Performance indicators and targets should be set to measure the success of library authorities in their attempts to tackle social exclusion. These should include a requirement to specify amounts spent on disadvantaged groups and deprived communities. *Open to All?* also advocated Annual Library Plans and an Oflib (Office for Library Standards) which could inspect public libraries as part of the best value process.

The Working Together Project (WTP) found that there need to be various types of evaluation of community-led service planning and implementation. For each of the people involved in the process evaluation should take place. This will include an overall evaluation of the impact upon an organization, staff and the community. Community-based evaluation should be open-ended, where the community defines the success measures and the questions which will be asked to determine if success occurs from their perspective. Evaluation does not just occur at the end of the process: it must be built into each stage of the community-led service planning process. Evaluation will occur when determining the target group, identifying need, planning service and programme-based responses, and when these services and programmes are delivered. By making evaluation part of the entire planning process, programmes and services should naturally evolve that incorporate community-based needs. This may actually lead to continual evolution of programme and service development.

Annual Library Plans

Universal community profiling and needs assessment only came about by compulsion when the government decided that every library authority should compile an Annual Library Plan (ALP) of what they intended to do over the next 12 months. This ALP had to be informed by a community profile and description of the local area and who lived in it. While this was a positive step forward, many libraries continued to rely on outdated and unreliable official data, and the views of local communities were not sought when ALPs were being compiled. In some cases the ALP was written by the Chief Librarian in glorious isolation, without even consulting staff. The voice of users, and of course non-users, was missing within these ALPs, which were often just a description of the local community rather than an assessment of needs. Also, after the ALPs were written and submitted to the government there was no monitoring mechanism to ensure that their contents were being delivered.

Public Library Service Standards

This lack of evaluation was addressed when the government introduced a set of Public Library Service Standards (PLSS), which each library service was encouraged to achieve. After lengthy consultation with professional librarians this set of standards was finalized and adjusted in the light of implementation. Unfortunately the PLSS were almost exclusively quantitative measures which monitored the number of inputs and outputs created by a library service. There were no real qualitative measures which assessed the impact and outcomes of library services on local communities. There was also no requirement to seek the views of local people to ask them about the effect which libraries had on their lives.

Public Library Users Survey

Another positive development was the launch of an annual Public Library Users Survey (PLUS) and later a version for young people. This was a useful mechanism for getting the views of service users on a wide range of subjects including book stock and information services. It could also be used to measure their satisfaction with the services they received so it was a qualitative step forward from ALPs and PLSS. But PLUS suffered from the halo effect whereby service users would give only positive feedback about their library, partly because they liked the staff and partly because they were fearful that negative feedback could lead to library closures. The major flaw in the PLUS methodology was that it only sought the views of regular library users who made up, at best, 20 per cent of local communities. The voice of passive/lapsed users (who made up another 20 per cent) and non-users (at

60 per cent, the majority of local people) was not heard. As a result, PLUS often led to library services being tailored even more closely to the needs of existing users while the needs of potential and non-users were completely ignored.

Despite the many faults of ALPs, PLSS and PLUS they were at least attempts by central government to ensure that libraries were meeting minimum national standards which addressed local needs. In some cases PLSS created a business case for library services to lobby for more resources, for example if the standard for books purchased per 1,000 local population was not met. But many library authorities did not even try to meet the standards and there were no effective sanctions or interventions that central government could make. The default position was always the 1964 Public Libraries Act which required every local authority to provide a 'comprehensive and efficient' library service to its local people. But 'comprehensive and efficient' was never defined and was open to wide interpretation by local councils. This created a postcode lottery whereby where you lived determined the quality and quantity of the library services which you could hope to receive.

Many professional librarians played the ALP, PLSS and PLUS games because they had to and not because they wanted to. They would rather have been left alone with their assumptions and second-guesses of community needs. After all, they knew best. With this lack of pull from the profession and a decreasing push from central government, ALPs, PLSS and PLUS were slowly watered down and finally removed altogether.

Improving Data and Research

The Modernisation Review of Public Libraries recognized that:

> If we are to understand the value of libraries we must research and analyse their take up and their impact. To examine how libraries can contribute to meeting local needs, library services need a radical change in data and research collection. Data exists at national level but may not be being used by local decision makers and practitioners effectively; national and local research initiatives have been undertaken without sufficient coordination and small scale local evaluations and research have limited application nationally. (DCMS 2010a: 47)

Data

There are concerns about the type of data being collectively used by libraries, and a number of library authorities have expressed frustration that local statistics are extremely positive whilst the national picture does not reflect those changes. While measuring book issues and visits may still be relevant, there is a need for more outcome- and impact-focused monitoring. Community satisfaction is an important measure and there should be better measurement of digital participation.

CIPFA Statistics

CIPFA statistics are the independent source of data about local government services. Established as a partnership between local authorities and CIPFA (the Chartered Institute of Public Finance and Accountancy), the annual public library statistics have been collected for many decades and present a consistent picture of library use as evidenced by loans, acquisitions, visits, etc. They are used by library authorities as a management information tool in benchmarking and self-assessment. The data is collected from local authorities annually at the end of the financial year. Given the quantitative nature of the CIPFA statistics it is inevitable that they are more useful for measuring the cost, rather than the quality, of library services and whether or not libraries are meeting community needs.

CIPFA surveys provided information about the number of public library users and of visits made, but there was little data gathered regarding other aspects of library usage. For example, there was no attempt to find out why some people did not use library services. In order to fill this gap in knowledge DCMS commissioned Ipsos MORI to carry out research into public library usage involving face-to-face surveys with a representative sample of 5,000 people aged 15+ in England.

The *Libraries Omnibus Survey* (Ipsos MORI 2009a) was designed with two main aims: to find out what people visit public libraries to do; and to investigate the level of latent demand – that is, how many people are doing activities elsewhere that could potentially be done in a library. Of those surveyed, 41 per cent had been to a public library in the previous 12 months. The activities undertaken by these library users included:

- borrowing a book – 81 per cent
- researching for own interest – 30 per cent
- participating in children's activities – 20 per cent
- borrowing music, films or computer games – 19 per cent
- using a computer – 16 per cent
- finding information on jobs, health, training, local events, etc. – 15 per cent
- using as a quiet place to study – 13 per cent
- other – 9 per cent.

The *Survey* found that there was a high degree of potential demand – that is, people who had not been to a public library in the previous 12 months, but who would have taken part in an activity which could have been undertaken in a public library. Therefore there was the potential that these people could become library users. For instance, of the 48 per cent of the people who had not visited a library in the past 12 months, 31 per cent had either borrowed or wanted to borrow a book. That was 15 per cent of the total sample.

Of those who accessed the Internet via a public place (4.8 per cent of the sample), just over half had done so in a public library. So there was potential for a rise in the number of people using public libraries for Internet access. Computer usage in library reduces as income rises, suggesting that this provision is serving the lower-income members of the community. Twelve per cent of the sample had used the Internet to look at public library websites.

CIPFA has also considered evaluating 'alternative' use of the library service that would track a visitor's journey through a library. From this, questions could be developed to more effectively collect valuable information relating to digital technology, use of the Internet/e-books and services provided by libraries outside their traditional scope, such as crèches, reading groups etc.

Taking Part *Survey*

The DCMS *Taking Part* survey (2011a) measures the percentage of the population using public libraries. It comprises face-to-face interviews and provides both national and regional figures for library participation, including a picture of usage outside the library premises such as website use, home visits, outreach work and mobile library attendance. The *Taking Part* survey measures library use for leisure purposes and therefore excludes visits for the purpose of academic study or paid work. It shows an increase in the proportion of children using libraries but a year-on-year decline in adult use. It also reported that between 2001 and 2010 the proportion of people visiting a public library in the UK fell from 56 per cent to 40 per cent. Participation rates continue to be significantly higher among those in the upper socioeconomic groups and in the least deprived areas of England. Public libraries are used by 44 per cent of people in the upper socioeconomic groups compared to just 33 per cent in the lower socioeconomic groups.

National Indicator for Libraries

The government tried to redress the balance between quantitative and qualitative performance measures by introducing a National Indicator Set (NIS) for all services provided by local authorities, including public libraries. These indicators would form the basis of Local Area Agreements (LAAs) which would be local strategic plans drawn up by Local Strategic Partnerships (LSPs) and monitored by central government. These new structures became driven by process, governance and bureaucracy rather than community needs. The community was represented on the LSPs and had a voice in the LAAs, but they were small players compared to organizations and institutions such as local authorities who did not want to give up or share their decision-making powers. As a result the LSPs and LAAs were top-down and not informed by grassroots opinion. In the horse trading which went on to select NIs for inclusion in the LAAs, public libraries came very far down the priority list. Even if the NI for public libraries (NI 9) was included in the LAA (only ten local authorities included it in 2010) it was of very limited value because all it measured was the number of local adults who had visited a public library in the past 12 months. It completely excluded children and young people and it made no attempt to measure user satisfaction or whether community needs had been met. Because of the inadequacy of NI 9 many public libraries chose instead to position themselves within the LAA by providing evidence of how they were contributing to more relevant and meaningful National Indicators, including:

- **NI 1** Percentage of people who believe people from different backgrounds get on well together
- **NI 2** Percentage of people who feel that they belong to their neighbourhood
- **NI 3** Civic participation in the local area
- **NI 4** Percentage of people who feel they can influence decisions in their locality
- **NI 5** Satisfaction with local area
- **NI 6** Participation in regular volunteering
- **NI 7** Environment for a thriving third sector
- **NI 9** Use of public libraries
- **NI 11** Engagement in the arts
- **NI 13** Migrants' English language skills and knowledge
- **NI 15 & 16** Violent and acquisitive crime rates
- **NI 17** Perceptions of anti-social behaviour
- **NI 19** Young offenders – reduced rate of re-offending
- **NI 23** Perceptions of respect and dignity
- **NI 45** Young offenders engaged in education, employment, training
- **NI 50** Emotional health of children
- **NI 72–117** Children and young people – Enjoy and Achieve and Positive Contribution
- **NI 119** People's overall health and well-being
- **NI 120** Mortality rate
- **NI124** People with a long-term condition supported
- **NI 138** Satisfaction of people over 65 with both home and neighbourhood
- **NI 139** People over 65 receiving information, assistance and support to live independently
- **NI 140** Fair treatment by local services
- **NI 141 & 142** Vulnerable people achieving and maintaining independent living
- **NI 144** Offenders in employment at end of order/licence
- **NI 146** Adults with learning disabilities in employment
- **NI 148** Care-leavers in employment, education or training
- **NI 150** Adults in contact with secondary mental health services in employment
- **NI 161** Learners achieving a Level 1 qualification in literacy
- **NI 162–165** Contribution to outcomes
- **NI 179** Value for money

We know that libraries can change lives, help learning and improve community cohesion. That is why it is essential that we measure the impact on library users. If we are to convince local and national leaders and partner organizations of the value of public libraries we must produce evidence which connects library use to local and national priorities.

Impact and Outcomes

In November 2008 DCMS and its Capturing Impact Reference Group commissioned BOP Consulting to undertake a study of the existing evidence base on the impact of public libraries. The resulting report, *Capturing the Impact of Libraries*, was published by DCMS in March 2009 (BOP Consulting 2009). This research confirmed that public libraries contribute to a number of policy priorities. For example, 78 per cent of Bookstart coordinators who distribute Bookstart packs in nearly every local authority in the country are funded by library services. Bookstart has been found to impact positively on parental reading habits and children's progress in early years.

The BOP Consulting report points to strong correlations between literacy levels and a variety of physical and mental health and well-being outcomes. For instance, the Reader Organisation's Get Into Reading initiative has been found to have significant potential to increase feelings of well-being in participants. Links between libraries and a number of other public policy agendas are also identified in the BOP report. Libraries' ability to engage with excluded groups, such as refugees and asylum seekers or children in care, can contribute to building stronger and safer communities, for example.

Libraries' work with preschool children – through Bookstart Rhymetime, Baby Bounce and storytime sessions particularly – makes a valuable contribution to language and literacy development. Research has shown that these are accurate predictors of educational attainment later in the life of the child.

Despite these valuable examples, the impact of libraries is not often evaluated effectively. This is predominantly because of the incredible complexity and high number of variables which make it difficult or impossible to prove the 'library effect'. In addition, the projects being appraised are usually pilots with small sample groups, because baselines against which to monitor improvement are not available, or because the studies are limited in their reach.

Model of Impact

Building on the BOP research DCMS have proposed a Model of Impact which makes a link between public library activities and resources, immediate personal benefits, intermediate outcomes and long-term outcomes (see Figure 10.1).

Public library activities and resources	Immediate personal benefits
Free book loans Journals and newspapers Reference collections Access to ICT and Internet Information, advice and guidance Dedicated expert staff Council information and guidance Reading groups Study support Formal and informal learning, including basic skills Job-hunting support Outreach Public space Activities and events Third sector information Community information Health and well-being information, signposting and support Personalized service Access to partner and shared services MP and council surgeries Volunteering	EMPOWERED INFORMED ENRICHED SAVING MONEY ENJOYMENT
Intermediate outcomes	**Long-term outcomes**
SOCIAL CAPITAL Involvement in democratic process, service design, participation and volunteering Supporting the development of social networks and relationships Capacity building the third sector Awareness of rights, benefits and external services	Stronger communities Increasing 'pro-social' behaviour and reducing anti-social behaviour Enhanced local democracy and legitimacy Reduced prejudice and hate crimes Reduced crime and fear of crime
NON-COGNITIVE SKILLS DEVELOPMENT Personal, social and emotional skills	Improved employability Improved ability to maintain stable relationships
COGNITIVE SKILLS DEVELOPMENT Speech, language and communication Literacy and language development Other adult basic skills (such as ICT, numeracy, health literacy) Business support and career management skills	Social mobility Higher earnings Improved employability Better physical and mental health Reduced offending
WELL-BEING AND HEALTH Increased health information Enable better choices about health Self-management abilities Reduced boredom and social isolation Improved mental and physical well-being Access to online transactions such as appointments booking	Increased life expectancy Better quality of life Better health and well-being Increased self-management and independence Reduced costs of health and social care

Figure 10.1   Model of impact

The contribution of local services to local well-being has also been considered by a number of other studies.

Libraries and Local Well-Being

Well-being is increasingly recognized by central government, local government and their strategic partners as being of key relevance to people's lives and a vital consideration for improving local area policy and service delivery decisions. This higher priority means it is now important to develop robust measures of well-being.

The concept and language of well-being was first introduced at the local level through the Local Government Act 2000. The Act included a new power of well-being, providing local authorities with the power to do whatever they consider necessary to promote or improve the economic, social or environmental well-being of their area. Following this, useful indicators aimed at measuring quality of life were developed and are now widely used by local authorities and their partners to track changing conditions of life at the local level.

In 2006 the UK government's Whitehall Wellbeing Working Group developed a statement of common understanding of well-being for policy-makers:

> Wellbeing is a positive physical, social and mental state; it is not just the absence of pain, discomfort and incapacity. It arises not only from the action of individuals, but from a host of collective goods and relationships with other people. It requires that basic needs are met, that individuals have a sense of purpose, and that they feel able to achieve important personal goals and participate in society. It is enhanced by conditions that include supportive personal relationships, involvement in empowered communities, good health, financial security, rewarding employment, and a healthy and attractive environment.
>
> Government's role is to enable people to have fair access now and in the future to the social, economic and environmental resources needed to achieve wellbeing. An understanding of the combined effect of policies on the way people experience their lives is important for designing and prioritising them. (Steuer and Marks 2008)

This powerful statement goes to the heart of developing needs-based and community-led library services. It encompasses collective goods (which can include the public library), meeting needs and empowered communities. It recognizes the role that government has in providing fair access to resources and that people's experiences should be used to design and prioritize services. Measuring well-being is useful for local authorities and their strategic partners to:

- understand local needs – to enable resources to be targeted to areas and population groups where they are most required
- measure outcomes – to assess performance and shape future priorities
- track progress – capturing 'distance travelled' and the extent to which some of the leading indicators for achieving local area outcomes are being met
- encourage partnership working and the pooling of budgets – between public libraries and other public service providers, linked to the cross-cutting nature of many well-being measures
- demonstrate *positive* local change – so that public libraries' energies to achieve change through initiatives which focus on developing human potential and enhancing lived experience are recognized and rewarded
- facilitate a shift from an emphasis on service provision to community-focused outcomes.

Measuring well-being can also support public libraries and their partners to measure 'real' progress by directly capturing people's experience of their lives rather than using proxy indicators. Given its immediate relevance to people's lives, this may also provide greater opportunity for better engagement with the community on shaping local policy and local service delivery.

A three-tiered approach is recommended for measuring well-being at the local level: universal level, domain level and targeted level. These levels are not mutually exclusive. Deciding at which level to measure will depend on the rationale for collecting new information and the potential for decisions and actions to be taken as a result of the findings in each local area.

Level 1: Measuring Well-Being at the Universal Level

The universal level provides an overall, cross-cutting measure of people's experience of life. It provides headline findings at a community (universal) level and a basis from which more detailed exploration and analysis can take place (for example, by exploring different domains – satisfaction with health, employment, family, etc. – or by asking how overall well-being could be improved). It would typically be captured by a single-item measure (or small group of measures) asking people to rate their overall satisfaction with life. Universal level well-being data could be used:

- to assess differences in overall well-being between population groups and/ or geographical neighbourhoods within a local authority area, as a basis for further exploration and targeted action
- to analyse universal well-being data against existing subjective and objective data to identify the key determinants or predictors of people's well-being at a local level (for example, good physical health, being economically active, level of income, residents' feeling a sense of belonging in relation to where they live, quality of open spaces, etc.).

Level 2: Measuring Well-Being at the Domain Level

The domain level measures different aspects or dimensions of people's well-being; for example, in relation to health, community safety, economic circumstances and so on. It moves beyond providing an overall assessment of outcomes to explore differences and variations within a local authority area, drilling down into some of the key components of people's life experience. Domain-level well-being data could be used:

- to explore how a community's well-being varies across different domains of life (health, family and relationships, neighbourhood, etc.) to inform the targeting of local resources
- to 'drill down' to provide a more detailed understanding of a community's well-being in relation to a particular domain already identified as a local priority (for example, social support and engagement), as a basis for future service planning and delivery
- to assess how different community groups and/or geographical neighbourhoods experience different aspects of their life, to provide an evidence base for how activities and services can best be tailored to meet different needs (for example, by ethnicity, by age, by gender, by neighbourhood).

Level 3: Measuring Well-Being at the Targeted Level

The targeted level measures some of the underlying or protective factors affecting people's overall well-being. This could include, for example, autonomy, resilience, self-esteem, feelings of competency, and strength of relationships. This approach could be used across entire local communities; however, over the short to medium term it is likely to be particularly useful for measuring the well-being of people whose circumstances make them vulnerable and who use services locally, such as specific population groups (for example, vulnerable older people over 75), targeted neighbourhoods and service users (for example, looked-after children). Targeted level well-being data could be used:

- to improve understanding of local needs, particularly of vulnerable groups or specific service users, to help inform the design and delivery of public library services and interventions
- to review performance and inform local action in relation to 'closing the gap', where efforts to improve psychological feelings and functioning (around building self-esteem, confidence, aspirations, autonomy and so on) might be needed to reduce inequalities and achieve better outcomes for more people
- to measure the well-being impact of specific initiatives or services being delivered at a local level, through tracking progress and capturing 'distance

travelled' in relation to how people feel and function

- to assess and highlight the importance of targeting resources by public libraries and their partners, towards the enabling/protective factors for people's well-being, to encourage a shift towards more preventative approaches and to improve local area outcomes over the longer term.

It is clear that public libraries can make a major contribution to improving the well-being of local communities. They can provide greater opportunities for communities to influence decisions affecting their library services. They can facilitate regular contact between communities. And they can help communities gain the confidence to exercise control over local circumstances.

Community-Led Approaches to Standards and Monitoring of Services

Evaluation is one of the most fundamental and important components of library services. It helps library systems legitimize their very existence to funders, provides a tool for improving programmes and services, and informs policy decisions. Most importantly it should be used to ensure library-based services are having the desired outcomes and impacts, as anticipated by both library staff and community members.

Working Together took an inductive approach to working with the community. Instead of creating, adapting and maintaining services based on internal discussions amongst library staff, the focus shifted to ensure that targeted communities and individuals in each of the four sites were involved in the monitoring of services. This implies a shift to narrative-based outcome and impact measurement tools, to complement traditional quantitative-based measures.

Traditional Approaches to Standards and Monitoring of Services

Initially, it was important to contextualize the current approaches used within library systems to evaluate services, to determine whether traditional approaches work for all community members. Project staff quickly recognized that existing techniques and approaches to evaluation were not adequate for accurately capturing the impact of services on some existing library users and socially excluded community members. A number of issues were observed with traditional monitoring techniques, including the following:

- They focused solely on services targeting existing library users and services:
  - Evaluation processes developed by library staff were primarily textual or written, thus presuming that the respondents have a high level of literacy.

- They were primarily passive in nature, where participants were asked to fill out forms and give them back *to staff* for interpretation.
- Numeric output measures (such as gate counts, check-out statistics, programme attendance, staff, time, etc.) were the primary data being used to determine failure or success. 'Output measures provide a onetime snapshot, but they do not provide library staff with an in-depth understanding to other important questions such as why, what, how or who' (Working Together 2008: 138).
- The collection, use and [often incorrect] causal connection of output measures were used to set policy, funding, and service directions. They were viewed as objective measures.
- Monitoring was occurring at the beginning and end of a programme or service, through passive or consultative-based means. This created little or no opportunity for adaptation throughout the implementation phase. By primarily limiting community input to the front or back end of a service, community influence was effectively constricted. Leaving evaluation to occur at the end of a programme or service nullifies community-based input into making it more relevant to meeting their needs.
- Many of the evaluation techniques were quantitative in nature. Close-ended surveys narrowly focused community responses to 'fit' within the predefined response categories determined by library staff. The following questions arose from this type of evaluation:
  - Are the responses provided in the evaluation form exhaustive?
  - Are the questions asked reflective of issues relevant to the community?
  - Since evaluation is only occurring at the end of the process, how will it be used to impact future services?

The traditional techniques for monitoring services did not reflect or work for non-library users and socially excluded communities. Many of the current evaluation methods only includes those already involved in a service, thus usually lending themselves better to those with the confidence and literacy skills to complete the measurement tool.

These issues were additionally compounded by the fact that:

- many socially excluded individuals do not use existing services, and
- many approaches employed to reach non-library users, such as telephone surveys, assumed that people lived at a physical address and had access to a phone line.

The Importance of Testing Community-Led Approaches to Standards and Monitoring of Services

As a Canadian federal government-funded project, each of the four WTP sites documented the vast majority of activities which took place over the course of the four-year project. Much of this documentation took the form of both quantitative and qualitative measures. Additionally, a number of different evaluation techniques were employed to ensure that the outcomes of the project could be substantiated. These included, but were not limited to:

- A 'traditional' qualitative interview schedule with four participants from each site. The national independent analysis showed the impact of a community-led approach on employability, the impact of the social conditions socially excluded people faced on employment uptake, and the central role that relationship-building plays in building linkages between underserved communities and the library.
- Monthly, quarterly and annual reports from each of the four sites, consisting of quantitative and qualitative measures. A number of the qualitative-based narratives sources in the Working Together *Toolkit* (2008a) were drawn from these reports.
- An independent and annual external site evaluation conducted by the Social Planning Council and Research Council of British Columbia. These evaluations consisted of interviews with socially excluded community members, library branch staff and managers, CDLs, site supervisors and senior management in each of the respective library systems.

These project-based evaluations continue to serve as a legitimate source of narrative-based impact and outcome measures. Additionally, it should be noted that senior WTP staff submitted reports to the federal funder which included narrative-based outcomes.

How to Use Community-Led Evaluation in Your Library System

Community-led evaluation is tied to each stage of the service planning process. This implies that there is a constant state of evaluation which will be occurring between library staff and members of the community. Additionally, and this can be challenging at times to contemplate, community members should be central in setting success measures. While it is still possible for library staff to set success measures and define positive outcomes, the community you are engaging also needs to be centrally and collaboratively involved in defining these outcomes.

When carrying out each phase of a community assessment – developing relationships, identifying needs, planning service, delivering services – community members should be asked for their evaluation-based feedback. *Evaluation should not just come at the end of the project. It should also take place from the very beginning and throughout the process.* This provides community members with the ability to influence the development and implementation of relevant services and programmes that will have the greatest impact on their lives. If it is not having an impact, community members are active participants to create change, to ensure that it does have an impact. It is very difficult to measure impact which should be defined and agreed by all concerned.

This is likely to both increase the complexity of evaluation and make it more meaningful. When initially developing clear and pre-determined outcomes and impacts (as in traditional evaluation), this is based on what library staff feel and determine will be important for community members at the beginning of the process (and may also reflect what community members initially feel should happen).

However, the entire community-led service model is a process. People change with experiences. The people involved in the process may change. The community's interests and needs may also change. Therefore, by building evaluation into the entire process, the programme and service development will also have to change in order to maintain its relevance.

This method or approach allows library staff to hear community-based need, interpret the feedback they receive in a library context, and discover the direction in which the community wants the process to proceed. The need that was initially identified may change!

It is our responsibility as librarians when following the community-led approach to constantly talk with community members to ensure that the need has been correctly identified within a library context, and is still relevant to the people we are working with. When evaluating it may be important to ask yourself and the community:

- What is the role of evaluation (reword when talking with the community!)?
- How will you know when or if there is a difference in your life?
- How do you know that what we are doing is working? What is working?
- How do you know that what we are doing is not working? What is not working?
- How involved are you in the process (community members and staff – self-reflection)?
- Is or will the programme/service become self-sustaining (ensuring community-based capacity building)?
- How can or should staff/community facilitate the process?

Ultimately, library staff and the community have to trust the community-led approach. This process, based on relationships, allows library staff to observe and begin to understand needs. Evaluation enables libraries to ensure that we stay on the correct path or the need to forge a new path, as determined by communities, when moving into service and programme development.

Best Practice Case Study: Edmonton Public Library

Soleil Surette and Pilar Martinez

Edmonton Public Library (EPL) has begun moving towards a community-led model of evaluation which complements traditional library evaluation. Community-led evaluation is an iterative process that is driven by community and library priorities, which are informed through community feedback, research and funder expectations.

At EPL evaluation takes both informal and formal forms. Informal community-led evaluation occurs through the constant gathering of data and stories by the community librarians in the form of their monthly reports highlighting the challenges and successes of their community work. Initial areas of community interest and trends can be flagged from these reports.

More formal community-led evaluation occurs through an evaluation of the relationship between various community organizations and the library. These are conducted yearly on a rotating basis by community librarians. EPL has engaged in two rounds of organizational reviews, where community librarians, using an interview schedule, engage community organizations in dialogue about the library and community members and the relationship between the organization and the library.

Obtaining meaningful data that can inform potential policy change has been a challenge. One significant barrier is that organizational representatives do not want to say anything negative for fear that this will lead to a discontinuation of the relationship. This was discovered in the initial round of reviews and may point to a failure on the part of EPL to fully engage the organizations in the review process (that is, it was not sufficiently community-led). There is great need to stress that the goal of the evaluation is to improve the relationship, to make it more responsive and meaningful for both sides and that the process should be an ongoing dialogue.

In response to this experience, EPL revised its initial questions, reduced the number and made them more open-ended. EPL has also found that approaching the review with a logic model that explains the library goals in terms of community-led work is very beneficial, as many organizations also use logic models and this helps them to situate the request for feedback.

Staff from community organizations are often very busy, and the relationship with the library is just a small part of what they do, so diverting resources to engage in community-led evaluation of library services can be a challenging request.

Engaging individual community members in formal evaluation can also be problematic. Mindful of issues around traditional forms of library evaluation (literacy levels, capturing mostly users), EPL is piloting the use of small focus groups made up of members or clients of the community organizations with whom EPL has formed relationships. The aim of these groups is to explore what impact, if any, the work of the community librarians has had on these individuals' relationship with the library; what services would these individuals like to access through the library; and what the library would need to do so these individuals felt welcome or involved in using library services.

In terms of engaging current users in community-led evaluation, EPL will be recruiting for focus groups about programming using a customer satisfaction survey. If this pilot is successful, focus groups will become a regular part of evaluation at EPL.

Basic Logic Model

A basic logic model provides a visual means of showing relationships among the resources available to run a programme and the desired outcome of the programme. It illustrates how resources (demand on resources) and activities are linked to outcomes. As shown in Figure 10.2 its elements are resources/inputs, activities, outputs, outcomes and impact.

Resources/ Inputs	Activities	Outputs	Outcomes	Impact
Librarian Travel Programme supplies	Visit a New Moms' group	Number of people visited Number of new moms who came to SSLL programme for the first time	Build relationships Library becomes a 'place' for new moms Child develops early literacy skills	Child has skills to do well in school Moms are connected with other people
Librarian Travel Programme supplies	Conduct computer training at the Welcome Centre for Immigrants (WCI)	Number attending	Enhanced relationship with WCI and with individuals in the community Individuals developed basic computer skills such as ... Individual created resume	Will follow up (cannot measure impact at this point – but it does not mean it was not successful!) What are the stories?

Figure 10.2   Basic logic model

This model assumes that a need or asset has been identified in collaboration with the community. EPL has begun implementation of a logic model to assess whether the library is meeting the needs of its communities. The logic model includes the involvement of the community in assessing the library's ability and success in meeting identified needs and what outcomes and impacts have been achieved. As this model has expanded to programme evaluations, it is expected this will become more integrated into the evaluative processes the library undertakes with the communities it serves.

Within EPL's shared values and 'one library, one staff' approach, leadership support is critical to success. Ultimately we want to answer one simple question: How will you (the community member) know how/when we are making a difference in your life? How will we measure what we have done and why we have done it? How do we know if we are effective?

Success is hard to define in community-led services because it cannot be predetermined; it can, however, be measured at any point on a continuum from demand on resources to impact:

- Resources include staffing, financial, organizational resources. Evaluating the demand on resources will give an indication of efficiency and productivity.
- Outputs are direct products of a programme or event such as the number of people in attendance.
- Outcomes are changes in the behaviour of participants. For example, an outcome of Sing, Sign, Laugh and Learn (an early literacy programme) is that children develop early literacy skills. Outcomes may be immediate, or may take time to achieve.

There are various types of outcome:

- Programme focus: goals for the programme are stated in terms of service delivery; for example, increase the number of teenagers who come to the Library.
- Client focus (answers the question 'So what?'): how customers' lives will improve as a result of the programme; for example, youth develop assets as engaged community members.
- Impact often takes time and is a consequence of the outcome; for example, the impact of Sing, Sign, Laugh and Learn is that as a result of developing early literacy skills, a child does better in school.

Measuring Impacts through a Programme Logic Model

Developing and using a logic model provides a visual means of showing connections between the available resources we have, the activities we plan and any changes or results we hope to achieve. We can see how resources and activities are linked to outcomes and understand how initiatives affect short-term outcomes that lead to impacts. The model helps focus the evaluation on measuring each element to see what happens, what works, what does not work, and for whom. Documenting initial and/or interim steps shows whether the initiative is on track and shows success along a continuum. Ideally we want to be able to indicate impact; however, we recognize that impact is often intangible and complex and may not be realized for several years. This means that success may be determined at the output or outcome level. Most of our evaluation will be based on outcomes.

A challenge for EPL has been that time constraints are a considerable issue for the community in practising community-led evaluation. Equally challenging is the fear that the library will cut or change services based on the evaluation. This reflects more on the difficulties of communication in attempting to practise community-led evaluation, where not all members of the community may understand the evaluation process. While community-led evaluation is time-intensive for the library, it has been established as a priority in implementing the community-led library service framework and is well positioned within an organization that is striving to be evidence-based.

Helpful Hints

#1: There need to be various types of evaluation of community-led service planning and implementation. For each of the people involved in the process, evaluation should take place. This will include an overall evaluation of the impact upon an organization (such as the logic model provided by EPL in this chapter), staff and the community.

#2: Community-based evaluation should be open-ended, where the community defines the success measures and the questions which will be asked to determine if success occurs from their perspective.

#3: Evaluation does not just occur at the end of the process. Build evaluation into each stage of the community-led service planning process. Evaluation will occur when determining the target group, identifying need, planning service and programme-based responses, and when these services and programmes are delivered. By making evaluation part of the entire planning process, programmes and services should naturally evolve that incorporate community-based needs. This may actually lead to continual evolution of programme and service development.

#4: Service standards should be established for public libraries' activities related to social exclusion. Such standards should be both quantitative and qualitative.

#5: Performance indicators and targets should be set to measure the success of library services in their attempts to tackle social exclusion. These should include a requirement to specify amounts spent on disadvantaged groups and deprived communities.

Chapter 11
The Community-Led Library Service: A Blueprint for Change

Failure to implement the recommendations of *Open to All?* and the learnings of the Working Together Project may have dire consequences for libraries in North America and Europe. With tightening budgets, there is a real danger that library management and decision-makers will react by re-trenching in traditional service approaches.

Libraries are what people in positions of authority within each organization choose to make them. Community-led approaches to library services, developed through Working Together, provide libraries with a framework to work with local communities to expand the roles and approaches to service development. Librarians can either continue to speculate about community needs, or the spectrum of possibilities can expand beyond the 'professional librarian' to include community members who are the experts on their own needs.

During economic downturns, it may be tempting to take the easy path and revert to our old ways of working. However, the relevancy of the library service is directly related to its relevance to the public tax base and the local communities in which it functions. Continuing to work without innovation to ensure community needs are correctly understood and addressed, in the same way as lack of innovation in the private sector leads to the demise of private companies, may ultimately lead to the demise of the public library.

There is already evidence of this happening in the UK since the formation of a Conservative-Liberal Democrat (Con-Dem) coalition in May 2010 which is committed to drastically reduce public expenditure. Similar attempts to cut back public services are also starting to emerge in Canada and the time is now right to start advocating for community-led library services.

Great Libraries for Everyone

Soon after coming to power the Con-Dem alliance abolished a whole range of quangos (quasi-autonomous non-governmental organizations), including the Museums, Libraries and Archives Council (MLA). The strategic responsibility for libraries was transferred to the Arts Council who published *Culture, Knowledge and Understanding: Great Museums and Libraries for Everyone* (2011), a framework for decision-making for museums and libraries during the current spending period (2011–15):

The role museums and libraries play in relation to a broader range of public outcomes (health, education, return to work) is likely to take on a new importance in a context of widespread public reform, as well as strengthening the case we can make for the importance of cultural services to civic life. It will be very valuable for the arts to draw on the partnering skills that museums and libraries have developed and their experience of innovating in the face of change. It is this context of change that requires a new emphasis on dynamic sector leaders and a willingness to embed responsiveness into governance, delivery and management structures. Whilst the Arts Council is committed to promoting the specialist expertise that sits at the heart of museums and libraries, we recognise that we must also support these sectors to embrace new skills and knowledge and greater capacity to adapt to change.

> A further challenge for museums and libraries will be to ensure that their workforces are more reflective of the communities they serve. Whilst these sectors have concentrated to great effect in broadening audiences, the diversity of the workforce remains a challenge. Pockets of best practice have the potential to show the way; we will be seeking to identify and promote these examples as we tackle the shared challenges of pushing for equality of access to the training, work and career opportunities that our funding supports. (Arts Council 2011: 11)

The Arts Council also launched a wide-reaching consultation exercise *Envisioning the Library of the Future*. The initial research looked at changes to society and how these may affect the way libraries are run and what services they deliver. The Council followed up this research by consulting a wide range of stakeholders:

> It's essential that we gather a wide range of views from people that run libraries, fund and use libraries, to help us develop a shared vision of what the library service of the future may look like. This consultation will be invaluable in helping us to envisage the shape of that library, sitting at the heart of its community, providing services that local people value and enjoy. (*CILIP Update* 2012a: 6)

Some commentators have conjectured that the public library may not have a future because of the cuts in public expenditure which have put 600 public libraries at risk of closure. In addition, 3,000 opening hours a week have been cut since 2011. There are also concerns about large-scale job losses – particularly of qualified librarians – when paid staff are replaced with community volunteers as part of David Cameron's Big Society agenda. CILIP figures suggest that staffing levels have been cut back by more than 10 per cent. There has been a loss of 2,159 staff posts from a total of 20,924. One quarter of these were professional posts.

Public Library Inquiry

In response to these concerns the Parliamentary Culture, Media and Sport Committee launched a new inquiry into library closures in November 2011. The Committee requested views on the following issues:

- what constitutes a comprehensive and efficient library service for the twenty-first century
- the extent to which planned library closures are compatible with the requirements of the Libraries and Museums Act 1964 and the Charteris Report (which recommended that Library Needs Assessments be carried out in advance of any planned library closures)
- the impact library closures have on local communities
- the effectiveness of the Secretary of State's powers of intervention under the Public Libraries and Museums Act 1964.

It is difficult to predict what the outcome of this inquiry might be. On the one hand, the Public Libraries Act may be strengthened to protect libraries and save them from closure. On the other hand, the 1964 Act may be amended (for example, to allow councils to charge for book borrowing and information) or abolished completely (to free local councils from their statutory duty to provide library services). The most likely outcome is some kind of compromise which will enable library closures without government intervention. Here is a snapshot of some of the threats to UK public libraries as of April 2012:

- Bolton – five out of 15 libraries closed. More than 70 people staged protest in February 2012.
- Gloucestershire – cuts of £1.8 million by Conservative council went ahead.
- Somerset – plan to withdraw funding for 11 libraries was reversed after it was judged unlawful by the High Court in November 2011.
- Croydon – five companies tendering to run library services.
- Oxfordshire – council decided in December 2011 that 43 libraries would remain open: 22 fully staffed and 21 run by volunteers. But a High Court judge said in April 2012 that volunteers could not be used because they did not have equality training.
- Isle of Wight – decided to hand the running of five libraries to community groups in September 2011, saving £500,000 per year.
- Brent – authors Philip Pullman and Zadie Smith stepped in to fight closures. Campaigners lost appeal to save six branches and have lobbied the Secretary of State to investigate.
- Essex – opening hours cut in 2011, plus five managerial positions. In January 2012 it promised to keep all libraries but another reduction in opening hours seems likely.

- Surrey – campaigners fighting plans to hand over control of 10 public libraries to community groups wait to find out what action will be taken following victory in a judicial review.

An observer of the campaign to save Friern Barnet Library noted that 'Scenes like this are being played out around the country as disparate people unite to try to protect threatened libraries. It is happening, they argue, because of cost-cutting, but also because of a Localism Act that has thrown the future of libraries into the hands of councils' (Dutta 2012).

It is important to make a distinction between being anti-cuts (protesting against the reduction in public library funding) and anti-closures (because, on some occasions, it is the right decision to close a library).

Localism

The aim of localism was to shift power away from central government to the people, families and communities of Britain:

> Radical decentralisation means giving local people the powers and funding to deliver what they want for their communities – with a particular determination to help those who need it most. The Big Society is what happens whenever people work together for the common good. It is about achieving our collective goals in ways that are more diverse, more local and more personal.

> The best contribution that central government can make is to devolve power, money and knowledge to those best placed to find the best solutions to local needs: elected local representatives, frontline public service professionals, social enterprises, charities, co-ops, community groups, neighbourhoods and individuals. (DCLG 2010: 3)

This shift from Big Government to the Big Society would be achieved by taking six essential steps:

- Lift the burden of bureaucracy – by removing the cost and control of unnecessary red tape and regulation, whose effect is to restrict local action.
- Empower communities to do things their way – by creating rights for people to get involved with, and direct the development of, their communities.
- Increase local control of public finance – so that more of the decisions over how public money is spent and raised can be taken within communities.
- Diversify the supply of public services – by ending public sector monopolies, ensuring a level playing field for all suppliers, giving people more choice and a better standard of service.

- Open up government to public scrutiny – by releasing government information into the public domain, so that people can know how their money is spent, how it is used and to what effect.
- Strengthen accountability to local people – by giving every citizen the power to change the services provided to them through participation, choice or the ballot box.

The ideological thrust behind localism was the perceived failure of centralization:

> Our country has become one of the most centralised in the western world. In nations as diverse as America, Sweden, Japan, Spain, Canada, Germany and France, citizens are trusted to make decisions over a greater proportion of public expenditure – and at more local level – than our citizens are allowed to. We need to catch up. (DCLG 2010: 6)

The 'community right to buy' will give communities powers to save local assets threatened with closure, by allowing them to bid for the ownership and management of community assets. In reality, this has given the green light to cash-strapped local authorities to transfer public libraries into 'community ownership'. But, as councils such as Oxfordshire and Surrey have discovered, simply dumping unwanted library buildings on local communities is not the answer. Library services also need trained and qualified staff who can work with local communities to identify, prioritize and meet community needs.

Of more potential interest to community-led libraries is the 'community right to challenge' which will give communities a right of challenge to run local authority services. This means that local communities will be able to get more involved in the delivery of public services and shape them in a way that will meet local preferences: 'Citizenship isn't a transaction – in which you put your taxes in and get your services out. It's a relationship – you're part of something bigger than yourself, and it matters what you think and you feel and you do' (BBC News, Politics 2010).

Librarianship is not a transaction between library workers and 'customers'. It is a meaningful and sustained relationship with local communities. It is about library staff and local people working together to co-produce library services. The Institute for Public Policy Research North has put forward *Five Foundations of Real Localism* (Cox 2010) which can be used to develop community-led library services:

- Localism must be effective and efficient and there should be a clear and transparent rationale for decision-making.
- Localism must be properly funded to enable community capacity-building and the devolution of power and resources to local people.
- Localism must sit at the heart of a drive for social justice, with a clear set of community outcomes and a transparent approach to the allocation of resources to meet community needs.

- Greater devolution of power and responsibility to the local level must be accompanied by a step-change in the transparency and accountability of local decision-making across all service areas.
- Any drive for localism must ensure that decentralized services have genuine autonomy but also remain part of an integrated network.

Citizen-Powered Library Services

The Institute for Public Policy Research also produced *Capable Communities: Towards Citizen Powered Public Services* (IPPR North 2010), which found that there is appetite from local people to get more involved in delivering public services across different communities and different service areas:

Willing to keep an eye on an elderly neighbour	46%
Willing to attend a regular meeting with their neighbourhood police team	42%
Would regularly drive an elderly person to the shops	33%
Willing to make a regular commitment to mentor a child struggling through the education system	20%
Willing to become a school governor	18%
Willing to volunteer at a police station	18%

However, over 90 per cent of people believe that the state should remain primarily responsible for delivering most key public services. According to the *Taking Part* survey (DCMS 2011b), the appetite for volunteering is not as strong in the cultural sector, where only 7.3 per cent of people have volunteered in the past 12 months:

Has volunteered in Sport	18.8%
Has volunteered in the Arts	8.4%
Has volunteered in Heritage	5.1%
Has volunteered in Museums/Galleries	1.4%
Has volunteered in Libraries	1.1%
Has volunteered in Archives	0.6%

The number of volunteers in libraries is still comparatively low, despite a significant increase in recent years. It is estimated that there are around 21,500 volunteers in libraries, each working for an average of just 31 hours per year, doing the equivalent work of 341 full-time posts. CILIP is somewhat ambiguous in its opposition to any job substitution and the creation of community-run libraries that are not supported by a professional management team. CILIP recognizes the positive role volunteers can play while acknowledging services need to be professionally managed.

Library volunteers are predominantly female, white and middle-class, which reflects the dominant demographics of both library staff and users. There are barriers that affect the demand for greater participation by the community, such as a lack of confidence, time and skills. There are also barriers that result from the way public services are organized and operated – for example, rules, professional attitudes and red tape:

> Government at both central and local level needs to embrace a major shift in its role and purpose and rethink the means of producing public outcomes by placing people and communities in the driving seat. A transformation in attitudes, delivery models and levers will be required. This includes a major change in the role of professionals. Many of the professionals we spoke to were sceptical about handing responsibility over to citizens. Sometimes this was for good reason because they were concerned about falling standards if 'amateurs' were to take over. But often this was because they simply saw certain tasks as being part of their professional territory. There needs to be a culture change across the professions if this agenda is to be unlocked. (Cox 2010: 2)

Neighbourhoods

Neighbourhoods are a key focus for the Coalition's localism policies to decentralize control and create a 'Big Society'. Delivering good partnership working, generating more active citizenship and civic responsibility, maximizing the opportunities in devolution, and getting local councillors to play strong community leadership roles are not simple. However, neighbourhood working can help to make this happen. The Joseph Rowntree Foundation (2012) has identified a number of ways forward:

- Neighbourhood workers are key to coordinate partners and services, broker agreements and solve problems creatively.
- Structures for neighbourhood working need to be proactive, consistent yet flexible. They rely on skilled individuals, with 'local knowledge' and strong personal relationships.
- Organizational culture change can help to nurture creative problem-solving and empower frontline neighbourhood staff.
- Active citizenship could be strengthened by tapping into the pool of 'willing localists'.
- Transferring more control to communities requires new mechanisms to share risk and reward between public sector bodies and communities.
- Citizen behaviour change can be facilitated through redesigning systems, and specific tools such as 'nudge'.
- Inclusion in and between neighbourhoods, in devolution, needs careful brokering, facilitation and greater transparency.
- Councillors can play a community leadership role, and must be honest with constituents, tackle difficult issues head on, and mobilize the wider community.

- There is a shared desire by local councillors and communities to develop more open, honest, trusting and communicative relationships with each other.
- Central government could offer support, guidance and leadership for action at the local level on the shared challenges facing local public sector organizations and local government.

These are also ways forward for public libraries to develop needs-based and community-led services, which we will now examine.

Moving Community-Led Work Forward

Throughout the life of the Working Together Project (WTP), findings and learnings were widely shared at regional and national level. By sharing community-led approaches throughout the project, there was an increased level of awareness about community-led library service development, both within the participating library systems and nationally.

At the conclusion of the WTP a substantial number of findings and learnings were shared through the publication and free dissemination of the *Community-Led Libraries Toolkit* (Working Together 2008a). This publication has been a key document for public library systems trying to create new approaches to working with socially excluded populations.

The four years dedicated to the WTP have provided library systems around the world with a strong context, understanding, and starting point for using community-led service planning. While a solid foundation has been laid for future work from a community-led perspective, each library system will need to develop its own approach to suit its individual context. Unlike those outreach approaches where programmes and services are regularly created by one library system or branch, and placed into a number of other branches or community contexts, community-led planning ensures that the needs and interests of local communities are central. It is neither linear nor prescriptive, as there are no definitive steps which need to be taken. For library systems which want to actively engage and innovate services to meet the identified needs of underserved communities, community-led planning is the best approach.

Considerations

In addition to a number of considerations which have been highlighted throughout this book, there are some other issues of importance that should be briefly mentioned. In order to incorporate community-led work within a library system, it is essential that the library profession and library systems:

- Build an internal understanding of the non-prescriptive approach and develop multi-phased plans (Williment et al. 2011a) which engage both internally with staff to increase capacity and externally with existing library users and non-library users.

- Adapt to what they hear from their communities. The shifting nature of library work, for example the growing popularity of e-book readers, is accepted by library staff. The same culture of change also needs to be accepted by library staff when it comes to working with communities. Library services should be willing to be humbled. Not only will library staff learn about systemic barriers faced by library users, but also library policy and the ways in which library staff do their work will need to adjust, in order to address these issues.
- Library schools must provide students with the theoretical background and tools which will ensure that library systems can incorporate community-led services. These skills need to be taught in library schools and reinforced by employers.

Risks

On a national level, if the ultimate goal is to have the community-led library service integrated into Canadian public library systems, there is a significant amount of work to be completed. There are a number of risks which can inhibit the uptake of community-led library services. These will either need to be addressed, or at a minimum should be acknowledged. *Some* of these risks include:

- Ensuring that community-led library services are not seen as an add-on service, which can come and go based on budgets or the whim of decision-makers.
- Adopting the language of community-led work but not changing library work, approaches and behaviours!
- Ensuring discussions around community-led library service development enter the mainstream library community. As a generalization, public libraries in Canada have been relatively open to this approach but there have been relatively few discussions in academic and special libraries. The same could also be said of most MLIS programmes.
- The power of collaborative work was quite apparent with Working Together, where learnings and approaches were shared across library systems. It is tempting and at times logically easier to work within the silos of independent library systems, but unfortunately this decreases the likelihood of shared opportunities, shared learnings and increased capacity.
- For library systems beginning to adopt the community-led approach, momentum can wane, or come in waves. It is vital to involve senior managers and ensure the approach is integrated into mission and value statements. The risk remains in every system that if only a few staff are advocating this approach, a few significant staffing changes can de-rail the process.

- The inability of some library staff to look past Working Together: this was a starting point for community-led library services, and each system needs to take this approach and adapt it to fit both their needs and abilities.
  - Some librarians may jump to conclusions about community-led work without fundamentally understanding it. As information management experts, it is important that library staff educate themselves, before dismissing community-led work.
  - This includes taking the Working Together *Toolkit* and adapting WTP learnings to fit the local context (for example, the branch, the targeted community, etc.).
- Public library systems looking to other mechanisms or tools to try to legitimate the profession.
  - As the e-book revolution takes hold and significant changes in technology impact public library services, it may be tempting to try and rationalize public library services through tools such as these, without trying to address the underlying systemic issues inherent within the service planning process.
  - Professionalism and focusing on legitimizing the 'role' of the professional librarian can be confused with librarians becoming spokespersons for communities. Professionalism can actually increase the division between public library services and their relevance to the community. Instead, librarians need to ensure that their roles as experts in information sorting, retrieval, and facilitation are leveraged to assist communities – who are the *experts on their own needs*.

This is not a comprehensive list of potential threats to the adoption and uptake of community-led service planning. However, it is a starting point which decision-makers in library systems in Canada and other countries should be aware of.

Momentum

On a very positive note, there are significant numbers of activities which have taken place since the conclusion of the WTP. Each of these indicates that community-led service planning is being mainstreamed in library systems across Canada. Some highlights include:

- The development of a the Community-Led Libraries Network through the Canadian Library Association in 2011: this is key in ensuring shared learnings across library systems.
- A number of library systems have adopted elements of community-led library service: this includes some major library systems in Canada such as Vancouver Public Library, Halifax Regional Library (Williment et al. 2011b) and Edmonton Public Library (Edmonton Public Library 2012).

- The use of community-led service planning in an academic context (Singh 2010).
- The use of community-led approaches in rural public library service development (Somers and Williment 2011).
- The use of community-led service planning in children's services (Prendergast 2011).
- The use of community-led service planning in the development of services to current mainstream library users and underserved community members.
- Library systems starting to collect 'narrative'-based evidence and presenting this information, along with traditional measures such as statistics, to justify funding levels (Martinez et. al. 2012)

It has been four years since the conclusion of Working Together. As initially discussed, the timing of the WTP could not have been better. Tightening public budgets make it more important than ever that public libraries demonstrate their worth to policy-makers, funders and the general public. A retrenchment into 'traditional' library service planning will only lead to more of the same services, just marketed and justified in a new light. It is only through transformative approaches like community-led service planning that public libraries will be able to innovate and ensure their future and sustained relevance. This has been best summarized by Martinez and Williment (2011):

> The traditional service development process provides a number of ways in which library staff can internally generate programs and services to meet library staffs' perceptions of community needs. Community-led service development provides a new set of tools which library staff can build upon to ensure the continued relevance of public libraries that truly meet community needs. Unfortunately, systems which continue to guess at community needs will run the risk of being left in the twentieth century. This may lead to the development of two-tiered library service development, where (1) dynamic library systems respond to community needs beyond those of traditional library users while (2) other systems minimally engage users and try to maintain their relevance to community by marketing and informing communities of 'their' services.

> As with all other professions, industries and organizations, public libraries need to embrace innovation, thus ensuring that their services are relevant to both funders and the people they are meant to serve. The discussions and innovative practices occurring in Canadian public libraries are exciting because – ultimately – change will occur. The question will always remain – who will determine how public libraries will adapt? It will either happen proactively and internally, and hopefully based on collaborative decisions made with library staff and their communities – or else passive public libraries will be at the mercy of the outside forces imposing the change. (Martinez and Williment 2012)

Towards the Community-Led Library Service

The ideas put forward in *Open to All?* have stood the test of time and are as relevant today as when they were first proposed in 2000. Indeed, given the threats and challenges faced by public libraries (closures, staff cuts, privatization) and socially excluded communities (unemployment, welfare cuts, scapegoating), these ideas are more important than ever. *Open to All?* had a direct impact on all of its target stakeholders:

- National public library policy and strategy has been significantly influenced as evidenced by the focus on community and civic values in *Framework for the Future* (DCMS 2003) and library needs assessments in *The Modernisation Review of Public Libraries* (DCMS 2010a).
- Professional associations, particularly CILIP, have encouraged the development of more inclusive library services, through *Making a Difference: Innovation and Diversity* (SIEAG 2002) and the Body of Professional Knowledge.
- Research institutions and research funding bodies such as the Local Government Association and the Laser Foundation have funded research into the library-related needs of excluded groups and published their findings in *Extending the Role of Libraries* (LGA 2004) and *Public Libraries: What Next*? (Laser Foundation 2007).
- Training organizations, especially schools of information and library studies, have made their courses and programmes more relevant to public library work for social inclusion to ensure that their students become *The Right 'Man' for the Job?* (Wilson and Birdi 2008).
- Public library authorities have joined The Network to share good practice in developing strategies, structures, systems and organizational cultures which enable public libraries to tackle social exclusion.
- *Open to All?* ideas have also been tested by public libraries in Canada via the WTP (2004–08) which produced the *Community-Led Libraries Toolkit* (Working Together 2008a) and the *Community-Led Service Philosophy Toolkit* (Edmonton Public Library 2012).

The synthesis of *Open to All?* recommendations and WTP learnings has created the following blueprint for developing needs-based and community-led public library services.

Blueprint

- As librarians we learn from, adapt and evolve techniques used in the community development field. We do this in order to better work with socially excluded communities.

- Librarians are not the experts on what our communities need or want in terms of library services – the community is the expert. It is our job to ensure that we develop a library service that reflects the community's needs and vision. We do this *with* them, not *for* them.
- The type of relationships we are building and the framework for how we are working with socially excluded community members can also be applied to socially included community members.
- Community development in a library context represents a different approach to working with our communities: it represents a philosophical and practical shift from being a service provider for our communities to being a partner with our communities in service development and provision. This approach shifts the emphasis from our staff to our communities as the key initiators and/or drivers of service innovation and enhancement.
- Consultation is the necessary first step toward community development-based librarianship. Consultation must evolve into collaborative service prioritization, development, planning and evaluation.
- Reaching socially excluded community members and learning from them means meeting them in the places they are most comfortable and being open to learning from them. This means leaving the library and building trusting, respectful and equitable relationships. Only then will we be able to learn what socially excluded people need and want from their communities and library.
- A community development approach necessitates working directly with, and building relationships with, socially excluded individuals in the community. Libraries often have relationships with service providers (for example, through informal and formal partnership arrangements) but service provider goals and objectives should not be confused with direct consultation and collaboration with community members themselves. Nor should service provider priorities be substituted for priorities defined by community members. The priorities and needs expressed by our community members must drive our library services.
- Public libraries need to change how they interact with socially excluded people. It is not the role of public libraries to teach people to be 'responsible' or 'good citizens'. Rather their role is to make services more welcoming, supportive and responsive to the needs of socially excluded people. Public libraries need to change for communities. Communities should not be expected to change for public libraries. Libraries should provide a wide range of unbiased and non-judgemental resources which enable people to make informed personal choices.

Helpful Hints

#1: When using a community-led approach, target groups can extend beyond the socially excluded. If library staff begin to use this approach with a group they are comfortable working with first – then challenging them to engage the underserved – success and buy-in is much more likely.

#2: Selecting a group to engage can be identified based on a number of different rationales, which will vary in each community and library system context:

At times it may be based upon political reasons, staff comfort levels, library board or senior management decision, etc.

It is always beneficial to initially internally engage library staff and involve them in identifying and selecting an underserved group or community which they think could be consulted at a minimum.

#3: Be aware of the various rationales you will hear from library staff about why *not* to implement a community-led approach. These can include (1) the lack of resources, (2) the role of library services, and (3) the unknown. There are a number of practical responses which can be made to each of these points, including the following.

Resources

Everything we do in libraries takes time and money. When thinking about the potential cost of implementing the approach, also re-evaluate where time and money is currently being spent. A serious evaluation of current activities should at a minimum allow a library system or branch to re-allocate (within the current budget) a portion of current staff time and money towards working with the community.

Time is always in short supply. If a gap is identified, it is always easy to fill it with another activity. The question becomes: 'Is it filled with an activity libraries identify internally, or activities that are identified with the community as a priority/ need?' If the community is involved from the beginning of the service process, time may actually be saved – since relevance to community is ensured.

Role of Services

'It doesn't fit our mandate.' Overcoming this objection might employ a mixture of the following strategies:

- Working with the community, especially the public, in public libraries is part of our mandate. If it is not, be an advocate for changing your library systems mandate/vision/goals, etc.

- It makes good business sense to engage with as many community members as possible. A business model which only meets the needs of a minority of people is not value for money or sustainable. The collective public resources which are used to fund library services should be shared as widely as possible with all sections of the community.
- 'Library staff are not social workers.' As information specialists it is our obligation to inform and educate ourselves before making statements like this. Have library staff look up the definition of a social worker and compare it to their job descriptions.
- 'Our library staff are already doing it.' Since the approach was developed in 2008, it would be great to learn from one another. Urge staff to collaboratively share and discuss best practices.
- 'We are already serving our current users well.' Great, this approach will ensure that the library system will serve current users even better. For example, by building evaluation into each component of the service planning process, the community will inform the system if something is relevant to them before the programme or service is launched.
- 'It doesn't work.' Four major urban library systems across Canada used this approach extensively from 2004 to 2008 and the approach is being integrated by different systems in different ways. This process was constantly externally evaluated and won national recognition and awards. It has since been adopted and applied in other library systems and many other systems have expressed an interest in learning about the approach. The only way to know if something does or does not work is by trying it.

The Unknown

When approaching a community and learning to listen and hear community-identified need in a library context, the unknown is the most important part of the process. This is where learning and innovation occurs.

- This is not a prescriptive approach to work, nor a repetitive task-orientated approach to work. One of the future trends of library work is moving towards service- not task-orientated work. This approach will lead to innovation – which, in the current environment of rapid changes to the publishing and information management field, can only be beneficial to public libraries.
- 'How will it impact my work? I am unsure.' The good thing about community-led work is that it is a two-way process. Library staff, along with the community, will be involved in these decisions. Library staff can become more empowered by participating in this change management process.

Chapter 12

A Road Map towards the Community-Led Library Service

By integrating community-led service planning into the way in which library staff do their work, it provides them with additional tools and approaches to working with the community. Community-led service planning is usually implemented by focusing on a specific targeted community (such as teens, older adults, homeless, immigrants, etc.) and walking library staff through the service planning process. This includes having staff develop relationships with community members (community assessment), discovering community need (needs identification), developing programme or service responses with community, implementing a programme or service (with community), and evaluating throughout the entire process.

Traditionally, service planning was a very insular and internal process, where library staff would develop services based on their perceptions and speculation about community need. Services were also created 'for' community and delivered by library staff in-house or as outreach to the community.

The community-led approach acknowledges the important role traditional approaches can still play in serving community – but it also provides additional approaches that involve working *with* community. Using a community-led approach, library staff actively listen to people talk about their library-based needs, plan collaboratively with community members, and modify and reshape activities based upon community input. Community is actively involved in defining and measuring outcomes.

Most importantly, community-led approaches shift the role of library staff so they are the facilitators of knowledge exchanges between community and the library. Each has something to learn from and contribute to the other. The community teaches the library about the community – its assets, its challenges and its needs – while, library staff inform the community about library systems and where change can most readily happen.

This can be a humbling change management process for library staff to undertake. It requires a collaboration of equals between community members and the library. It requires a shedding of the personas of the librarian as educator and expert, and adopting a new identity – librarian as facilitator. To clarify, librarians do maintain their professional expertise as information managers, while community is acknowledged for its expertise in its own needs.

Ultimately, this approach will ensure that library programmes and services will continue to be relevant to local communities. Instead of building something and waiting to see if people will come (we like to refer to this as the 'Field of Dreams' model), this approach ensures that the community will come, since they are involved throughout the entire process.

Consultation

Consultation – the different approaches used to engage with local communities to ensure that they are fully involved in the design, planning, delivery and evaluation of library services:

1. The library service should be committed to move from informing the public to working with local communities to plan services. Consultation should be based on the development and maintenance of relationships which are not passive or one-off meetings with community members, but active, ongoing and sustained interactions. The initial assessment of communities should be achieved by library workers walking and moving about in the community, literally knocking on doors. Other methods to access community members should include: partnership working with service providers; 'hanging-out' in community spaces; informal and formal group discussions; advisory committees; attending regular meetings and events; and taking existing services into the community. In doing so, library workers must be skilled in selecting the communities to work with, based on needs identified through local Library Needs Assessments. This will ensure that those with the greatest needs are identified and prioritized and will guard against people who push themselves forward but are not representative.

2. The library service should have a consistent and widespread internal and external awareness of the range of different citizens within the area. The library service should listen to and engage with diverse communities, with honesty and transparency, inclusivity, fairness and reality as core values which underpin its work. The library service's commitment to engagement should be evident in library strategies, structures, systems, cultures and service plans, and community engagement should be integral to the work of the service. There should be good local intelligence and good relationships with different communities which enable effective facilitation and community leadership.

3. The library service should fully understand the different aspirations of different communities and successfully balance these. The library service should develop a dialogue with communities and groups differentiated by such issues as social class, ethnicity, gender, sexuality, disability, religion/faith, language, age, migration patterns and locality in order to understand their needs, priorities and concerns. The library services engagement with communities should mean it is able to keep track of changes that may lead

to community tensions and can respond to these accordingly (for example, when Lincolnshire Libraries was the first service on the ground to respond to community tensions during Euro 2004). There should be clarity about the type of engagement with users of services, local people and communities, which is relevant and meaningful to those communities.

4. Methods of engagement should meet the different communication preferences of local communities. Outreach work (as a first step towards community development, rather than as simply a service delivered outside the library) should be targeted to reach disadvantaged or marginalized groups and should result in greater involvement of diverse groups of citizens. Effective engagement should lead to change and recognizable improvement in library service provision and delivery.

5. Comprehensive information about the take-up of library services across diverse communities and localities should be routinely collected and should be sophisticated enough to enable partners to profile and identify unmet needs. Library systems and processes should demonstrate a full understanding of the community's different needs and aspirations, reflected in policy and service delivery.

6. The library culture should be strongly focused on improving outcomes for local people. This should be shared and supported by staff and elected councillors. Benefits to communities should be increased through increased trust of library services, a greater sense of inclusion and a willingness to participate in the future. Complaints should be listened to, taken seriously, handled sensitively and used to generate improvement for diverse local communities. Locally elected councillors and staff should receive training on how to engage with communities.

7. When working with library staff, introduce them to the public involvement continuum. Ask library staff individually to write down at least two different activities they are currently doing which involve the community. Have them place their answers along the involvement continuum. Most responses will probably fall on the giving/getting information end of the continuum. Ask staff how the activities could be changed so they can be moved towards the engaging/partnering/collaborating end of the continuum.

8. A number of key questions can be used to determine how well library staff are engaging with community. It is important to identify where ideas are initiated. When working with a targeted community: How were they engaged? Who identified the community need? Who placed the identified need in a library context? If it was library staff, did they re-engage the community to verify if they were interpreting the library-based need correctly? How was the community involved in the identification and then developing the service response?

9. After relationships are established with individual community members, ask them if they would be willing to walk through the community with you, and introduce you to other community members.

The discomfort that librarians may initially experience being in an unfamiliar place where socially excluded community members gather should be viewed as having only one tenth of the discomfort that socially excluded members face when entering libraries.

Needs Assessment and Research

Needs assessment and research – the methods by which community needs can be identified, prioritized and met:

1. When assessing what resources are available and how these match the needs of the community, consider: Have you analysed and considered need and demand? What are the specific needs of adults, families and young people of all ages? Would members of the community be able and willing to contribute to the delivery of library services as volunteers or joint managers? What are the needs of those living, working and studying in the area?
2. When assessing community needs, evaluate: How accessible is the service? Is public transport appropriate? Are there barriers to physical access of library buildings that should be removed? Have local people been consulted? How? What are the views of users and what are the views of non-users? Have you carried out an Equality Impact Assessment? What implications are there for other strategies, such as educational attainment, support for those seeking work, digital inclusion, adult social care? Are there other partnerships that can be explored – for example, with the third sector, community and development trusts or town and parish councils?
3. When developing a programme or service, ask yourself where the evidence has come from for the activity you are proposing in your library system. If you cannot provide evidence from direct consultation or collaboration with the community, ask yourself: How was the programme or service identified? Where did the need come from? Was the need identified by library staff or the community?
4. Broad generalizations about how socially excluded people access services and information can be presented to library staff, so they can start to contextualize the differing approaches people take to address their needs.
5. There are a number of issues which library staff should be aware of when engaging and listening to conversations. These include being sensitive to the context in which the conversation is occurring, using plain language, and being wary of the Hawthorne Effect.
6. If the community or target group does not continue to work with library staff beyond the needs assessment, and you find just yourself or other library staff developing and implementing the programme/service, alarm bells should be sounding that something may have gone amiss.

7. When working with library staff there are a number of different issues which should be addressed when starting and going through a needs identification process: define who the target is; determine the skills which staff need to develop; provide structural support, for example, developing policies or procedures which support 'non-traditional' needs assessments.

Library Image and Identity

Library image and identity – how public libraries are perceived as a reflection of their buildings, staff and services:

1. Local communities should be actively involved in all stages of library service design, planning, delivery and evaluation. Imaginative approaches should be adopted to engage local communities, particularly young people and socially excluded people. This engagement should seek to combine all four key elements to today's public library: the people for whom the library service is intended (along with the staff providing the service); the programme of services, events and activities required to deliver that service; the partners which the library service wants to work with; and the library itself, along with the spaces it offers to meet community needs.
2. Marketing and publicity campaigns should be used to shift the popular public perception of libraries as static, passive repositories of books to an image of dynamic, community-focused and people-friendly services. These efforts should go beyond superficial rebranding exercises and the simple grouping of related services under one roof. These publicity campaigns should also make the library offer to the community clear and visible to all the citizens in the area – on the website, in library buildings and through any other local marketing opportunities.
3. All library systems and processes should be reviewed to ensure that any real and potential barriers to library access – institutional, personal and social, environmental, and those related to perceptions and awareness – are identified and reduced or eliminated. Libraries should be open at convenient times which match community lifestyles. The impact of loan periods, overdues, borrowing limits, fees and charges should be assessed and mitigating action taken where necessary.
4. Communities should have access to welcoming, high-quality library buildings located in the right places and open at the right times for their users. These buildings should have iconic designs, innovative services and inventive links to local people. Traditional library architecture should be replaced with modern and contemporary features such as street-level retail entrances, open-plan design and circulation, and domestic furniture to create 'the living room in the community'. The role of small community

libraries, mobile libraries and 'library access points' in community spaces should also be considered.

5. Stand-alone library buildings should be replaced with co-located library services which can be used as community hubs and which help to widen usage and make valuable links for the users. Co-location should be used to bring together complementary services on an equal footing. Effective co-location of libraries with other services – such as health or employment services, post offices, leisure services, schools, early years settings and children's centres, universities or other educational institutions – will enable innovation, offer value for money and deliver a coherent, joined-up approach to the community.

6. Ask library staff in your branch to identify library jargon which they find is confusing or they would not expect members of the general community to understand. Ask staff in the library system to expand on this list. Circulate the list to all library staff and title it 'Words Banned for Use with the Public'!

7. Ask library staff to identify interactions they are having with the public where there is confusion. These could be conversations at the checkout, at the information desk, etc. Ask staff to identify if this confusion is centred on specific policies, procedures or the language that library staff are either explaining or using.

8. One activity which library staff can do, and was tried through Working Together, is to have non-library users take library staff on a silent tour of the library (silence is only required of library staff). This is a great activity to do with larger groups which do not regularly use the library space because it allows them to tell library staff how they navigate the library, what their perceptions are of the library collection and space, and to point out issues and perceptions of the library which staff and regular library users do not see, since they are using it every day.

Outreach, Community Development and Partnerships

Outreach, community development and partnerships – the differences between outreach and community development in the context of traditional and community-led service planning:

1. Outreach activities are developed and assessed by the librarian. Outreach creates unequal power dynamics between library staff and community members, which are exacerbated in socially excluded communities. Despite its limitations, outreach can be used to take services to those who cannot access a library, such as the elderly, the disabled and those with mobility problems. Outreach can also be used as a conduit, leading to community-led service development.

2. Libraries should work in partnership with a wide range of organizations who share a common goal of meeting community needs. These partnerships should be based on a set of principles including equality of power and resources. Partnerships should not be opportunistic or short-term or used just to acquire funding. Partnerships should be long-term, sustainable and grounded in shared objectives and values.

3. Community development is not an end product, but a means to an end – how library staff will engage with the community to build relationships, and begin to hear community-based needs. Community development combines public library resources with local community resources to identify, prioritize and meet community needs. Community development requires a culture change whereby professionals develop sustained relationships with local communities.

4. Every community is different and every community has different needs and so community development work cannot be prescriptive. The techniques used by library staff to enter a community or to explore need may be similar in different communities, but the programme or service will always be different because community need drives the library response.

5. Co-production is an advanced form of community development whereby library services are delivered in an equal and reciprocal relationship between library workers and local people. Co-production transforms the dynamic between the library and its community, putting an end to 'them' and 'us'. Instead, people pool different types of knowledge and skills, based on lived experience and professional learning.

6. Outreach activities tend to focus on the end product, the delivery of the service to the community. When entering a community, ask yourself if a service or programme has already been determined for that community. If it has, this is not community-led service planning, it is outreach. Shift the focus from the end product (the programme or service which will be delivered to a community) to how library staff will engage with the community to build relationships, and begin to hear community-based needs.

ICT and Social Exclusion

ICT and social exclusion – the role of new technology in tackling social exclusion:

1. There are some significant barriers to the use of ICT by socially excluded communities, including lack of disposable income, limited experience or use of new technology and lack of access to ICT. In order to address these barriers ICT in libraries should be available free at the point of need. There should be unfettered access to online information without any filtering or

censorship. Hardware and software should be regularly updated so that the latest equipment and programmes are available.

2. ICT initiatives should be targeted at socially excluded communities. New and innovative approaches to marketing these initiatives should be employed to prevent the ICT being dominated by existing users. Staff should be trained in how to deliver ICT programmes in an appropriate way to excluded communities. These programmes should focus on the individual needs of participants and specific targeted benefits, rather than a 'one solution for all' approach.

3. ICT is a means to an end and not an end in itself. Simply providing new technology will not automatically make public libraries more socially inclusive. ICT is a means to creating relationships and as a potential entry point for building more inclusive library services.

4. ICT creates opportunities for library staff to work with community partners to develop truly inclusive ICT services by reaching community members who may be hesitant about entering library spaces, while at the same time assisting community agencies to meet their objectives.

5. E-books pose both an opportunity and a threat to public libraries. They provide a platform for attracting lapsed and non-users into the library, but these tend to be people who are already ICT-confident and can afford the e-book technology. The threat comes from charges for e-books which undermine the principle of free book loans and the provision of staffed public libraries.

6. Many library staff may be unsure of their own skills in using technology and have varying levels of comfort delivering IT training outside a scripted training course. Delivering community-led ICT instruction means that the content and approaches used to deliver the instruction will need to be adapted to best meet each individuals needs.

Materials Provision

Materials provision – the development of holistic collections policies to ensure that library stock reflects the needs of local communities:

1. Public libraries should be agents of social change and not social control. Materials provision must be informed by community needs. Stock selection should not be the sole preserve of professional librarians. The local community should be actively involved in deciding the size, range and content of library stock.

2. The local community should also be able to influence how stock is displayed and promoted. For example, should there be integrated or special collections? What type of classification or categorization schemes should be used?

3. Public libraries have a major role to play in literacy and reader development which should be positioned as a key function of the service. There should be an egalitarian ethos between reader development staff and emergent readers. There should be a range of self-motivated and independent activity including choosing and finding appealing books, reading, analysing and discussing them with others, recommending and writing about them and visiting and using libraries.
4. Reader development should be embedded at a strategic level and a full range of effective resources should be provided in partnership with adult learning services. An evaluation framework should be developed with emergent readers to measure the impact of improved literacy. Longitudinal evaluation should also take place with individual learners.
5. The library offer should include clear and firm commitments around materials provision, including: free access to a range and quality of stock to browse and borrow and online resources and information that meet local needs; a community of readers, connecting people to other readers through reading groups, activities and recommendations; and family activities, including family reading and learning activities, homework clubs, links to family information services, holiday reading challenges.
6. It is important to include the library systems collection development/access team in the process. In one case, a CDL discovered a library staff member in the collection department was selectively weeding out materials that youth had purchased. The collections librarian objected to the theme being added to the collection – only to discover within the next year, it was one of the 'hottest' trends in Hollywood and youth services.

Staffing, Recruitment, Training and Education

Staffing, recruitment, training and education – the skills and competencies that library workers must have to build relationships with excluded communities:

1. Staffing structures should be aligned with social exclusion strategies. This will require job titles, job descriptions, person profiles and competencies which recognize the importance of outreach, partnerships, community development and proactive ways of working.
2. Library staff should reflect the demographics of the local community in terms of age, gender, ethnicity, faith/belief, sexual orientation, disability and social class. This will enable library workers to understand and be empathetic towards community needs.
3. Library staff should be aware of social inclusion policies and how these relate to their day-to-day work. These policies should not be presented as mere compliance with legislation or a tickbox exercise. Quickfix solutions

should be avoided and services to excluded communities should be mainstreamed and not 'added on'.

4. Frontline staff should feel empowered concerning the development and delivery of services for socially excluded groups, which requires an inclusive approach to service planning and an attempt to avoid the presentation of decisions that are perceived to have been made on an executive basis. This can be achieved via the formation of lateral communication groups, more one-to-one meetings between individual staff members and line managers, and the sharing of information on an interpersonal basis via team meetings or seminars, facilitating the opportunity for response and discussion.

5. Staff should receive *relevant* training and information on groups affected by social exclusion, in an attempt to significantly raise levels of awareness and cultural sensitivity amongst all staff.

6. Staff should also be trained in the skills required to work with socially excluded communities. This training should include: communication skills; listening skills; influencing relationships; reflective practice; improved confidence and assertiveness; negotiation skills; and dealing with conflict.

7. The most important elements in library staff training include:
   – Providing library staff with an opportunity to express their perceptions or pre-conceived notions of the community.
   – Providing library staff with training and an overview of community-led service planning and tools. Try to build in interactive activities, where library staff can apply principles with the community.
   – Providing opportunities for library staff to be constantly exposed to socially excluded or underserved communities, either inside the library or in the community. Relationships can only be established and sustained through continuous interactions.
   – Displaying organizational support. Ensure messages are coming from senior management, so all staff understand that the organization is advocating that library staff work from a community-led approach.

8. Library services should work in partnership with local training and skills providers, including library and information schools, to develop the training they need. Libraries should also work with early years settings, schools and youth workers to help library staff benefit from professional development in working with children and their families. Mentoring and work-shadowing opportunities should also be developed.

9. Volunteers play an important role by building bridges to local communities and supporting staff in the library team. Volunteers often have skills which complement (but should not replace) staff expertise. Volunteers from socially excluded communities can help to identify needs, break down barriers and misunderstandings, tackle prejudice and discrimination and foster empathy and community cohesion.

Mainstreaming and Resourcing for Social Exclusion

Mainstreaming and resourcing for social exclusion – how to place community needs at the heart of public library strategy, structures, systems and organizational culture:

1. Social exclusion should be mainstreamed as a policy priority across all aspects of the library service including strategies, staff and service structures, systems and organizational culture.
2. The social exclusion strategy should be driven by community needs and reflect organizational and national policies and priorities. The social exclusion strategy development process should be open and transparent and should include all key stakeholders including the local community, staff, politicians, board members, suppliers and partners.
3. The staffing structure should be aligned with the social exclusion strategy. A 'whole service approach' should be taken to ensure that all staff take ownership of social exclusion and that services to excluded communities become embedded and sustainable and not vulnerable to changes of policy or budget reductions.
4. The service structure should be aligned with the social exclusion strategy to ensure that the right services are in the right places and at the right times to meet community needs. Resources should be re-directed from building-based services to fund community-based services.
5. Library systems should be aligned with the social exclusion strategy to ensure that there are no barriers to access.
6. The organizational culture should be focused on community needs via a set of values, attitudes and behaviours which are owned and consistently enacted by every member of staff. Culture change should be accelerated through service planning, performance management and workforce development.
7. Staff must have the authority to create change. Networks and support mechanisms should be created to ensure that staff who are working with the socially excluded can share their experiences and strategies and key learnings can be disseminated.
8. Develop community engagement or community-led statements to clarify to senior management, staff, and the community the approach the library will be taking. Integrate community-led wording into the libraries' mission and vision statements.
9. Educate senior management. Explain the rationale and teach community-led language, while also ensuring that buy-in moves beyond 'speaking community-led'. The focus should be on actions not adoption of language. Determine and implement system-wide and branch-based plans. Ensure accountability, timelines and levels of authority. Make it a part of everyone's job.

Standards and Monitoring of Services

Standards and monitoring of services – how to work with local people to create meaningful performance indicators and evaluation systems:

1. Service standards and monitoring should be based on a wide range of quantitative and qualitative data to provide a holistic, accurate and contemporary view of public library performance.
2. Library performance should be measured in terms of impact and outcomes rather than inputs and outputs. The desired or intended impact and outcomes should be identified in partnership with local communities.
3. A model of impact should be developed which can demonstrate the impact that public library activities and resources have in terms of immediate, intermediate and long-term community outcomes.
4. Library impact measures should be used to assess the contribution that library services are making to major policy objectives such as skills, learning and the local economy; children, young people and families; stronger communities; and health and well-being.
5. Library impact indicators should be used as one of the tools to measure community well-being at universal, domain and targeted levels.
6. Performance monitoring should take place at every stage in the planning, design, delivery and assessment of library services. Clear measures should be agreed at the beginning and these should be reviewed and amended throughout the process. Evaluation should not be left until the end of the process.

References

ADP (Advice Development Project). 2004. *Welcome To Your Library: An Evaluation Report*. Available at: http://www.welcometoyourlibrary.org.uk/ listDocuments.asp?page_id=70&page=3.

Arts Council. 2011. *Culture, Knowledge and Understanding: Great Museums and Libraries for Everyone*. Available at: http://www.artscouncil.org.uk/media/ uploads/pdf/culture_knowledge_and_understanding.pdf.

Atkey, Jill. 2008. *Working Together: Library–Community Connections – Final Project Evaluation, February 2004–April 2008*. [Social Planning and Research Council of British Columbia] Vancouver: Prepared for Vancouver Public Library and partners.

Audit Commission, *Knowing Your Communities Toolkit*. Available at: www.audit-commission.gov.uk.

BBC News. 2012. Could teenagers be stopped from looking at porn? Available at: http://www.bbc.co.uk/news/magazine-17826515, 26 April.

BBC News, Politics. 2010. David Cameron's speech to the Conservative Party conference, 6 October. Available at: http://www.bbc.co.uk/news//uk-politics-11485397.

Bird, Viv, and Akerman, Rodie. 2005. *Literacy and Social Inclusion: The Handbook*. London: National Literacy Trust/Basic Skills Agency.

BOP Consulting. 2009. *Capturing the Impact of Libraries*. London: DCMS.

Boyle, D., and Harris, M. 2009. *The Challenge of Co-Production: How Equal Partnerships between Professionals and the Public are Crucial to Improving Public Services*. London: NESTA (Discussion Paper) [Online]. Available at: http://www.neweconomics.org/sites/neweconomics.org/files/The_Challenge_ of_Co-production.pdf.

Bryson, Jared, and Usherwood, Bob. 2002. *Social Impact Audit*. Taunton: South West Museums Libraries and Archives Council.

CABE (Commission for Architecture and the Built Environment). 2003. *Better Public Libraries*. Available at: http://webarchive.nationalarchives.gov. uk/20110118095356/http:/www.cabe.org.uk/files/better-public-libraries.pdf.

CABE (Commission for Architecture and the Built Environment). 2004. *21st Century Libraries: Changing Forms, Changing Futures*. Available at: http:// webarchive.nationalarchives.gov.uk/20110118095356/http:/www.cabe.org. uk/publications/21st-century-libraries.

Cahn, E. 2001. *No More Throwaway People: The Co-Production Imperative*. Washington DC: Essential Books.

Campbell, Brian. 2003. *Libraries in Marginal Communities: A Demonstration Project*. Unpublished Working Together document.

Campbell, Brian. 2005. 'In' versus 'With' the Community: Using a Community Approach to Public Library Services. *Feliciter*, 51(6): 271–3.

Canadian Library Association. 2011. *Community Led Library Service Network*. Available at: http://www.cla.ca/Content/NavigationMenu/CLAatWork/Networks1/CLLSN_ToR_final_aug11.pdf.

Charteris, Sue. 2009. *A Local Inquiry into the Public Library Service Provided by Wirral Metropolitan Borough Council*. Available at: http://webarchive.nationalarchives.gov.uk/+/http:/www.culture.gov.uk/reference_library/publications/6485.aspx.

CILIP Update. 2012a. Arts Council consults, March.

CILIP Update. 2012b. Refurbs attract more visitors, April.

Corrigan, Philip, and Gillespie, Val. 1978. *Class Struggle, Social Literacy and Idle Time*. Brighton: John L. Noyce.

Cox, Ed. 2010. *Five Foundations of Real Localism*. Institute for Public Policy Research North. Available at: http://www.bcise.com/Reports/Nov-2010/five-foundations-for-real-localism.pdf.

DCLG (Department for Communities and Local Government). 2006. *Strong and Prosperous Communities*. Available at: http://www.communities.gov.uk/documents/localgovernment/pdf/152456.pdf.

DCLG (Department for Communities and Local Government). 2008. *Understanding Digital Exclusion Research Report*. FreshMinds. Available at: http://www.umic.pt/images/stories/publicacoes2/Understand_Dig_Inclusion.pdf

DCLG (Department for Communities and Local Government). 2009. *Communities in Control: Real People, Real Power*. Cm 7427. Norwich: The Stationery Office. Available at: http://www.communities.gov.uk/documents/communities/pdf/886045.pdf [accessed October 2011].

DCLG (Department for Communities and Local Government). 2010. *Decentralism and the Localism Bill: An Essential Guide*. Available at: http://www.communities.gov.uk/documents/localgovernment/pdf/1793908.pdf.

DCMS (Department for Culture, Media and Sport). 1999. *Libraries for All: Social Inclusion in Public Libraries*. Available at: http://webarchive.nationalarchives.gov.uk/+/http://www.culture.gov.uk/images/publications/Social_Inclusion_PLibraries.pdf.

DCMS (Department for Culture, Media and Sport). 2003. *Framework for the Future: Libraries, Learning and Information in the Next Decade*. Available at: http://webarchive.nationalarchives.gov.uk/+/http:/www.culture.gov.uk/reference_library/publications/4505.aspx.

DCMS (Department for Culture, Media and Sport). 2010a. *The Modernisation Review of Public Libraries*. Available at: http://www.official-documents.gov.uk/document/cm78/7821/7821.pdf.

DCMS (Department for Culture, Media and Sport). 2010b. Culture Minister launches support programme for libraries. 1 July. Available at: http://www.culture.gov.uk/news/media_releases/7216.aspx.

DCMS (Department for Culture, Media and Sport). 2011a. *This Cultural and Sporting Life: The Taking Part 2010/11 Adult and Child Report*, August. Available at: http://www.culture.gov.uk/images/research/taking-part-Y6-child-adult-report.pdf.

DCMS (Department for Culture, Media and Sport). 2011b. *Taking Part 2011/12 Quarter 3: Statistical Release*. Available at: http://www.culture.gov.uk/publications/8938.aspx.

DeFaveri, Annette. 2005a. *Breaking Barriers. Libraries and Socially Excluded Communities*. Information and Social Change 21. Available at: http://www.libr.org/isc/articles/21/9.pdf.

DeFaveri, Annette. 2005b. *The Culture of Comfort*. Information for Social Change 22. Available at: http://libr.org/isc/issues/isc22/22-2.pdf.

DIUS (Department for Innovation, Universities and Skills). 2009. *The Learning Revolution*, White Paper. Cm 7555. Available at: http://www.bis.gov.uk/assets/biscore/corporate/migratedd/publications/1/learning_revolution.pdf.

Dutta, Kunal. 2012. Keep on borrowing: libraries refuse to die, in *The Independent on Sunday*, 15 April.

Dutton, W., and Helsper, E.J. 2007. *The Oxford Internet Survey (OxIS) Report (2007): The Internet in Britain*. Oxford Internet Institute, University of Oxford.

Edmonton Public Library [Canada]. 2012. *Community-Led Service Philosophy Toolkit*. Available at: http://www.epl.ca/sites/default/files/pdf/CommunityLedServicePhilosophyToolkit.pdf.

HM Government. 2009. *Putting the Frontline First: Smarter Government*. Government White Paper, Cm 7753. Available at http://www.hmg.gov.uk/media/52788/smarter-government-final.pdf.

Horne, M., and Shirley, T. 2009. *Co-Production in Public Services: A New Partnership with Citizens*. London: Cabinet Office, Strategy Unit [Online]. Available at: http://webarchive.nationalarchives.gov.uk/+/http://www.cabinetoffice.gov.uk/media/207033/public_services_co-production.pdf [accessed: October 2011].

IPPR North (Institute for Public Policy Research North). 2010. *Capable Communities: Towards Citizen Powered Public Services*. Available at: http://www.ukmediacentre.pwc.com/imagelibrary/downloadMedia.ashx?MediaDetailsID=1829.

Ipsos MORI. 2009a. *The Libraries Omnibus Survey*. Available at: http://www.culture.gov.uk/images/research/Libraries_omnibus.pdf

Ipsos MORI. 2009b. *Most Britons Feel They Can Make It in Life – but Little Change over Past Decade* [poll summary]. London: Ipsos MORI [Online] Available at: http://www.ipsos-mori.com/researchpublications/researcharchive/2299/Most-Britons-feel-they-can-make-it-in-life-but-little-change-over-past-decade.aspx [accessed: October 2011].

Joseph Rowntree Foundation. 2012. *Working in Neighbourhoods, Active Citizenship and Localism: Lessons for Policy-Makers and Practitioners.* Available at: http://www.jrf.org.uk/sites/files/jrf/neighbourhoods-localism-citizenship-full.pdf.

Laser Foundation. 2006. *Destination Unknown: A Research Study of 14–35-Year-Olds for the Future Development of Public Libraries.* Define Research and Insight Ltd, (commissioned by the DCMS and funded by MLA and Laser Foundation). Available at: http://www.bl.uk/aboutus/acrossuk/workpub/laser/publications/projreports/publiclibraries.pdf.

Laser Foundation. 2007. *Public Libraries: What Next? Final Report on the Work of the Laser Foundation.* London: Laser Foundation. Available at: www.bl.uk/aboutus/acrossuk/workpub/laser/artwork.pdf.

Leicester City Libraries. 2000. *Achieving Inclusion ... Review Report 2000.* Leicester: Leicester City Council, Arts and Leisure.

Lines, Ann, Savory, Christopher, and Reakes, Angharad. 2004. *Extending the Role of Libraries.* London: Local Government Association.

LGA (Local Government Association). 2004. *Extending the Role of Libraries.* London: LGA.

Löffler, E., Bovaird, T., Parrado, S., and van Ryzin, G. 2008. *'If You Want to Go Fast, Walk Alone. If You Want to Go Far, Walk Together': Citizens and the Co-Production of Public Services.* Paris: Ministry of Finance, Budget and Public Services [Online] Available at: http://www.govint.org/fileadmin/user_upload/Who_we_are/Co-Production_Citizen_Survey_2008.pdf [accessed: October 2011].

McLeod, Patti-Lynne. 2006. Entry into the community: community asset mapping. Ontario Library Association Super Conference. 2 February 2006. Available at: www.accessola2.com/superconference2006/thurs/419/mapping.doc.

Martinez, Pilar, and Williment, Kenneth. 2011. Canadian libraries: innovating and creating inclusive services. *Bis*, 4: 26–9. Available at: http://foreningenbis.com/bis-pa-engelska/public-libraries/canada/.

Martinez, Pilar, Bird, Amanda, Olsen, Anne, Lukasik, Laura, and Muirhead, Laura. Are we making a difference? Evaluating community-led approaches in public libraries. Canadian Library Association Conference Presentation. 2 June 2012. Available at: http://www.cla.ca/conference/2012/day4.html.

Marx, Karl, and Engels, Frederick. 1848. *The Communist Manifesto.*

Maslow, Abraham. 1943. A theory of human motivation. *Psychological Review*, 50(4): 370–96.

Mayo, Marjorie, et al. 2008. *Community Engagement and Community Cohesion.* Available at: http://www.jrf.org.uk/sites/files/jrf/2227-governance-community-engagement.pdf.

Muddiman, D., Durrani, S. Dutch, M., Linley, R. Pateman, J., and Vincent, J. 2000a. *Open to All? The Public Library and Social Exclusion.* London: Resource.

Muddiman, D., Durrani, S., Dutch, M., Linley, R., Pateman, J., and Vincent, J. 2000b. *Open to All? The Public Library and Social Exclusion. Volume 1: Overview and Conclusions.* London: Resource (Library and Information Commission Research Report 84) [Online]. Available at: http://www.seapn.org. uk/content_files/files/ota_volume_1_final_version_sept_211.doc [accessed: 10 July 2009].

Muzzerall, Darla, McLeod, Patti-Lynne, Pacheco, Sonia, and Sharkey, Karen. 2005. Community Development Librarians: starting out. *Feliciter*, 51(6): 265–7.

Office for National Statistics. 2012. *Internet Access Quarterly Update.* Available at: http://www.ons.gov.uk/ons/rel/rdit2/internet-access-quarterly-update/2012-q1/stb-internet-access-quarterly-update-2012-q1.html.

Prendergast, Tess. 2011. Beyond storytime: children's librarians collaborating in communities. *Children and Libraries*, Spring: 20–6, 40. Available at: http://www.ala.org/ala/mgrps/divs/alsc/compubs/childrenlib/index.cfm.

Pask, Russell, and Wilkie, Sarah. 2011. *Opening up a New World: Public Libraries Connecting Housebound People to the Networked Nation.* Available at: http://www.artscouncil.org.uk/media/uploads/pdf/OpeningUpANewWorldFullReport.pdf.

Pateman, John. 2003. *Developing a Needs-Based Library Service.* Leicester: NIACE.

Pateman, John, and Vincent, John. 2010. *Public Libraries and Social Justice.* Aldershot: Ashgate.

SIEAG (Social Inclusion Executive Advisory Group to CILIP). 2002. *Making a Difference: Innovation and Diversity: The Report of the Social Inclusion Executive Advisory Group to CILIP.* London: CILIP.

Singh, Sandra. 2010. *Librarians as Information Providers and Facilitators: The Irving K. Barber Learning Centre as a Model for the Expansion of the Role of Academic Libraries in University–Community Engagement.* Available at: http://www3.ul.ie/dllo/pdfs&powerpoints/Sandra%20Singh.pdf.

Singh, Sandra, and DeFaveri, Annette. 2005. *Community Development in a Library Context.* Internal Working Document from the Working Together Project.

Singh, Sandra, and DeFaveri, Annette. 2007. *Key Messages.* Internal Working Document from the Working Together Project.

Singh, Sandra, Campbell, Brian, and DeFaveri, Annette. 2008. Toward an inclusive library service: the Working Together National Demonstration Project, in *Reaching Out: Innovation in Canadian Libraries.* Laval, Quebec: Presses de l'Université Laval, 52–6.

Somers, Denis, and Williment, Kenneth. 2011. Community-led library service in a rural community: Musquodoboit Harbour Branch. *Feliciter*, 57(2): 50–2.

Steuer, Nicola, and Marks, Nic. 2008. *Local Wellbeing: Can we Measure it?* The Young Foundation. Available at: http://www.youngfoundation.org/files/images/YF_wellbeing_measurement_web.pdf

Stonewall. 2003. *Profiles of Prejudice*. Available at: www.stonewall.org.uk/documents/profiles.doc.

Usherwood, Bob. 2007. *Equity and Excellence in the Public Library: Why Ignorance is Not Our Heritage*. Aldershot: Ashgate.

Vincent, J. 2009. Inclusion: training to tackle social exclusion, in *Handbook of Library Training Practice and Development. Volume 3*, edited by A. Brine. Farnham: Ashgate, 123–46.

Vital Link, The. 2005. *Confidence All Round: The Impact on Emergent Adult Readers of Reading for Pleasure through Libraries*. Manchester: The Vital Link.

Williment, Ken. 2009. It takes a community to create a library. *Partnership: the Canadian Journal of Library and Information Practice and Research*, 4(1): 1–11. Available at: http://journal.lib.uoguelph.ca/index.php/perj/article/viewFile/545/1477.

Williment, Ken. 2011. People who can and should influence change in libraries. Social Justice Librarian Blog. 9 November 2011. Available at: http://sjlibrarian.wordpress.com/2011/11/09/people-who-can-and-should-influence-change-in-libraries/.

Williment, Ken, Gatley, Randy, and Jones-Grant, Tracey. 2011a. *Putting the Public Back in Public Libraries: Community-Led Libraries*. OCLC Webinar, 26 September 2011. Available at http://resourcesharing.webjunction.org/events/webinars/webinar-archives/articles/content/125355837.

Williment, Ken, Jones-Grant, Tracey, and Somers, Denise. 2011b. From project to branch integration and sustainability: community-led work at Halifax Public Library. *Public Libraries*, 50(2). Available at: http://www.publiclibrariesonline.org/magazines/featured-articles/project-branch-integration-and-sustainability-community-led-work-halifax.

Wilson, Kerry, and Birdi, Briony. 2008. *The Right 'Man' for the Job? The Role of Empathy in Community Librarianship*. Sheffield: Department of Information Studies, University of Sheffield. Available at: http://www.shef.ac.uk/polopoly_fs/1.128131!/file/AHRC-2006-8-final-report-04.08.pdf.

Working Together Project. 2008a. *Community-Led Libraries Toolkit*. Vancouver: Working Together Project [Online]. Available at: http://www.librariesincommunities.ca/resources/Community-Led_Libraries_Toolkit.pdf.

Working Together Project. 2008b. *Proposed Community Development Course for Library Schools*. Internal Working Document from the Working Together Project.

Young, Michael, and Willmott, Peter. 1957. *Family and Kinship in East London*. Harmondsworth: Penguin.

Index

Page numbers in *italics* refer to figures and tables.